Christian Haas

Incentives and Two-Sided Matching

Engineering Coordination Mechanisms for Social Clouds

Studies on eOrganisation and Market Engineering 12

Karlsruher Institut für Technologie (KIT)

Herausgeber:

Prof. Dr. Christof Weinhardt
Prof. Dr. Thomas Dreier
Prof. Dr. Rudi Studer

Incentives and Two-Sided Matching

Engineering Coordination Mechanisms for Social Clouds

by
Christian Haas

KIT Scientific Publishing

Dissertation, Karlsruher Institut für Technologie (KIT)
Fakultät für Wirtschaftswissenschaften, 2014
Referenten: Prof. Dr. Christof Weinhardt, Prof. Dr. Steven O. Kimbrough

Impressum

KIT Scientific Publishing

Karlsruher Institut für Technologie (KIT)
KIT Scientific Publishing
Straße am Forum 2
D-76131 Karlsruhe

www.ksp.kit.edu

Print on Demand 2014

ISSN 1862-8893
ISBN 978-3-7315-0237-1
DOI 10.5445/KSP/1000041861

Incentives and Two-Sided Matching

Engineering Coordination Mechanisms for Social Clouds

Zur Erlangung des akademischen Grades eines
Doktors der Wirtschaftswissenschaften

(Dr. rer. pol.)

von der Fakultät für
Wirtschaftswissenschaften
am Karlsruher Institut für Technologie (KIT)

genehmigte

DISSERTATION

von

Dipl.-Wi.-Ing. Christian Haas

Tag der mündlichen Prüfung: 17. Juni 2014
Referent: Prof. Dr. Christof Weinhardt
Korreferent: Prof. Dr. Steven O. Kimbrough

Karlsruhe, 2014

Abstract

An unprecedented variety of resources are shared, exchanged and traded within (social) networks of users. In this context, the Social Cloud framework leverages existing relationships between members of a social network for the exchange of resources. The design of a Social Cloud comprises several challenges that need to be addressed to create a sustainable platform. This ranges from the identification and provisioning of relevant incentives for user participation to achieve a critical mass of users, the understanding and modeling of the underlying trust concepts, the design of market mechanisms for resource allocation, to implementation details that ensure the technical feasibility of the platform.

This thesis focuses on the design of coordination mechanisms to address two of these challenges, namely user participation incentives and resource allocation mechanisms. The thesis applies a simulation-based approach to design incentive schemes and allocation mechanisms. In the first part, based on the survey-based identification of relevant participation incentives and their dependency on certain factors, two case studies show the usefulness of applying simulations in the engineering of contribution schemes for Social Clouds. The second part of the thesis advocates the use of two-sided matching for resource allocation due to the social setting of the considered scenario. For this preference-based allocation, heuristics are proposed and evaluated for one-to-one matching as a means to provide flexibility with respect to diverse user preferences and objective functions, and to find high quality solutions in settings for which no efficient exact or approximation algorithms exist.

The case studies and results of this thesis for user participation exemplify that a simulation-based approach can be leveraged as complementary methodology to analytical modeling and prototyping to find useful results with respect to the effects of contribution schemes on different user types. Considering resource allocation, the proposed algorithms provide an increased solution quality compared to existing algorithms, and have the advantage of inherent flexibility with respect to changing requirements and matching goals as they can be easily adapted to different preference or goal settings. The study of preference manipulation shows that while there are cases where manipulation is beneficial, the expected reward is comparably small, which indicates little space for practical manipulation in real scenarios. Furthermore, the thesis considers a dynamic allocation scenario showing that continuous reallocation is necessary if the amount of supplied and demanded resources fluctuates.

This work contributes to the field of incentive engineering by providing new insights in relevant incentives for social resource sharing and through the application of simulation-based approaches to design contribution schemes. The field of two-sided matching is advanced by showing that the proposed heuristics provide superior performance and flexibility for preference-based resource allocation.

Acknowledgements

The completion of this work was enabled by the support of many people, to whom I own my deepest gratitude. First of all, I want to thank my supervisor Prof. Dr. Christof Weinhardt for his ongoing support, advice, and encouragement throughout the PhD at the Institute of Information Systems and Management (IISM) as well as the Karlsruhe Service Research Institute (KSRI). Furthermore, I am very thankful to my co-advisor Prof. Dr. Steven O. Kimbrough (University of Pennsylvania, USA) for the insightful discussions and helpful comments that guided this research. I also want to particularly thank Prof. Dr. Thomas Setzer and Prof. Dr. Kay Mitusch for serving on my thesis committee.

My sincere thanks go to all my former and current colleagues from IISM and KSRI, which have been a fundamental factor that made the thesis such an interesting and enriching endeavor. In particular, my special thanks go to Dr. Simon Caton for his friendship and the numerous professional and personal meetings that we had over the years. I also want to thank Margeret Hall, Alexander Schuller, and Anuja Hariharan for reading and improving parts of the thesis, and who together with Anders Dalén, Axel Kieninger, and Tim Straub made the PhD time much more enjoyable through various social events.

For the ability to pursue a research stay at the University of Chicago and Cardiff University as well as having very fruitful collaborations I owe my honest gratitude to Dr. Kyle Chard and Prof. Dr. Omer Rana. I also gratefully acknowledge the financial support by the Karlsruhe House of Young Scientists (KHYS) that enabled this research stay.

Finally, I thank my family, Hermann, Elisabeth and Michael Haas, for their continuing support and love throughout my entire life. I also thank Magie for her emotional support, love and constant encouragement. Without them, this work would not have been possible.

Contents

List of Figures

List of Tables

List of Abbreviations

EFC	Enforced Fixed Contribution
GA	Genetic Algorithm
GATA	Genetic Algorithm with subsequent Threshold Accepting Algorithm
IP	Integer Program
LP	Linear Program
P2P	Peer-to-Peer
QoS	Quality of Service
RSMA	Requester-Optimal-Stable-Matching
SC	Social Cloud
SES	Social Exchange Simulator
SLA	Service Level Agreement
SM	Stable Matching
SMT	Stable Matching with Ties
SMTI	Stable Matching with Ties and Incompleteness
TA	Threshold Accepting Algorithm
TIPI	Ten Item Personality Inventory
VC	Volunteer Computing
VFC	Voluntary Fixed Contribution
VM	Virtual Machine
VVC	Voluntary Variable Contribution

List of Symbols

α_i	Availability of user i
β	Convexity parameter for utility function
$\chi_{r,j,i}(t)$	Feedback of user j about user i for resource type r
δ	Percentage of transactions requiring resources at the same time
$\delta_{i,r}$	Percentage of resources user i shares
η_r	Relative scarcity of resource type r
i, j, k	User indices
κ_1, κ_2	Weight of score $s_i(t)$ components
κ_T	Threshold value for scarcity
λ	Degree of altruism
$\omega_{i,r}$	Initial resource endowment of user i and resource type r
ω_{min}	Minimum number of provided resources
$o \in O$	Outcome based on the set of possible outcomes O
p	Relative price for sharing resources
$\Pi_{i,o}$	Provisioning of resources from user i
$\Pi_{i,s}$	Consumption of resources from user i
P_i	Preference Profile of user i towards other users
$P_{i,j}$	Preference rank that user i has towards user j
$\succsim_i$	Priority structure of user i, where $\succ_i$ denotes strict priority and $\sim$ denotes indifference
r	Resource type
$R(n)$	System requirements function
$s_i(t)$	Score of user i at time t
$s_{quantity,i}(t)$	Score (Quantity) of user i at time t
$s_{scarcity,i}(t)$	Score (Scarcity) of user i at time t
$\sigma_{i,r}$	Percentage of resources user i reserves for own purposes
σ_{min}	Minimum level of resources reserved for own usage
S_i	Strategy set for user i
$\tau_{i,r}$	Utility of user i for sharing resource type r
ϑ	Trust scores
θ_i	Type of user i

U_i	Utility of user i
$u_i\,(\theta_{i,o})$	Utility of user i given its type θ_i and outcome o

Part I.

Introduction and Foundations

Chapter 1.

Introduction

"The Internet and especially Web 2.0 has brought about many new ways of sharing as well as facilitating older forms of sharing on a larger scale."

(Belk 2013)

RESOURCE allocation has always been one of the core foci of economic research. Whenever one group of people has access to, or can provide certain resources, and another group is interested in consuming these resources, (economic) mechanisms can facilitate such an exchange. Over the years, several types of allocation mechanisms have emerged as principle ways to trade, share and exchange resources, such as fixed-price markets, auctions, and negotiations. In general, they can be categorized into mechanisms where the exchange involves monetary transactions, and non-monetary mechanisms.

The advent of computers had drastic effects on resource exchange mechanisms. On one hand, the emergence of computer-based and computer-mediated exchange platforms fundamentally changed the ways that resources are traded or shared, affecting the speed, complexity and transparency of resource allocation in many areas. This ranges from a rapid increase in speed through algorithmic traders on stock markets to internet-based sharing platforms where cars[1], skills[2], travel accommodation[3], and other resources are shared between members of the platform. On the other hand, besides facilitating the exchange, computing resources (storage, computational power, etc.) represent a commodity that is becoming increasingly

[1] `http://www.zipcar.com/`; `https://www.stadtmobil.de/` – last accessed May 2014
[2] `http://www.skillshare.com/` – last accessed May 2014
[3] `http://www.couchsurfing.com/` – last accessed May 2014

important. As the generated data from research and businesses increases and computational models become more complex to solve, the demand for computational resources changes accordingly. The evolution of distributed computing paradigms such as Cluster Computing within an organization and Grid Computing across organizations (Foster and Kesselman, 2003) reflect the necessity to provide access to a larger set of computational resources. Over the last years, Cloud Computing emerged as the dominant paradigm to provide various types of computational resources (such as computational power or storage) on-demand (Armbrust et al., 2010). A multitude of different exchange mechanisms have been suggested and are used for these paradigms. Especially when the resource exchange involves different organizations, monetary mechanisms are commonly used to gain access to the resources (see Buyya and Murshed (2002) for Grid Computing and the large Cloud Computing vendors such as Amazon Web Services[4] and Rackspace[5]).

A prevalent economic argument for the Cloud Computing principle of on-demand access to third-party computational resources is the "Capex to Opex" principle (converting capital expenses to operating expenses; Armbrust et al. 2010, p.53). Yet, it also exemplifies the change from a property-dominated paradigm in which resource ownership was considered important, to an access- and service-based paradigm (Rifkin, 2000; Vargo and Lusch, 2004). This paradigm change is in line with the observation that the importance of the *resource sharing* concept, although being far from new, has steadily increased over the past years and receives considerable renewed interest in both research and media (see e.g. Levine 2009; Belk 2010). With the introduction of Web 2.0 technologies that facilitate the online communication and interaction between people, the last years have seen a rise in the number of platforms that facilitate the sharing of certain resources. This ranges from the previously mentioned sharing of physical resources (cars, travel accommodation, etc.), to digital or virtual goods as well as computation resources (files[6], storage[7], computational power[8], knowledge artifacts[9], etc.). Two important concepts for online resource sharing in this context are Peer-to-Peer (P2P) (sharing) networks in which resources are exchanged directly between users of the network in a decentralized

[4] `http://aws.amazon.com/` – last accessed May 2014
[5] `http://www.rackspace.com/` – last accessed May 2014
[6] `https://www.dropbox.com/` – last accessed May 2014
[7] `http://friendstore.news.cs.nyu.edu/` – last accessed May 2014
[8] `http://boinc.berkeley.edu` – last accessed May 2014
[9] `http://www.myexperiment.org`, `http://nanohub.org` – last accessed May 2014

manner, and Volunteer Computing where computational resources are donated to (scientific) projects.

As social connections and the trust inherent to them is a facilitator of economic exchange (Granovetter, 2005), a potential reason for this renewed interest in sharing is the increasing prevalence and importance of (online) social networks in people's everyday lives. This not only manifests itself in the rise of social network platforms such as Facebook with over a billion users, but also in other (socially-driven) Web 2.0 driven platforms (such as YouTube, Twitter, etc.) which thrive on user interaction and contributions. Considering resource exchanges, the increasing importance of social connections (in contrast to the mostly anonymous Web and platforms that emerged in the early years of the Internet) also does not go unnoticed. The mentioned platforms for sharing physical or virtual goods are example of platforms which leverage the social connections of users to facilitate resource exchanges. In contrast to monetary-based markets in which resource exchange necessarily involves certain types of payments, these new types of exchange platforms often implement non-monetary based allocation mechanisms as a means to allocate resources. In particular, the social context might induce incentives such as reciprocal or altruistic participation (Fehr and Schmidt, 2006).

Combining these aspects, and considering the increased interest in security aspects, many exchange platforms begin to focus on social, non-anonymous resource sharing. Examples are P2P cloud computing (Babaoglu et al., 2012), the sharing of computational storage among friends (Tran et al., 2008), and even the sharing of insurance policies.[10] Similarly, Swamynathan et al. (2008) proposes a "social marketplace" which combines traditional online marketplaces with social network features to enable purchases between friends and friends of friends.

This amalgamation of online resource exchange and social networks is also the background of this work. The *Social Cloud* paradigm (Chard et al., 2012) serves as the main use case of this thesis, and is explained in detail in Section 2.1. In particular, a Social Cloud (SC) is defined as the sharing of (computational) resources and services between members of an underlying social network. The design of such a platform is far from trivial, and several challenges need to be addressed for the creation of a successful Social Cloud platform. These challenges are outlined in the next section.

[10] `https://www.friendsurance.de/` – last accessed May 2014

1.1. Design Challenges

A Social Cloud is a form of electronic marketplace where users share and exchange resources. As such, there are several design decisions that have to be addressed: the interaction of users with the platform, the mechanism to exchange resources, the underlying technical infrastructure, etc. The methodology of *Market Engineering* (Weinhardt et al., 2003; Neumann, 2004) provides the means to structure this design process. In particular, it focuses on the design of institutions to implement and facilitate the resource exchange. Starting with the definition of the transaction object of the market (i.e., the types of resources that are exchanged), Market Engineering considers several viewpoints of institutional design: the definition of a market *microstructure* that specifies the economic mechanisms used to determine resource allocations and transactions; the specification of an *IT infrastructure* to host the electronic marketplace and its functionality; and a *business structure* that addresses aspects such as business models and data ownership. The goal of Market Engineering is to define these institutions such that they incentivize a certain user behavior that results in a desired market outcome.

Using the Market Engineering approach, several challenges can be identified in the design of a Social Cloud. This section provides an overview of the most relevant design challenges, gives an extended description of the respective challenges and specifies which of the challenges are addressed by this thesis.

Trust

In the context of resource sharing, or online cooperation in general, the existence of trust is a fundamental factor that facilitates the exchange (Granovetter, 2005). Arrow argues that "[v]irtually every commercial transaction has within itself an element of trust, certainly any transaction conducted over a period of time. It can be plausibly argued that much of the economic backwardness in the world can be explained by the lack of mutual confidence" (Arrow, 1972, p.357).

Trust and its relation to exchange platforms has been studied in various disciplines. Computer science mainly focuses on the application of trust concepts in platforms for resource exchange. Examples are the calculation of trust scores between users of a social network (Golbeck, 2005), and various reputation systems that aim at establishing the trustworthiness of users involved in resource exchanges (e.g., PeerTrust (Xiong and Liu, 2004), PowerTrust (Zhou and Hwang, 2007), EigenTrust (Kamvar et al., 2003)). In economics, the concept of social or other-regarding preferences tries to incorporate the effects of trust on user behavior in resource exchanges, mainly through interpreting reciprocal actions as signs of trust between users (Berg et al., 1995; Fehr and Schmidt, 2006). In sociology, trust is mainly perceived as calculated risk taking in decision situations within social interactions (e.g., Coleman (1990)), and several layers of trust are distinguished (Endress, 2012). From an interdisciplinary perspective, the roles of institution-based trust in the design of (online) marketplaces are of importance (Pavlou and Gefen, 2004).

Whereas trust is modeled as a single score in the previously mentioned reputation systems, Endress (2012) argues that trust has multiple layers. There can be a baseline trust between two users depending on their relationship, yet this can be superimposed by context-specific trust, e.g., the perceived capability of providing a certain outcome or action. It might also depend on the prior expectations of the interacting users. Hence, trust is a multi-faceted concept that needs careful elaboration in the context of social resource sharing. Although first steps into this direction have been taken by Caton et al. (2012), this challenge is not focus of this thesis.

Volatile Resources and User Availability

Social resource sharing differs from both ownership-based resource usage as well as traditional payment-based resource usage. In contrast to resource ownership, users who request resources have to take into account that resource availability depends on the user providing the resource, e.g., if the resource is currently already used, how long it can be used, etc. Also, especially for computational resources the requested resources might not be as available and as reliable as resources provided by professional companies, and often involve a best-effort type of usage policy. For example, storage or computational power provided by users on a voluntary basis depends on how much storage is available on their system, how long their machines are online, etc.

User availability and the corresponding volatile resources have certain consequences for participating users. For example, if a user requests computational resources to store data or use computational power, the unavailability of the providing user can cause serious consequences. This challenge is also relevant from a technical point of view. If, for example, users exhibit a pattern of availability and unavailability, and the platform wants to guarantee that data stored on other users' machines is available at any time (or with a certain probability), then techniques such as data replication have to be considered.

This challenge is partially addressed in the thesis. In particular, the thesis studies the effects of user availability and unavailability on the platform reliability in a case where the resources required to run the platform are provided by the users themselves.

Technical Implementation

Every online platform depends on a sound technical implementation to ensure reliable performance, achieve a high availability, and provide the necessary functionality for user management and user interaction. This basic functionality includes databases to store relevant data about users, transactions, and other information, as well as the definition and implementation of the user interface through which users interact with the platform. From the perspective of a sharing community, the platform also has to facilitate the actual exchange of (computational) resources. This is a non-trivial technical challenge, as it requires the consideration of different device technologies (e.g., mobile vs. static access), operating systems, and changing network addresses.

For a Social Cloud, Chard et al. (2012) and Caton et al. (2014) provide examples how such a platform can be implemented, and Seuken et al. (2010) specifically considers user interface design for a computational storage sharing market. In this thesis, the implementation challenge is partially addressed by the description of an implemented Social Compute Cloud for sharing Virtual Machines. Usability aspects, on the other hand, are not the focus of this thesis and can be considered an interesting opportunity for future work.

User Participation

Once the technical infrastructure for the platform is implemented, the next challenge is to attract users to participate on the platform. For online communities in general, and sharing communities in particular, a commonly agreed upon challenge is to gain a critical mass of participating users (Markus, 1987; Van Slyke et al., 2007; Westland, 2010) at which point network effects can be harnessed. With an increasing number of users, the available resources and thus potential utility from using the platform generally increases as well. The design of appropriate incentives is specifically targeted to increase user participation. The potential motivations of users to join and participate on an online (sharing) platform can be diverse and heterogeneous, and not all users can be expected to exhibit the same behavior when presented with particular incentives. Hence, an incentive scheme targeted at increasing the number of actively participating users has to be aware of the potentially heterogeneous user pool, and provide appropriate incentives (Vassileva, 2012).

Participation incentives encompass the first main part of this thesis. In the context of Social Clouds, relevant motivations and incentives will be identified and discussed. Furthermore, two case studies are presented that highlight the usefulness of a simulation-based approach in the design of incentive schemes.

Resource Allocation

Platforms for resource sharing or exchange are characterized by the fact that some users have resources to offer that can be used or consumed by other users. In such a context, the decision about the type of (economic) mechanism that facilitates this exchange is fundamental. Platforms, in general, have a variety of options for such mechanisms. One possibility is to allow users to contact, negotiate and share resources in a decentralized manner, leaving the decision process which users to contact solely to the users themselves. Another possibility is to provide a certain form of centralized mechanism that determines the transactions and potential remunerations between users.

There are two main challenges in the design of a suitable resource allocation mechanism for Social Clouds, or online platforms in general. First, it has to be decided which type of allocation mechanism is to be used, i.e., whether a decentralized mechanism is used or a centralized mechanism with or without monetary transactions. Second, the chosen type of mechanism has to be adapted for the specific scenario in order to guarantee certain desirable criteria, such as efficiency or fairness. Ideally, the allocation mechanism is congruent with the platform philosophy and is chosen according to its ability to reflect what is important for the participating user types. For example, in social settings non-monetary mechanisms might be preferred as monetary remunerations can affect the non-monetary motivations of participating users (Frey and Jegen, 2001; Bénabou and Tirole, 2003).

The design of a suitable resource allocation mechanism is the second main focus of the thesis. For the first mentioned challenge, the findings of the relevant participation incentives are used to identify the suitable type of allocation mechanism. Building on this, for the second challenge of designing the mechanism according to the requirements of the platform, algorithms to find good allocations according to several performance criteria are introduced and evaluated.

User Behavior

Online communities generally have an etiquette that users should not engage in harmful or malicious activities on the platform. Especially when resources are shared or exchanged, the tampering or misuse of the resources can have serious negative effects on the resource providing users, the resources, as well as the platform itself (e.g., with respect to platform reputation). Besides misusing resources, the strategic provisioning of false information, for example in resource exchanges, might be beneficial for certain users if the respective exchange mechanism is not incentive compatible. As such misrepresentation of information can be harmful to other users and for the system as a whole, it is generally deemed desirable to implement mechanisms that do not allow users to gain through information misrepresentation.

Although users might have to sign community guidelines when joining the platform, this does not ensure that the rules are actually followed. Different approaches can be pursued to address this challenge. Through the design and provisioning of certain incentives, malicious or harmful behavior can be made less appealing for users. The design of formal agreements (similar to Service Level Agreements) is used by certain platforms to lay out the terms of the resource exchange, and to specify actions if the agreement is not adhered to. Furthermore, from a strategic point of view, if the expected gain from malicious behavior or information misrepresentation is negative, then (rational) users have an (economic) incentive to abstain from such behavior. Considering the technical implementation, additional security measures can be used to minimize the risk of exploitation.

Several aspects of strategic or malicious behavior are discussed throughout the thesis. Specifically, in the context of resource allocations the thesis investigates if users can gain from misrepresenting their private information.

1.2. Research Outline

For the design of a sharing platform such as a Social Cloud, the previously mentioned challenges have to be addressed. This thesis contributes to this field by focusing on two of these challenges: 1) User participation incentives, and 2) the design of non-monetary resource allocation mechanisms.

Considering user participation incentives and contribution schemes, the thesis aims to answer following research question:

RESEARCH QUESTION 1 ≺PARTICIPATION AND CONTRIBUTION INCENTIVES≻ *What are relevant user participation incentives for Social Clouds, and how can they be leveraged in the design of tailored participation and contribution schemes?*

The first step in the design of appropriate and effective incentive schemes is the identification of different participation stages that define how and to what degree (potential) users interact with the platform. The existence of several distinct stages with specific requirements for user integration and participation has already been identified for general online communities (Jones and Rafaeli, 1999; Iriberri and Leroy, 2009). This is an important consideration as the motivations and incentives might be different between stages. For example, the motivation to join a platform can be different from the motivation to actively contribute to the platform. However, Social Clouds have unique, potentially different requirements for user participation as other online communities. This stems from the fact that (bilateral) resource exchange between users on the basis of existing social connections might have an impact on the user behavior and the existing relationships. Therefore, research question 1.1 is posed to identify the relevant participation stages in which the user interacts with the platform.

RESEARCH QUESTION 1.1 ≺INCENTIVE ENGINEERING≻ *What are the stages of participation and the corresponding relevant incentives that users exhibit in Social Clouds?*

The results of research question 1.1 are necessary to design incentive schemes that take into account the specific requirements of the different participation stages. Chapter 3 addresses this research question by utilizing two approaches. On one hand, through a comparison of related platforms and exchange systems as well as participation studies in online communities, a conceptual model of the participation stages is constructed. Additionally, the specific challenges within the separate stages are discussed in the context of a Social Cloud. On the other hand, building on the previously derived model, a small-scale web-based survey aims to identify the relevance of certain incentives within the mentioned participation stages. In particular, its goal is to find relationships between user characteristics and the relative importance of certain incentives.

By design, the introduction of an incentive scheme can affect how users interact with other users and the system, for example by providing incentives to increase one's sharing activity. Before being applied in practice, the effects of such a (potentially novel) incentive scheme on the overall platform have to be predicted to ensure that the scheme achieves its goals. Often, analytic modeling is used to predict said effects, or the scheme is introduced for a subgroup of users and subsequently analyzed. However, both approaches are not always feasible. For example, a realistic analytical model might be too complex for formal evaluation, or the platform for which the incentive scheme is designed might not exist yet. For these reasons, this thesis proposes and applies a simulation-based approach as complementary methodology to study potential effects of incentive schemes on the system. In particular, such an approach can yield predictions which are unattainable by the other methods, such as dynamic effects on different user groups. To demonstrate how such a simulation-based approach can augment the incentive scheme design, research question 1.2 studies the effects that can be predicted by such an approach.

RESEARCH QUESTION 1.2 ≺INCENTIVE SCHEME DESIGN≻ *How can a simulation-based approach be leveraged in the design of incentive schemes for participation?*

As an example for the design of an incentive scheme, the introduction of a participation constraint in a Social Cloud is considered in a case study in Chapter 4. The aim of such a participation constraint is to provide incentives for users to contribute resources to the system. It is well-known that users might have different preferences to contribute resources and can be distinguished into different types (Andreoni and Miller, 2002). Although the potential effects of the constraint on the overall system have been studied before (see, e.g., Ranganathan et al. 2004), the implications on different user types, and the consideration of system performance depending on the distribution of such user types, is a novel scenario that requires investigation. Furthermore, from a purely analytical approach it is not clear how the participation constraint will affect the resource contribution of the users dynamically. Hence, research question 1.2 investigates the effects of such an incentive scheme on different user groups and determines if the participation constraint achieves its purpose.

User participation incentives, as studied in research questions 1.1 and 1.2, are necessary to create a sustainable platform with continuing and active user participation. From a technical point of view, such an online platform also requires certain technical infrastructure resources to host the platform itself, e.g., for services such as user registration and management. Besides using dedicated third-party resources for the infrastructure, it is also possible to let the users provide the necessary resources themselves. The concept of a *co-operative infrastructure*, in this case, is defined as a platform where the resources that host the platform are provided and owned by the users. As the feasibility of such an approach depends on the contribution of the users, an incentive scheme needs to be designed such that enough resources are provided to ensure a certain platform availability. Research question 1.3 considers this scenario and focuses on the feasibility of different incentive schemes.

RESEARCH QUESTION 1.3 ≺CO-OPERATIVE INFRASTRUCTURES≻ *What are the effects of different contribution schemes on co-operatively provided infrastructure resources for Social Clouds?*

To answer this research question, the previously described simulation-based approach is used in a second case study in Chapter 4 to examine several different contribution schemes for users. For example, a certain contribution to the infrastructure might be enforced for all users who want to participate, or the decision to participate can be completely left to the users themselves. Research question 1.3 studies how different contribution schemes and assumptions about user type distributions affect the feasibility of such a co-operative approach.

The first main research question considers aspects of user participation and resource contribution, which was identified as one of the key challenges in the design of a Social Cloud platform. Given that users participate on the platform and provide resources, the second key challenge is to find appropriate (matching) mechanisms that allocate resources in line with the goals of the platform. As discussed, in many economic settings the allocation of resources involves monetary transactions based on (private) valuations that the market participants have for the resources. While such monetary-based mechanisms might be useful for many exchange settings, there are also scenarios for which non-monetary mechanisms are considered more useful. This is especially the case in settings where monetary-based exchanges would be considered unsocial, unethical or illegal. Examples of such settings are the matching of children to schools (School Choice Problem, see e.g. Abdulkadiroğlu and Sönmez, 2003) and the matching of college students to college spaces (College Admission Problem, see e.g. Roth and Sotomayor, 1992).

Considering resource sharing platforms, especially ones with a social setting such as Social Clouds, the use of non-monetary mechanisms can be observed frequently. Examples are the use of credits and trophies on nanoHUB.org[11] and myExperiment.org[12] (called "nanos" and "reputation points", respectively) for sharing research artifacts as well as learning and teaching materials; P2P platforms where users can exchange electronic goods; or storage-sharing platforms where users can supply and use storage provided by other users without monetary compensation (see e.g. Seuken et al., 2010). In these platforms, participants (which can still be distinguished into resource providers and resource consumers) share and consume available resources without the immediate goal of monetary gain. A characteristic of such platforms is that in contrast to mostly anonymous platforms, users of such "social" platforms often value non-monetary incentives (such as reciprocity, altruism, etc.) higher than purely monetary remuneration when it comes to the sharing and exchange of resources (Bénabou and Tirole, 2006; Fehr and Schmidt, 2006).

In such a non-monetary setting, the theory of *two-sided matching* is well established as a means to allocate resources. The key aspect of two-sided matching is that users specify a preference ranking with whom they want to share and exchange their resources. Based on these preferences, a matching mechanism tries to find an allocation with certain properties (Roth, 2008). Depending on the structure of the preferences and the desired properties, several algorithms have been developed to compute such an allocation. However, there are some drawbacks with existing solutions: 1) there are scenarios for which the calculation of an optimal solution is NP-hard and no suitable approximation algorithms with a guaranteed quality bound exist (Halldórsson et al., 2003). 2) Existing algorithms are all developed for a given scenario and a certain combination of goals, thereby lacking the flexibility of being applicable in different scenarios. 3) Existing algorithms concentrate

[11] `http://nanohub.org` – last accessed May 2014
[12] `http://www.myexperiment.org` – last accessed May 2014

on achieving a *stable* solution, which infers that no user can be better of by deviating from the given solution; due to an impossibility results (Roth, 1982), the corresponding mechanisms are not *incentive compatible,* and the effects of strategic manipulation have to be considered. 4) Two-sided matching algorithms are often considered in a static context, where the allocation is calculated in a batch-like procedure, which does not reflect potential dynamics of a real platform such as a Social Cloud.

This is the focus of the second part of the thesis, which aims to address these drawbacks and considers algorithms for preference-based resource allocation[13] as a means to combine non-monetary mechanisms with the advantages of centralized, market-based allocation:

RESEARCH QUESTION 2 ≺RESOURCE ALLOCATION≻ *Which types of algorithms provide a good combination of performance, flexibility, and strategic properties for preference-based resource allocation?*

As the allocation mechanism should have a certain flexibility to adjust to different goals and scenarios, heuristics have been suggested to calculate allocations in preference-based matching (Vien and Chung, 2006; Kimbrough and Kuo, 2010). This thesis follows a similar direction and extends this work by developing heuristics that have the ability to handle a variety of preference structures and goal combinations. As there might be a trade-off between the flexibility and the achieved solution quality of such heuristics compared to existing algorithms, the performance of the heuristics is the focus of research question 2.1:

RESEARCH QUESTION 2.1 ≺ PERFORMANCE OF HEURISTICS ≻ *What is the performance of heuristics for preference-based matching compared to existing matching mechanisms?*

Chapter 5 compares the performance of different algorithms and heuristics in several standard scenarios. As heuristics allow for more flexibility over existing algorithms with respect to goals and preference structures, an equal or improved performance with respect to certain goal metrics would show the general applica-

[13]In the remainder of the thesis, preference-based matching and two-sided matching will be used interchangeably.

bility of said heuristics and provide a valuable contribution to the field of two-sided matching.

Besides pure performance and solution quality characteristics, there are additional considerations that are of practical interest in preference-based matching. One such aspect is the consideration of strategic behavior in a market. From the point of view of participating users, the question of how to interact with the matching mechanism arises. As the mechanisms calculate solutions based on the preference rankings that are provided by the users, they might have an incentive to manipulate their submitted preferences in the hope to benefit from manipulation. In fact, the impossibility result of Roth (1982) shows that for the standard set of goals in preference-based matching (if a stable solution has to be guaranteed), there can be no incentive compatible mechanism, i.e., for which it is the best strategy for all users to submit their true, non-manipulated preferences. This also applies for heuristics if a stable solution is of interest.

In general, the manipulation of the submitted preferences can have several effects. Besides the direct effects on the manipulating as well as non-manipulating users, which can either gain or lose by such manipulation, it might also change the quality of the solution with respect to the true preferences of users. For example, an optimal solution with respect to the submitted preferences might not be optimal under the true, non-manipulated preferences, and the effects of manipulation on solution quality is a largely unexplored field. Hence, the focus of research question 2.2 is the potential effects of such manipulation:

RESEARCH QUESTION 2.2 ≺INCENTIVE COMPATIBILITY≻ *What are the effects of preference manipulation on the manipulating users, non-manipulating users, and the solution quality?*

Chapter 6.1 studies the effects of manipulation for considered preference-based matching algorithms. In addition, it also considers the robustness of certain algorithms against potential manipulation. This aspect is particularly interesting if participating users want to learn a beneficial manipulation strategy. Both the likelihood of a successful manipulation, as well as the average gains from manipulation are considered.

Besides flexibility, performance, and incentive compatibility, the fourth aspect that needs to be addressed is the general setting of the matching calculation. Preference-based matching mechanisms usually assume that the allocation is calculated in a batch-like procedure, where participants submit their preferences to the algorithm once and are matched according to the resulting solution. In realistic settings, however, the scenario can be more complex. Instead of being matched only once, or at certain time intervals, requesting and providing users might join and leave the system dynamically. This creates situations where new supply and demand arrives in between the allocation time-slots. Research question 2.3 targets this issue and studies options to deal with such dynamic supply and demand.

RESEARCH QUESTION 2.3 ≺DYNAMIC ALLOCATIONS≻ *What are options to allocate dynamic supply and demand, taking into account potential existing matches?*

Two straightforward strategies to deal with such dynamic supply and demand are either recalculating the entire solution (taking into account the currently matched users), or leaving the new supply and demand unallocated until the next allocation time-slot. The first option might not always be possible for time- or technical constraints, e.g., if the calculation of the solution takes too long or breaking up matched pairs is technically not feasible. The latter option, however, will potentially leave a considerable amount of available resource idle. Therefore, research question 2.3 studies the effects of such dynamic supply and demand on preference-based resource allocation. Besides the two mentioned strategies, two heuristics are considered as an approach to match otherwise idle resources without breaking up currently matched users.

1.3. Structure of the Thesis

The research outline as described in the previous section reflects the structure of the thesis, which is comprised of four parts. Part I introduces the necessary concepts as well as the main use case and methodology which is applied in the subsequent parts. The design of participation incentive schemes is the focus of Part II, and Part III considers mechanisms for resource allocation. Part IV concludes the thesis and highlights future research directions.

A high-level illustration of this thesis' structure is shown in Figure 1.1. Chapter 2 lays the foundation for the subsequent chapters by establishing the common terminology and main concepts used throughout the thesis. In particular, Section 2.1

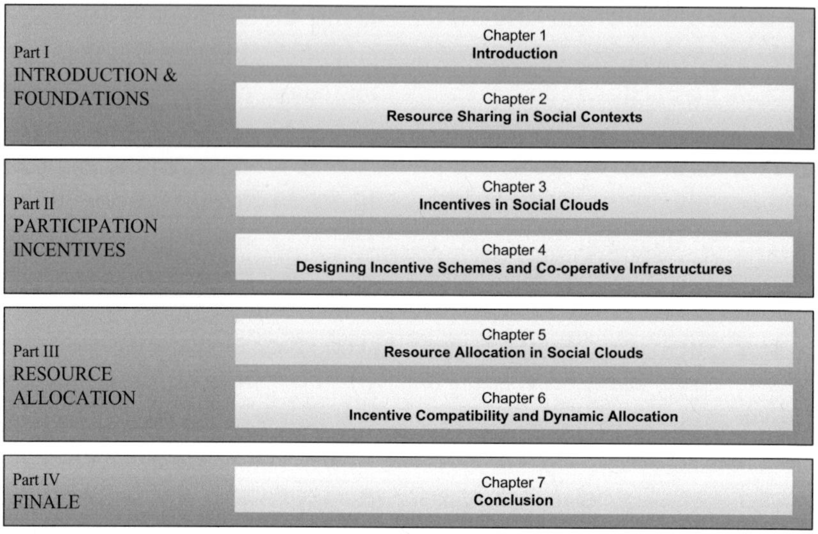

Figure 1.1.: Structure of this Thesis

describes the concept of Social Clouds and provides details on an implemented prototype thereof. Section 2.2 discusses a simulation-based approach and the corresponding simulation tool as main methodology in this thesis. The previously mentioned challenges of user participation and resource allocation are further detailed in Section 2.3.

Building on these foundations, Chapter 3 tackles the challenge of providing incentives for user participation by identifying different stages of user interaction and participation with the platform. Additionally, the results of a web-based survey on the importance of different incentives within these stages and their dependency on factors such as user type are presented. Chapter 4 consists of two case studies: the first case study investigates the effects of a participation constraint on system and user behavior and the dependency on user characteristics. The co-operative provisioning of infrastructure resources is focus of the second case study, which compares different contribution schemes and their effectiveness based on the distribution assumptions of user types.

In the third part of this thesis, Chapter 5 considers preference-based matching mechanisms as a means to allocate resources in Social Clouds. Starting with an outline of the main concepts and existing algorithms, it describes the proposed heuristics and evaluates their performance for different preference structures and goal combinations. Chapter 6 presents two additional topics of interest in the area of preference-based matching. First, the effects of strategic manipulation of preferences are evaluated and discussed. Second, approaches to handle dynamic allocations are considered. Chapter 7 summarizes the key contributions of this thesis, provides an outlook on future research and highlights complementary topics.

1.4. Research Development

Parts of this thesis have been presented and published at four peer-reviewed international conferences and workshops, as well as an international journal. This section provides an overview of the published material and simultaneously outlines the development of the work and the corresponding refinement and extension steps.

The identification and discussion of different stages of user participation during their interaction with a Social Cloud (Section 3.2) was presented in a workshop at the 11th IEEE/ACM International Symposium on Cluster, Cloud and Grid Computing (CCGrid 2011) (Haas et al., 2011).

The simulation tool described in Section 2.2 which is used to facilitate the simulation-based evaluations in the thesis, along with the case study about the introduction of a participation constraint and the corresponding evaluation (Section 4.2) were presented at the 8th IEEE International Conference on eScience (eScience 2012) (Haas et al., 2012). The description and implementation of the simulation tool was extended to capture additional scenarios, such as simulating preference-based resource exchanges. Furthermore, the case study as presented in Section 4.2 additionally considers the comparison of different user type distributions. The case study on co-operative infrastructures was presented at the 48th Hawaii International Conference on System Sciences (HICSS'48) (Haas et al., 2013). The corresponding Section 4.3 encompasses an additional contribution scheme that was added as an extension for this thesis.

Considering the evaluation of preference-based matching heuristics and their comparison to existing algorithms, the results for the first scenario (Section 5.4.3) were presented at the 10th International Conference on Economics of Grids, Clouds, Systems and Services (GECON 2013) (Haas et al., 2013). The evaluation was then extended to cover additional scenarios as well. The Social Compute Cloud prototype as described in Section 2.1.4, as well as the consideration of dynamic allocations in the context of preference-based matching in Section 6.2, was published in IEEE Transactions on Services Computing (Caton et al., 2014).

Chapter 2.

Resource Sharing in Social Contexts

"The recent changes in our economic landscape have notably exposed and intensified a phenomenon: an explosion in sharing, bartering, lending, trading, renting, gifting, and swapping."

(Botsman and Rogers, 2010)

THIS chapter introduces the concepts and methodologies used throughout the thesis. Section 2.1 introduces the concept of Social Clouds, a resource sharing paradigm in which resources are shared between members of existing social networks. The Social Cloud concept will be used as unified use case throughout the thesis. Additionally, a prototype of a Social Cloud for computational resources, along with its implementation details, is presented. In conjunction with the prototype, a simulation tool was developed as complementary methodology to study various aspects of a Social Cloud. Section 2.2 describes the simulation approach and corresponding tool that is used as the main evaluation methodology in this thesis. Applying literature reviews and a comparison to similar systems, Section 2.3 discusses two coordination challenges that have to be addressed in the design of such platforms. In particular the consideration of user participation incentives, as well as the type of (economic) resource allocation mechanisms, are identified as the key challenges which this work addresses. Finally, Section 2.4 closes the chapter with a summary of the described concepts.

2.1. The Concept of Social Clouds

This section describes the concept of a Social Cloud (Chard et al., 2010, 2012) as an example of a social resource sharing platform. It will be used as a unifying use case that shows the practical application of the mentioned topics and will serve as an example sharing platform throughout this work.[1] Section 2.1.1 defines the concept, describes the components and discusses use cases for the application of a Social Cloud. Section 2.1.2 provides an overview of related concepts, and Section 2.1.3 discusses challenges in the design and construction of a Social Cloud. Section 2.1.4 focuses on a prototype system of a Social Compute Cloud and provides implementation details.

2.1.1. Definitions

A Social Cloud is a dynamic environment through which (new) Cloud-like provisioning scenarios can be established based upon the implicit levels of trust that transcend inter-personal relationships digitally encoded within a social network (Chard et al., 2010, 2012). The concept of a Social Cloud is defined as:

Definition 1 (**Social Cloud, Chard et al., 2012**). *A Social Cloud is a resource and service sharing framework utilizing relationships established between members of a social network.*

The vision of a Social Cloud is motivated by the need of individuals or groups to access specific resources they are not in possession of, but that can be made available by connected peers. In simple words, Social Clouds use social networks as mechanisms for collaboration and resource sharing. Moreover, Social Clouds rely on social incentives to motivate sharing and non-malicious behavior, as users leverage their existing networks to share capabilities and resources (Haas et al., 2013). A Social Cloud is a form of Community Cloud[2], as the resources are owned, provided and consumed by members of a social community.

[1] Therefore, the terms "platform" and "Social Cloud" are used interchangeably.

[2] NIST defines a Community Cloud as: "[...] The cloud infrastructure is provisioned for exclusive use by a specific community of consumers from organizations that have shared concerns (e.g., mission, security requirements, policy, and compliance considerations)." (Mell and Grance, 2011)

There are several characteristics that distinguish a Social Cloud from other computing approaches. In contrast to Volunteer Computing (VC), which is defined as "a form of distributed computing in which the general public volunteers processing and storage resources to computing projects" (Anderson and Fedak, 2006, p.73), users in a Social Cloud cannot only donate but also consume different resources in exchange for their resource provision. Furthermore, contrary to traditional P2P resource sharing which "allow a distributed community of users to share resources in the form of information, digital content, storage space, or processing capacity" (Krishnan et al., 2006, p.32), the resources are provided by users with direct or indirect relationships in a social network. Hence, resources are no longer offered by anonymous providers but by socially connected users, where the existing relationships can be used to deduce some form of bi-lateral association or understanding of trust. Furthermore, it is also different from the definition of Cloud Computing:

Definition 2 (**Cloud Computing, Mell and Grance 2011**). *Cloud computing is a model for enabling ubiquitous, convenient, on-demand network access to a shared pool of configurable computing resources (e.g., networks, servers, storage, applications, and services) that can be rapidly provisioned and released with minimal management effort or service provider interaction.*

Whereas the NIST definition of Cloud Computing focuses on technical aspects such as on-demand access, rapid provisioning and configurable resources, the Social Cloud paradigm focuses on the utilization of the underlying social network for the sharing of a pool of resources. Common aspects between the definitions are having such a pool of different types of resources and services, and having (ideally) low management effort and interaction.

Another key aspect in the definition of a Social Cloud is the existence of an underlying social network between the users. This is crucial as it has implications about which mechanisms are used to facilitate resource sharing in such a system. As Granovetter (2005) shows, social networks have an impact on market outcomes, and trust emerges on the basis of a social network. Hence, the design of a Social Cloud has to take the social network of users into account. This is elaborated in more detail in Chapter 3.

Figure 2.1 shows an example SC where users provide (potentially heterogeneous) resources, and a clearinghouse determines the allocation of supply and demand.

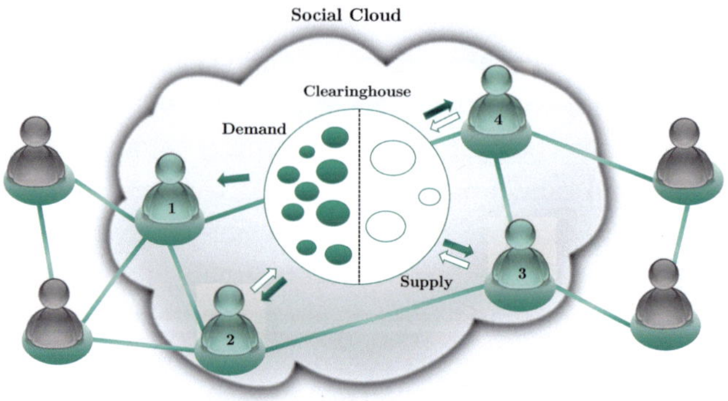

Figure 2.1.: Example of a Social Cloud

The connections between users show the underlying social network, and the numbered users indicate that these users are part of the Social Cloud. Note that not only the resources, but also the types of users, in a SC can be heterogeneous. Different types of users have different resource capabilities and requirements. The potential heterogeneity of users and resources also affects the interaction of the users with the SC clearinghouse as well as the appropriate choice of a market mechanism (which is not restricted to preference-based matching for general Social Clouds).

Architecture

The general technical architecture of a Social Cloud is shown in Figure 2.2. The main component is the Social Cloud platform, which consists of several modules. The Clearinghouse module includes the allocation mechanisms and relevant corresponding social and economic protocols (e.g., social service level agreements that provide a formal description of the exchanges). The Platform Manager provides administration functionality and is responsible for the tasks such as user management. Several databases are required to store relevant data about user resources, allocations, and user preferences. For the technical facilitation, a Resource Middleware component enables the execution of the Social Cloud platform on computational resources. The Social Cloud platform has two main interfaces. The socio-technical adapter enables the extraction of social network data, and the user interface defines how users communicate with the platform, e.g., through the specification of sharing preferences.

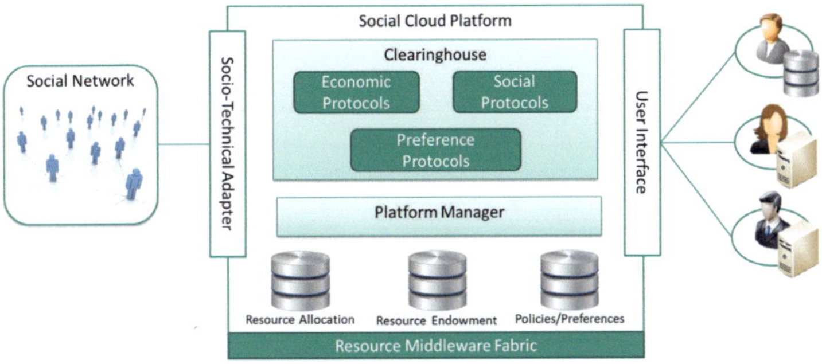

Figure 2.2.: General Architecture of a Social Cloud

Application Scenarios for Social Clouds

The definition of a Social Cloud is flexible and allows for a range of potential application scenarios. Based on Chard et al. (2012), the following list describes the potential scenarios.

Social Storage Cloud In this scenario, users of a Social Cloud share storage space, for example to backup data, share pictures, and store large data sets. Given certain security requirements, this scenario is perhaps the simplest to implement. A prototype of a Social Storage Cloud implemented as a Facebook application has already been developed in (Chard et al., 2012).

Social Compute Cloud Instead of storage, (virtualized) computational resources are shared in this scenario, which targets the potentially large un- or underused computing potential of personal computers. Such computational power can be used by other members of the Social Cloud, or provided to scientific communities for complex computations. This scenario is considered by John et al. (2011), who study different incentive schemes to encourage contribution to such public research projects. A prototype of a Social Compute Cloud is also presented in detail in Section 2.1.4.

Social Collaboration Cloud The mentioned platforms myExperiment.org and nanoHUB.org are examples for this type of scenario. Here, members of a Social Cloud participate due to some common collaborative task or goal, for example the sharing of knowledge artifacts within a scientific community. A potential use case is the sharing of large datasets within a scientific community using a social content delivery network (Chard et al., 2012).

Social Cloud for Public Research Closely related to Social Compute Clouds, this scenario considers Social Clouds for providing computational resources to Volunteer Computing-like projects. Specifically, not only could the provided computational power due to unutilized resources be potentially increased dramatically, research projects can also be propagated through the network to friends and other members in- and outside the network, thereby increasing the potential user base (Thaufeeg et al., 2011).

Social Enterprise Cloud In contrast to the previous scenarios which focus on private users, enterprises can also leverage specialized Social Clouds through their social networks. This would allow them to gain access to additional computational resources, and at the same time increase the awareness of the enterprise/company with participating users.

Trust

One of the fundamental assumptions of the Social Cloud paradigm is the existence of a certain level of trust between the members of the social network. As mentioned in Section 1.1, however, different scientific disciplines have their own version of what constitutes the notion of trust, which makes an interdisciplinary focus necessary. For this reason, Caton et al. (2012) define trust in the context of a Social Cloud from the perspectives of economics, computer science and sociology.

Definition 3 (**Trust in Social Cloud, Caton et al., 2012**). *Trust is a positive expectation or assumption on future outcomes that results from proven contextualized personal interaction histories corresponding to conventional relationship types and can be leveraged by formal and informal rules and conventions within a Social Cloud to facilitate as well as influence the scope of collaborative exchange.*

There are several important concepts addressed by this definition. The notion of positive expectation on future outcomes is related to economic aspects such as expected reciprocity, where another user is trusted to return a favor in the future. *Proven contextualized personal interaction* means that the specific trust depends on the prior social context of previous interactions, e.g., indicated by the relationship type between the users. *Formal and informal rules and conventions* is another relevant aspect which indicates that trust can be facilitated by explicit agreements (e.g., terms of collaboration), or informal norms that are enforced by the community.

2.1.2. Related Concepts

There are several concepts similar to a Social Cloud as previously defined. Using the same term, Mohaisen et al. (2011) propose a paradigm for trustworthy distributed computing on social networks. In the context of federated Cloud systems, Elnaffar et al. (2013) describe a model of a social network where several cloud systems form different types of relationships with other clouds. Kourtellis et al. (2010) present a P2P based service ("Prometheus") that collects social information from different sources and allows social-based mapping and to draw social inferences. Kourtellis (2012) argue that the vast amount of information present in social network (platforms) can be leveraged to build socially-aware distributed systems with various application scenarios, increasing aspects such as system response time.

From a technical point of view, several distributed computing approaches such as ASPEN (Curry et al., 2008) and PolarGrid (Guo et al., 2009) leverage information of social networks in their applications. OpenSocial (Häsel, 2011) provides interface specifications that allow access to social network information in order to create social web applications. P2P clouds (Ranjan et al., 2010) aim to create (private) clouds on the basis of peer connections, yet do not have the same assumptions about the underlying social network and the resulting trust between members as in the concept of Social Clouds.

In particular (academic) domains, social networks are also used to build and coordinate special-interest communities. Prominent examples are the previously mentioned platforms myExperiment (De Roure et al., 2009) and nanoHUB.org (Klimeck et al., 2008). myExperiment allows users to share (scientific) workflows, in order to determine commonalities and increase the dissemination of popular workflows (e.g., for scientific experiments) to the scientific community. nanoHUB.org is a large, world-wide community of researchers in nanotechnology, and users can share teaching and research material among each other.

Another related field is Volunteer Computing through systems like BOINC (Anderson, 2004). In projects such as SETI@home (Anderson et al., 2002), users donate computational resources to scientific projects which use the donated resources to run extensive calculations. In contrast to Social Clouds, Volunteer Computing is inherently unilateral as the concept does not involve the notion of bilateral exchanges. Furthermore, the participating users do not have to belong to the same social network and can remain completely anonymous, and social connections and relationships are not leveraged.

A prominent example of sharing computational resources is the exchange of electronic storage between participating users. Examples of such a scenario are platforms like FriendStore[3] (Tran et al., 2008), F2Box (Gracia-Tinedo et al., 2012), symform[4], P2P storage sharing (Seuken et al., 2010), or a Social Storage Cloud (Chard et al., 2010) in which registered users can provide free storage space on their own machines for data backup and other purposes to other users. In return, the contributing users are able to use the storage of other users for their own backup. Such systems are alternatives to third-party storage and backup solutions. Security measures such as encryption algorithms or sandboxing technologies are important in this scenario to avoid unauthorized access of one's data on other users' machines, as well as protecting storage-providing users from malicious data.

2.1.3. Design Challenges

There are many challenges in the construction of a Social Cloud that need to be carefully considered. The following discussion considers four key challenges: the technical facilitation of the cloud platform, the inclusion as well as interpretation of social (network) structures, the design and implementation of appropriate socio-economic models for the facilitation of exchange, and the sustainability of the platform infrastructure.

Technical Facilitation To facilitate the exchange of resources, i.e., both provision and consumption, the necessary technical infrastructure has to be provided. This includes the handling of different types of users (e.g., mobile users with non-static IP addresses) and resources (e.g., computational storage and Virtual Machines). In addition, even though the Social Cloud paradigm assumes a certain level of trust between users, certain security mechanisms such as sandboxing are required. Such security mechanisms aim at protecting resources from potentially malicious users and also protect user applications from potentially malicious resources. These aspects can be partially addressed by virtualization, which also enables the support for different operating systems.

[3] `http://friendstore.news.cs.nyu.edu/` – last accessed May 2014
[4] `http://www.symform.com/` – last accessed May 2014

Leveraging Social Structures Users of a Social Cloud are connected through an underlying social network. To utilize the underlying social network structure for resource sharing, Social Clouds rely on users to allow access to their social network and trust the platform with the corresponding data. The data that is accessible on many social network platforms, which often utilize a binary representation of a "friend" relationship, might not be adequate to capture the multitude and complexity of the specific relationships. Besides the relationship role, other factors such as (perceived) competency, the exchange context (i.e., being a provider or consumer), and trust also influence the relationships between users. Hence, a Social Cloud should provide the ability to augment standard social graphs with additional (meta-)data, which can then be used to model relationships more adequately and to potentially extract preferences of users towards one another.

Socio-economic Model The applied resource sharing mechanisms in Social Clouds have to consider the application scenario as well as the relationships between users. Depending on the scenario, different mechanisms might be suitable, and the Social Cloud should provide the necessary functionality to enable the respective mechanism. In non-enterprise settings, where the focus is on sharing rather than sale of resources, non-monetary mechanisms (in particular, preference-based matching) promise to align the social setting of the platform with the advantages of market-based allocation of resources such as allocation efficiency and stability.[5] Congruent to the previous challenge, a Social Cloud has to provide the means for users to express their sharing preferences.

Platform Facilitation A Social Cloud needs certain computational resources to provide a basic set of functionality (such as user management) and to facilitate the actual resource exchange. The use of third-party resources to host the platform would require a revenue model (or similar) to cover the expenses, and might contradict the concept of voluntary resource sharing. An option to alleviate this challenge is to follow a co-operative model which implies that users provide resources not only for sharing, but also to support the platform itself in the form of infrastructure resources. Such a co-operative infrastructure model is introduced in Chapter 4.3.

[5]This is the focus of the second part of this thesis. Chapters 5 and 6 introduce and evaluate concepts of preference-based sharing.

2.1.4. A Prototype Social Compute Cloud

In order to demonstrate the usefulness and viability of a Social Cloud, this section describes a prototype of a Social Compute Cloud in which participating users can share virtualized computing resources with friends of their social network (Caton et al., 2014). A Social Compute Cloud is designed to enable access to compute capabilities in the form of Virtual Machines provided by socially connected peers, and users are able to execute programs on these contributed, virtualized resources.

Architecture and Implementation of a Social Compute Cloud

Building on the previously described general architecture of a Social Cloud (Figure 2.2), and addressing the challenges mentioned before, Figure 2.3 shows the architecture of the Social Compute Cloud and its core components. The Social Cloud Platform provides the technical implementation details which are needed to facilitate the resource exchange. To enable the actual sharing of virtualized resources, the Seattle framework is used as resource middleware component as it largely provides the needed functionality such as sandboxing (Cappos et al., 2009; Zhuang et al., 2013). Seattle is an open source P2P platform designed to create a distributed testbed to easily create distributed applications. It was chosen as the basis for the implementation due to its lightweight virtualization middleware that is used to enable application execution on contributed resources, and its extensible clearinghouse model.

Considering the socio-economic model that governs the resource exchange, a social clearinghouse encompasses the implementation of preference-based matching algorithms, as well as a module to capture the user preferences. A new social clearinghouse that leverages these connections is implemented as the original Seattle clearinghouse did not consider social connections and did not provide the functionality for preference-based allocation of resources. The implemented algorithms are the matching algorithms described in Chapter 5. For the specification of sharing preferences, the implementation provides an interface that allows users to specify a preference rank for each user in their social network that is also part of the Social Compute Cloud. Given the outcome of the matching algorithms, users are assigned to contributed and available resources. For the access to underlying social network, the platform uses a Facebook application to access a users' social network data (as well as providing a means for authentication). The platform also provides databases to store social network data as well as data about the provided and requested resources.

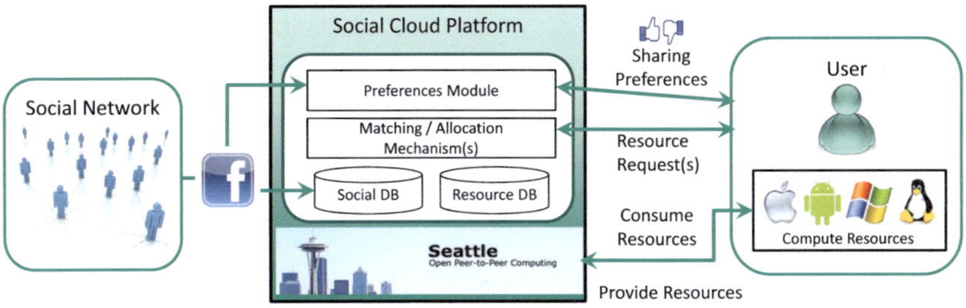

Figure 2.3.: Architecture of a Social Compute Cloud and its Core Components

The prototype has been evaluated in a proof-of-concept study in (Caton et al., 2014). As a next step, the prototype should be studied as a test system with real users. The feedback of the deployed system would then serve to potentially improve the implementation and design of the Social Compute Cloud, and also to get data about how users interact with the system and other users. Such feedback can provide additional insights in actual user behavior, for example considering their incentives to participate on the platform and the process how they specify their preferences.

A complementary methodology to study Social Clouds is to use a simulation-based approach. For this reason, the next section introduces a simulation tool that is used throughout the thesis to model, simulate and analyze aspects of a Social Cloud.

2.2. Simulating Social Clouds

As Social Cloud scenarios begin to become more commonplace, it is important to understand the intricacies of the corresponding exchange system. A primary example is the behavior of the system as a product of its users' actions and interactions, as these define how the system performs. This is important, as resource exchange systems naturally include a high level of complexity stemming from the dependencies between the decisions of single users and the behavior of their peers and extended peers, i.e. friends of friends. This challenge is aggravated by the different relationship types that can exist between users and the social context that is attributed to a given relationship type by a user. These contexts can also be different between users, but ultimately mean that a user's behavior strongly depends on the relationship types that exist within their resource sharing community and the users they interact with. Therefore, in order to adequately design Social Clouds, many experiments on user behavior and user management are required. Similarly, in the wider context of computationally supported science (e-Science), a tool that can help in the design and study of resource exchange communities will aid in the understanding of their dynamics, but also in the design of new mechanisms to improve different parts of their performance.

Given the social setting and myriad of potential user profiles for Social Cloud platforms, studying system behavior with a purely analytical approach may be inflexible or even unsolvable. Instead, a simulation environment can be a suitable methodology to study the behavior of complex systems. Doing so will allow not only the testing and analysis of new aspects of these systems. It also enables the investigation of which aspects of underlying social circles and communities are important in their design, and the identification of methods to capitalize upon these observations. A key opportunity that such a simulation tool opens up is the ability to merge observations of exchange situations from existing systems or lab experiments of usage. A simulation tool can help not only in the design of such systems, but also in identifying and pre-screening case studies and experiments to observe real users as well as further analysis of completed user experiments to test and form hypotheses about resource exchange in social settings. In other words, a simulation approach is a useful complementary methodology in the study of dynamic, complex resource sharing systems.

This section provides details of the simulation tool (Social Exchange Simulator (SES)) developed for this task. Application scenarios are described in Section 2.2.1, and Section 2.2.2 provides a discussion of related work. Finally, Section 2.2.3 describes the architecture of the simulation tool. The main parts of this section have been published in (Haas et al., 2012).

2.2.1. Purpose and Potential Applications

In the context of engineering, testing and introducing Social Cloud, the designer has to anticipate the behavior of the platform under certain conditions. Several standard methodologies are applicable for this task in general.

1. Theoretical analysis of system properties.
2. Prototypical implementation and simulation of expected system behavior.
3. Empirical observation of user and system behavior.

The simulator targets the second methodology: based on certain assumptions about user intelligence, behavior and certain system properties, it is able to study dynamic system behavior and, for example, the predicted response of users to certain changes on the system rules. It is necessary to emphasize that such a simulation tool derives its value by being complementary to other research methodologies. It cannot substitute the insights a system designer can get from using the other methodologies, but rather provide additional, complementary results that are helpful in the design of a resource sharing platform. For example, the simulation tool can be used in a system that is complex enough that analytical predictions are not feasible and at the same time is not implemented, leading to a lack of data about actual user behavior.

In the context of designing a Social Cloud, there are various apparent use cases how simulation can benefit the development process. In particular, the SES can be used to study following sample questions:

Incentive Schemes Do certain incentive schemes achieve more sharing activities? What attributes of an incentive scheme are most useful for certain user types? How does an incentive scheme have to be adjusted to reflect a change of user types in the system?

User Types and Network Structure What is the effect of user availability on system performance? How is the exchange affected by different utility function distributions of users (e.g., having more selfish users)? How does the network structure (e.g., random versus small-world structures) affect collaboration? How many links between users have to exist before the exchange activities are effective?

Co-operative Infrastructures Is it feasible to let the users of a Social Cloud platform provide its infrastructure? What is the influence of the user characteristics, such as their availability or inherent willingness to share, on the feasibility of this approach?

Resource Exchange and User Strategies How do users select if and how much they exchange? What effects have different exchange mechanism on the resource allocation? What is the effect of different learning strategies on the resulting exchange behavior?

Resource Allocation Mechanisms Given a certain supply and demand of resources, which allocation mechanisms yield the best outcome considering certain market objectives? What are the effects of different preference structures on the performance of the considered algorithms?

In particular, several of the mentioned scenarios are also applied in this thesis. Chapter 4 presents case studies concerning the design of incentive schemes and co-operative infrastructures, and Chapters 5 and 6 apply the SES in the context of allocation mechanisms.

2.2.2. Requirements and Related Tools

The incorporation of aspects such as social network connections and relationship types into resource exchange simulation yields specific requirements that the SES has to address. Therefore, this section first defines the requirements for such a scenario. The second part of the section compares relevant existing simulation tools and identifies why it is necessary to create a new simulator that is suitable for social resource sharing settings.

Requirements for the Social Exchange Simulator

In order to facilitate the engineering process of Social Clouds, the SES has to be able to correctly model and adequately represent such a system. This involves the representation of the users, their incentives, behavior, and relationships to other users; the underlying network with its (potentially dynamic) topology; and the interaction and resource exchange mechanisms that exist within the system.

Flexible User Model The scenarios of social resource sharing can be diverse, and this needs to be reflected by the user model. In some cases, a user model might include specific incentives for certain actions, in other cases characteristics such as user availability might be an important design aspect of the simulation. Hence, rather than predefining a certain type of user model, the

SES should allow for a flexible specification and at the same time provide the necessary classes to facilitate the modeling of various user characteristics (such as availability).

Integration of Social Network Topologies The topology of an underlying social network, and especially the position that a user has in the network, can have important consequences on the behavior of both the system and the user. For example, the importance of a user in a network can depend on the respective position, such as being a link between different groups that enables the dissemination of information. Another example is the implementation of different feedback mechanisms, which can also be affected by the specific network structure. For these reasons, the SES has to be able to model different network topologies (such as random, small world, etc.), and compute certain metrics based on the user position in the network.

Representation of Relationship Types As discussed earlier, relationships between users can be of various types, and the types might affect the interaction between them (and thereby affect the entire system). The relationship type, for example, can affect the respective preference for sharing specific resources with another person, or can influence the level of trust towards that person. Therefore, the SES should provide the means to model various types of relationships to study how specific types (or distribution of types) can affect the interactions between users.

Implementation of Different Resource Exchange Mechanisms The exchange of resources between users can be facilitated by many different mechanisms. The simulator has to either model or provide the means to incorporate different types of resource exchange mechanisms and allow for a seamless integration and switch of the used exchange mechanism. In particular, due to the focus on preference-based matching, it has to provide the means to compute allocations based on two-sided matching algorithms.

Comparison to Other Simulation Tools

The design and development of simulators as general-purpose tools has been prevalent in many adjunct areas. This section briefly outlines the most relevant work for the SES in general.

Simulation tools can be broadly divided into two categories:

1. *Multi-purpose simulation tools* that provide the tools and means to implement custom simulations.
2. *Specialized tools* that focus on certain use cases and provide specialized functionalities for these use cases.

Table 2.1.: Comparison of Simulation Tools

Tool	Flexible User Model	Social Network Integration	Relationship Type Specification	Resource Exchange Mechanisms
Multi-Purpose Simulation Tools				
Repast	●	◕	◑	○
NetLogo	●	◕	◑	○
MASON	●	◑	◑	○
Specialized Simulators				
GridSim	◑	○	○	●
SimGrid	◑	○	○	◕
CloudSim	◔	○	○	●
PeerSim	◕	◕	○	○
OverSim	◔	◔	○	○
SIGVerse	◑	○	○	○
This Approach				
Haas et al. (2012)	●	●	●	●

Table 2.1 shows an overview of the related simulation tools according to their category, and the degree to which they fulfill the previously introduced requirements. The tools of the first category all belong to the group of general-purpose simulation tools. Due to having the best match with respect to the mentioned requirements, the tools RepastSimphony[6], NetLogo[7], and MASON[8] are selected for comparison. These tools represent a system as collection of (often intelligent) agents with certain policies, and the system behavior is determined by the interactions between these agents. Most related simulation tools provide functionality for modeling networks, graphs, and interactions between users. The user model is usually quite flexible and can be extended by adding custom extensions. However, whereas Repast-Simphony, NetLogo, and MASON provide built-in social network functionalities (which are, however, restricted to the provided libraries and not easily extendable), the inclusion of relationship types for interactions is only partially supported and would need extensive customization. Furthermore, none of the three mentioned

[6] `http://repast.sourceforge.net/` – last accessed May 2014
[7] `http://ccl.northwestern.edu/netlogo/` – last accessed May 2014
[8] `http://cs.gmu.edu/~eclab/projects/mason/` – last accessed May 2014

simulation tools has built-in support for resource allocation mechanisms, which are a central requirement.

The second category includes specialized simulators such as GridSim (Buyya and Murshed, 2002), SimGrid (Casanova et al., 2008), and CloudSim (Calheiros et al., 2011) for the study of complex Grid and Cloud Systems, respectively. These simulators provide tools specifically catered for the needs to represent complex Grid and Cloud system, including resource allocation mechanisms. The extension of the user model would involve extensive customization in both cases, as this was not the primary purpose of these tools. Unfortunately, neither of these three tools provides support for including social network aspects or the integration of relationship types between users. PeerSim (Montresor and Jelasity, 2009) focuses on simulating (large) P2P systems. It provides modules to define the underlying network topology, yet the user model is not very flexible and resource exchange mechanisms are missing entirely. From a more technical point of view, OverSim (Baumgart et al., 2007) is able to simulate P2P overlay networks, and was developed for the simulation of overlay protocols. Although it provides functionality to model different types of underlying networks, due to the more technical use case it is not very suitable for simulating social exchanges. Furthermore, the tool SIGVerse (Inamura et al., 2010) was developed to model social interactions between humans. However, its focus is more on simulating direct interactions between single humans (or artificial agents), and does not consider resource exchange or underlying network connections.

From a comparison of the technical specifications of the mentioned simulation tools, as presented in Table 2.1, it is apparent that no single simulation tool fulfills all the necessary requirements for the given scenario. Based on this observation, two approaches can be pursued: either the extension and customization of an existing tool, or building a separate simulation tool. As the functionalities provided by existing tools is mostly limited to the included libraries and customization would have to take the dependencies between new and existing libraries into account, the design of a separate simulation tool was considered to be the best decision.

As an agent-based representation is a very natural approach to model social systems, where each user (agent) is assumed to have a certain level of intelligence, the principle of agent-based simulation is adopted for the SES. Using existing libraries for social network integration, it provides its own libraries to model different relationship types and resource exchange mechanisms, and is thus suited for addressing the design challenges for a simulator for social resource sharing. The next section provides details about the architecture and implementation of the SES.

2.2.3. Architecture

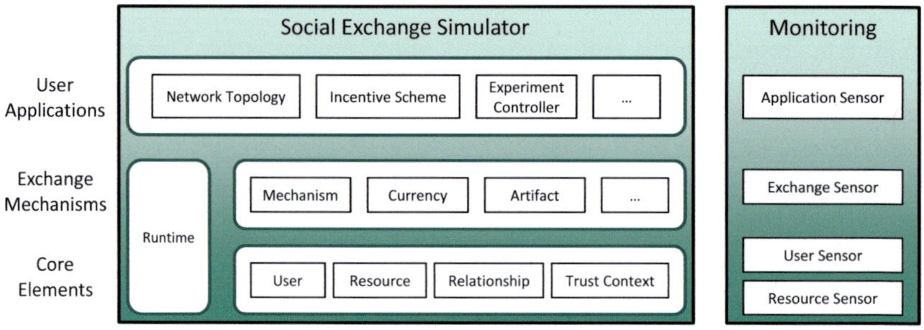

Figure 2.4.: Layered Structure of the Social Exchange Simulator

Similar to comparable simulation tools (e.g. Buyya and Murshed (2002); Calheiros et al. (2011)) the SES is built through a layered structure, as this permits the flexible usage and exchange of single components. The implementation language is Java. Figure 2.4 shows the package structure of the SES. The architecture distinguishes between three layers: the component layer, the exchange layer, and the application layer. In addition, the SES contains monitoring sensors in each layer to observe the state of the exchange network as a whole and its entities, e.g. users, resources, collaboration and exchange mechanisms, etc. Sensors can be triggered by events, such as a transaction on the market.

As a foundation, the component layer contains the core elements that are common to all social resource sharing platforms and necessary for their representation. Examples include the representation of users, resources, different relationship types and the ability to model trust between users. This can be, for example, implemented through a context-specific representation, i.e. considering the form of exchange as well as the real world relationship between participating users. The component layer addresses the requirements for a flexible user model as well as the specification of different relationship types. Above the component layer, the exchange layer targets the requirement for resource exchange mechanisms and defines how the exchange of resources in the platform takes place. Examples include the *Mechanism* for exchange (e.g., auctions, reciprocal exchanges, preference-based matching, donations, and forms of volunteer computing), the *Artifacts* that represent the exchanged resources (single resources, resource bundles, etc.), and the *Currency* of exchange (e.g. virtual/sharing credits, preferences, real world currencies, tokens, etc.). Along with a basic *Runtime* utility class, which manages the component and the exchange layers, these two layers form the base packages of the SES. On top of this base, an application layer contains classes to aid the implementation of applications and scenarios. This includes the implementation of different network types, such as small-world or random networks, in order to address the corresponding requirement. The code base is also not specific for a simulation environment, and has been designed such that it could also support a real world implementation of a Social Cloud through, for example, the inclusion of plugins for social network platforms.

Due to the hierarchical approach, all core and exchange components are designed to be interchangeable in a plug-and-play fashion. This is done via concrete interface definitions (specified in an API) and dynamic class loading of interface implementations by the Runtime. By doing this, users of the tool can flexibly exchange classes to study their dependencies and influences on the system. Key examples here are Mechanisms, which have a crucial impact on the resource exchange, and Users, who define whether exchange will take place and in what forms. However, the general interfaces permit the definition of any Mechanism or User type (e.g. free-rider or altruist, different utility functions, etc.), which are then managed by the Runtime as plug-and-play components.

Throughout the thesis, the simulation tool will be used to address research questions 1.2, 1.3, 2.1, 2.2, and 2.3 stated in Chapter 1. For example, in Chapter 4 the SES is used to study the effects of an incentive scheme on a given system, as well as on different user types. In the second part of the chapter, the feasibility of a co-operative infrastructure approach is studied through the SES. Finally, Chapters 5 and 6 use the SES to compare different algorithms for preference-based resource allocation, their dependency on certain factors and the effects of preference manipulation on the matching outcome.

2.3. Coordination Challenges in Social Clouds

Common to other sharing platforms, Social Clouds involve certain challenges that system designers have to be aware of and that need to be addressed to create a sustainable and successful sharing platform. Specifically, this thesis focuses on two key challenges: the incentivization of users, and the market-based allocation of resources. This section, therefore, introduces and discusses these challenges.

2.3.1. Participation Incentives

The task of identifying and engineering incentives for online-based collaboration and exchange systems is challenging and requires a thorough understanding of the related concepts. Active participation is crucial for the survival of a resource exchange platform, as computer-mediated communities (such as Social Clouds) require a certain minimum number of users (*critical mass*) for sustained activity (Markus, 1987). In contrast to anonymous platforms, Social Clouds can leverage the connections between users to provide incentives for continued participation.

To design participation incentives, it is necessary to understand the motivations for users to participate in the considered system. Motivation theories have been developed that aim at defining, categorizing, and explaining the types of motivations that act as underlying drivers of human behavior in certain situations. This understanding of underlying motivations is crucial for the design of incentives, as participants might have different motivations in different systems. For example, participants might be motivated through monetary payoffs in some systems, whereas more altruistically motivated in other systems, in which case an incentive scheme should concentrate on monetary incentive in the first, and more intrinsic (non-monetary) incentives (such as social comparisons) in the latter case. Thus, this section starts with an overview and categorization of motivation and incentive types. Subsequently, incentive issues in the context of different scientific disciplines are discussed.

Types of Motivation and Incentives

One of the most common categorizations of motivation types differentiates between the reasons that lead to a certain behavior or action. A prominent example, which has been used in a variety of contexts and will also applied in this work, is the classification of intrinsic motivation and extrinsic motivation. According to Deci and Ryan (1985), these two concepts can be described as follows:

- **Intrinsic Motivation** for a certain task means that users find the task itself enjoyable or interesting (often lacking a directly observable, or separable, reward).
- **Extrinsic Motivation** stems from situations where the reason for a certain action is based on a separable outcome, e.g. monetary gain.

Although this coarse distinction of intrinsic and extrinsic motivation is broadly used in the literature, it is often extended to include sub-types of motivation within the two categories. In contrast to the distinction of extrinsic and intrinsic motivations, the classification of sub-types of motivation and incentives into the two categories is not as clear and still subject to debate. Additionally, the meaning of different sub-types might differ between different disciplines and authors. For example, Ryan and Deci (2000) distinguish between four different types of extrinsic motivations depending on the "perceived locus of causality", i.e., based on the perception of where the motivation emanates from. To provide an overview of the motivation types that are most relevant for this work, Table 2.2 shows several sub-types and the their explanations.[9]

Table 2.2.: Overview of Incentive Classification and Types

Classification	Incentive Type	Sample Authors
Intrinsic	Altruism	Clary et al. (1998)
	Fun, Enjoyment	Deci and Ryan (1985); Nov (2007)
	Ideology	Hars and Ou (2001); Lakhani and Wolf (2005); Nov (2007)
	Interest, Curiosity	Ryan and Deci (2000); Bishop (2007)
	Exchange of Knowledge and Experience	Chan et al. (2004); Nov (2007)
	Understanding, Learning	Clary et al. (1998); Hars and Ou (2001)
Extrinsic	Reciprocity	Kollock (1999)
	Community Identity	Hars and Ou (2001); Lakhani and Wolf (2005)
	Reputation, Feedback	Kollock (1999); Hars and Ou (2001); Rafaeli and Ariel (2008)
	Finding of and Interaction with Friends	Antikainen (2011)
	Own Demand, Influence on Development/Growth	Hars and Ou (2001); Lakhani and Wolf (2005)
	Human Capital, Self-Marketing	Hars and Ou (2001); Lakhani and Wolf (2005)
	Monetary Reward	Hars and Ou (2001); Tedjamulia et al. (2005)

Within the intrinsic motivation types, altruism is one of the most commonly mentioned types. In economics, altruism refers to "costly acts that confer economic

[9]This classification is not exhaustive, yet provides an overview of the most relevant motivation types for this work.

benefits on other individuals" (Fehr and Fischbacher, 2003, p.785). An example of this motivation type is the provisioning of resources for volunteer computing projects, in which case the provisioning infers (energy and opportunity) costs for the providing users. Besides altruism, fun and enjoyment as well as ideology are often mentioned, for example in the case of the knowledge-sharing community Wikipedia (Nov, 2007). Other types of intrinsic motivation also include interest and curiosity in the activity itself, the intention to share and exchange experience, and the learning of new skills and knowledge (Hars and Ou, 2001).

Considering extrinsic motivation types, Table 2.2 splits this category into two subgroups. The first group (sometimes considered a distinct motivation type besides intrinsic and extrinsic: *social motivation*), subsumes motivations stemming from interactions with other users. This includes reputation-based incentives to increase one's standing within a community, the finding of and interaction with friends, and the identification with a particular community. Reciprocation also falls in this category and refers to situations where participants either take a certain action as response to a previous action of other users (such as lending a resource after borrowing another resource from this user), or in anticipation of actions in the future (considering expected behavior). The second group focuses on extrinsic motivations which are not directly community-based. This involves participating because one needs or benefits from the project (for example in case of open source projects), the marketing of one's skills for career reasons, the increase in human capital, and also monetary rewards from participation.

Considering the interplay of intrinsic and extrinsic motivations, there seems to be a complex and context-dependent relationship between the two concepts which is not necessarily linear. Having both types of incentives in a system, or adding additional incentives, does not have to result in an increase in overall motivation, but rather to a reassessment of the relative importance of the incentive types (Frey and Jegen, 2001; Bénabou and Tirole, 2003). A prominent example of this interplay is the *motivation crowding(-out)* effect, which shows that adding extrinsic incentives (such as money) can as well undermine the relevance of intrinsic incentives and thus affect the actions in an unexpected way (e.g., reducing overall participation, see Frey and Jegen (2001)). In the context of donating to charities, Ariely et al. (2009) study the interaction of intrinsic, extrinsic and "image motivation" (similar to social motivations), and focus especially on the interaction of image motivation and extrinsic motivation. They show that the relative importance of image motivation depends on the visibility of the specific action, and is higher if other users are able to perceive the actions of others. Furthermore, Tedjamulia et al. (2005) suggest a framework for user participation that considers both intrinsic and extrinsic incentives, yet do not provide an empirical evaluation of their model. Overall, however, the interplay of different types of motivations is still subject of further research.

After the introduction of different motivation categories and types, approaches and theories from different scientific disciplines as well as their specific focus and assumptions are discussed.

Motivation and Incentive Theories in Economics, Sociology, and Psychology

User participation is vital for many economic and social systems, and the incentivization to induce desired or proper participation and behavior has been a main research focus over a substantial period of time. Researchers from different fields and disciplines have developed models of motivation and participation theory that try to classify and explain the different types of motivations of users. Two views that are directly relevant to this work are economics and (social) psychology, which try to describe and explain user participation and behavior based on the respective theories.

The Economic View: From Traditional to Behavioral Economics

In traditional economic theory, users are modeled as fully rational agents that maximize their expected payoff/utility in a given scenario (*homo economicus*, Henrich et al. (2001)). If rational users engage in a certain (economic) mechanism, e.g. an electronic marketplace, in order to achieve a desired user behavior the mechanism has to provide appropriate incentives to the rational users. This is the subject of the economic area of *Mechanism Design*[10] which aims at designing mechanisms in a way that prescribes a certain behavior for rational users (Nisan and Ronen, 1999). For the modeling of such a mechanism, users are commonly assumed to have certain private information, e.g. their valuations for outcomes of the mechanism, and a certain range of actions they can take. They are able to formulate strategies about which action to take depending on the current state of the system. Depending on the mechanism, it might not be best for users to reveal this private information truthfully to the system. For example, they might not provide true information about their valuations for a certain outcome of the mechanism. An

[10] A formal notation of Mechanism Design is provided in Section 2.3.2.

important concept, closely related to the design of incentives, is *incentive compatibility*, which is achieved if it is the best strategy of a user to reveal their valuations truthfully. Hence, in Mechanism Design incentives are provided through rules of the mechanism and the strategies that these rules prescribe on the (rational) user.

There are various examples of the application of a Mechanism Design approach to provide certain incentives for participating users. For the design of online resource exchange platforms, it has been applied in the design of (virtual) credit- or money-based electronic exchange systems or marketplaces (Golle et al., 2001; Antoniadis, 2004; Anagnostakis and Greenwald, 2004; Feldman et al., 2004; Ranganathan et al., 2004). For example, Golle et al. (2001) introduce an exchange mechanism that uses micro-payments to incentivize users to contribute in the P2P network. As a certain amount of credits is needed to consume resources and credits can be gained by providing resources, such an incentive scheme aims to encourage participation and resource sharing while at the same time preventing users who only consume without contributing themselves (free-riders) from exploiting the system.

While such approaches fit nicely in the traditional economic theory and the corresponding mechanisms have certain (theoretical) properties, over the years it has been shown that there are several issues with these types of incentive schemes. On the one hand, despite their nice theoretical properties there seem to be several reasons why especially (micro-) payment-based schemes are not well accepted (Odlyzko, 2003). On the other hand, there is substantial critique on the perfectly rational model of users. This is further exemplified by various experiments that show that users do not act purely based on monetary preferences as usually assumed in traditional economics (see e.g. user behavior in economic games: Andreoni and Miller (2002); Fehr and Schmidt (2006)).

In contrast to pure self-utility maximization, users might also be contributing to a platform for other reasons, such as social or ideological reasons (Mowbray et al., 2006). The field of *Behavioral Economics* aims at explaining the discrepancy between assumed and observed behavior of participants in economic systems. Most theories in behavioral economics still use the concept of utility-maximizing users, yet acknowledge that non-monetary incentives might influence and explain the observed behavior. The most common approach is to augment the utility functions with additional factors that model non-monetary concepts. For example, (expected) *reciprocity* tries to explain how individuals incorporate the expected return from other users in their decision process, and *inequality aversion* assumes that users want to avoid highly unequal payoffs. Examples for these theories are the theory of equity, reciprocity and competition (Bolton and Ockenfels, 2000), the theory of fairness and reciprocity (Fehr and Schmidt, 2000, 2006), and the concept of social preferences (Charness and Rabin, 2000). These theories are successfully able to explain a large variety of observed user behavior in different economic settings, and acknowledge the fact that different users might put different emphasis on non-monetary motivations.

User Motivation Theories in Sociology and Psychology

Whereas economic theory commonly considers incentives based on the assumption of utility-maximizing (rational) users, over the past decades (social) psychology has developed its own set of different motivation theories. Although a comprehensive review of motivation theories is outside the scope of this section, some theories relevant for the problem at hand will be introduced.

One of the earliest works, which is still influential in incentive and learning theory, is the work by Thorndike (1927) and Skinner (1953). Thorndike (1927) describes the "Law of Effect", which states that given a certain set of potential actions, which are repeated over time, the actions that are beneficial are chosen proportionally more often over time, whereas actions that are detrimental are chosen less often. Skinner (1953) builds on this fundamental result, which is also the building block of *Reinforcement Learning* theory, and proposes the "operant conditioning" theory. It states that actions are motivated by (different types of) rewards, and differentiates whether the motivations are triggered exogenously (extrinsic motivations, e.g. money) or endogenously (intrinsic motivations, e.g. fun). Closely related is the "expectancy-value theory" which considers beliefs about abilities, expectancies for success as well as subjective task values as components determining motivation (Wigfield and Eccles, 2000). According to Ryan and Deci (2000), research that builds on the operant theory considers intrinsic motivation as a case where the task is the reward itself, and related research is mainly interested in studying what makes a task intrinsically interesting. In contrast, research building on the learning theory, which considers a needs-based characterization of motivations, aims at studying which (psychological) needs are addressed by intrinsically motivated tasks.

Beside reward-based theories, another branch of motivation theory considers the social fabrics involved in the resource exchange setting. The theories of social comparison (see e.g. Festinger (1954) and Suls et al. (2002)) try to explain how the motivation of participants depends on their comparison with their peers. The theory of "social loafing" argues that users within groups tend to work less (have lower motivation to contribute) than if they would work individually (Karau and Williams, 1993). Furthermore, the "Common Identity Theory" and the "Common Bond Theory", which describe the motivations of individuals based on their connection to the (social) group, or other members of the (social) group, respectively, have been applied in the context of designing online communities as well (Ren et al., 2007). Other theories from sociology include the *Resource Theory of Social Exchange* (Foa and Foa, 2012) which provides a framework for analyzing the exchange of several types of resources, e.g. money or services, in social contexts. Similarly, the *Social Exchange Theory* with its focus on organizational behavior considers issues such as reciprocity and negotiations in social contexts (see e.g. Emerson (1976); Cropanzano and Mitchell (2005)).

Lastly, considering the participation in volunteer scenarios, the volunteering motivations scale of Clary et al. (1998) distinguishes between six functions that help to explain volunteer behavior in various settings. Given a volunteer task, *value* is related to altruistic concerns, *understanding* addresses the ability to gain new skills and learning experiences, *social* considers reputation and social comparison, *career* targets career-relevant beneficial effects of participating in the task, *protective* is ego-related and explains volunteer participation to avoid negative feelings and guilt, and *enhancement* focuses on personal development.

Summary

The focus of this section was to provide an overview of concepts and theories relevant for user participation. First, different motivations to participate and contribute in sharing and exchange scenarios were categorized. Afterwards, relevant theories from the field of economics, sociology and psychology were discussed.

Overall, it can be seen that the incentivization of user participation and the understanding of underlying motivations is a multi-faceted topic with various theories in different research fields. In particular, there seems to be a complex interrelationship between incentives and their relative importance in different scenarios. This also motivates that the relevant user motivations and incentives have to be identified for the specific scenario at hand.

Several of the important concepts described in this section will be used in Chapters 3 and 4, which study user incentives in Social Clouds. In particular, several of the mentioned motivation types will be used to identify relevant incentives in such a setting.

2.3.2. Resource Allocation

Mechanism Design

From the perspective of economic theory, the general Social Cloud setting with users requesting and providing resources is an example of a microeconomic system. Given the *economic environment* which consists of the participating users, their available resources and preferences, a humanly-devised *institution* provides rules how participants can interact with each other and the institution, and determines how the exchange of resources is structured. Such an institution prescribes a certain *behavior* on participants and leads to an *economic outcome*, e.g., how resources are allocated. The *performance* of the considered institution can then be evaluated through certain system performance metrics (Smith, 1982; Weinhardt et al., 2003).

The previously mentioned task to find allocation mechanisms for Social Clouds is equivalent to designing an institution that governs this exchange process. The field of *Mechanism Design* provides the means to formalize this institution design process. A *mechanism* is defined as "specification of a message space for each individual and an outcome function that maps vectors of messages into social decisions and transfers" (Jackson, 2003, p.2). In the realm of resource exchanges, the message space defines how the participants interact with the market, e.g., how they specify their valuation for a certain resource. The outcome function then determines a certain allocation of resources, which is often accompanied with the determination of certain transfers between participants (e.g., monetary transfers).

Formally, adopting the notation by Jackson (2003), participating users i, $i \in \{1,...,N\}$ have private information (e.g., about motivations relevant to them). User i's private information is represented by its type θ_i, which is in the set Θ_i. This type determines agent i's preference for a certain outcome $o \in O$, where O is the set of possible outcomes. The preference (or valuation) is often modeled as utility function, where $u_i(\theta_i, o)$ determines user i's utility for a given outcome, given its type

θ_i. For the comparison of two different outcomes, o_1 and o_2, $u_i(\theta_i, o_1) > u_i(\theta_i, o_2)$ indicates that outcome o_1 is preferred to outcome o_2.

From a system perspective, the allocation of resources would determine a certain outcome which optimizes a desired goal, e.g., the maximization of total welfare. In other words, given the (potential) types of users, the system designer can define a function $f : \Theta_1 \times \ldots \times \Theta_N \rightarrow O$ that finds the best outcome given the user types (also referred to as Social Choice Function). As the user types are private information, the system designer has to find a way to incentivize users to reveal this private information in order to be able to find the best outcome. This is the goal of the mechanism, which defines rules how users can interact with the system. More specifically, the mechanism prescribes a certain *strategy set* S_i on user i, which represents the actions available to user i. It also defines an *outcome rule* that maps the strategy set to a certain outcome. A mechanism is said to implement a social choice function if, in equilibrium, the mechanism yields the same outcome as the social choice function. A *transfer function* t:$\Theta \rightarrow R^n$ determines the transfers that result from a given outcome. As described subsequently, this transfer can have different implementations, including monetary and credit transfers as well as the complete absence of transfers.

Types of Exchange Mechanisms

The allocation of resources is one of the key aspects of market design. Given a certain supply and demand of resources, an *allocation mechanism* determines which request is matched to a given offer and vice versa. There are many examples where such mechanisms are applied, ranging from technical applications such as job and Virtual Machine (VM) scheduling on compute infrastructures, to economic applications such as the allocation of products to consumers. The types of allocation mechanisms that are used in the various settings can be diverse as well. They range from monetary-based mechanisms like auctions or fixed-price markets to dynamic negotiation that determines the details of the allocation and exchange of goods and resources. The most relevant mechanisms can be categorized as follows:

Monetary-based Mechanisms If the exchange and sharing of resources involves monetary payments, traditional market-based approaches are often used. Examples are fixed-price systems (such as Cloud Computing marketplaces like

Amazon Web Services[11]) where resources are offered for a specified price, and auction mechanisms where the price is determined dynamically depending on the current supply and demand (such as auctions on eBay[12]). Such mechanisms assume that participating users have a certain valuation for the resources they are interested in, and interact with the mechanism according to this valuation.

Credit-based Mechanisms Similar to monetary-based mechanisms, platforms with (virtual) credit-based mechanisms use valuation-based matching procedures. The difference between the two approaches is that credit-based systems do not necessarily involve real money. For example, users can gain credit by providing resources for other users, and use that credit to consume resources in return. A key challenge of such credit-based systems is the management of the currency with respect to credit value, specifically inflation and deflation due to leaving or arriving users (see e.g. Irwin et al. (2005)).

Preference-based Mechanisms In many systems where the use of monetary mechanisms is not feasible, not wanted, or morally/ethically not possible, preference-based mechanisms are applied to retain some of the advantages of a market-based resource matching approach (Roth, 2008). In this case, resources are shared on the basis of preferences that users have for other users, and the mechanism allocates the resources with respect to certain criteria (e.g., overall welfare).

Best-effort and Volunteer Mechanisms In such mechanisms, resources are essentially shared without involving credits or monetary exchanges, or even preferences for other users. Examples are volunteer platforms without direct reward for resource provisioning, and Trophy-based systems in which users can gain certain trophies for sharing resources (such as the volunteer computing project BOINC, see Anderson (2004)). In contrast to credit-based systems, however, such trophies or other rewards are not used for the resource exchanges, but rather for the personal gratification and satisfaction of the users.

Decentralized Approaches Another option is to leave resource allocation to the users themselves, for example via distributed communication protocols (see e.g. Streitberger and Eymann (2009)). The downside of a decentralized self-organizing approach, however, is that users would most likely have to invest

[11]`http://aws.amazon.com/` – last accessed May 2014
[12]`http://www.ebay.com` – last accessed May 2014

a significant amount of time in the system trying to get "good" deals, negotiate and in general manage their exchanges. The resulting emergent user behavior would be unpredictable and potentially inefficient at the system level.

Note that the differentiation of mechanism types considers different implementations of transfer functions. In monetary mechanisms, the transfer function specifies the monetary amount that users have to pay or receive, given the determined allocation. For credit-based systems, instead of monetary transfers the amount of exchanged credits is determined. In case of preference-based mechanisms, there is no actual transfer of money, credits, or other remuneration. Best-effort and Volunteer mechanisms also do not involve transfers, yet also do not provide a market-based type of mechanism. The last example, decentralized allocation approaches, does not fall into the above categorization as no central mechanism is designed.

To decide which approach is promising in case of a Social Cloud, the advantages and disadvantages of the approaches can be compared. As mentioned before, the social context and the complex interactions between monetary and intrinsic or social motivations suggest that non-monetary mechanisms are most suitable. Furthermore, decentralized allocation systems can be problematic in terms of user interaction and feasibility, and can lead to market failure (Roth, 2008). This leaves centralized, managed market mechanisms as potential options. Considering credit-based systems, their ability to match resources according to the valuations of users and relative supply and demand stands in contrast to the significant challenges of managing the credit currency. The potentially high interaction of users with the system to determine and submit their valuations for resources can also be seen as a drawback. In contrast, volunteer or best-effort mechanisms which do not encompass common market criteria such as system welfare or fairness might be easier to manage, yet produce allocations that can be sub-optimal with respect to these criteria. Finally, preference-based matching can be seen as a compromise between market efficiency and ease of use, which not only addresses the resource allocation problem, but also considers the social context of allocations.

Two-Sided Matching for Preference-based Resource Allocation

The field of two-sided matching markets is a successful and established means to allocate resources based on preferences rather than monetary or credit-based valuations. Instead of monetary valuations, it assumes that users have an ordinal preference ranking with whom they want to share, i.e., both sides have preferences for the other side. Each side ranks participants of the other side in an ordinal ranking (with rank 1 being the most preferred choice). The objective of two-sided matching is to guarantee that the solutions given by such a market mechanism satisfy certain desirable characteristics, such as stability, fairness, or (social) welfare.[13]

In the context of the previously introduced Mechanism Design notion, a two-sided matching mechanism specifies a message space (users submit their preference rankings and get the final match), and the outcome function (matching algorithm) matches the preferences to a certain outcome (specifies which users are matched). The transfer function, in this case, is not further specified as the mechanism does not use monetary transfers.

Overall, the designer of a Social Cloud platform has the objective to guarantee certain performance criteria for the exchange. This raises an important question: Which economic systems can be implemented for social resource sharing such that certain economic properties are still fulfilled? As the described two-sided matching approach is in line with the social context of the resource exchange in Social Clouds, preference-based matching mechanisms will be the focus of Chapters 5 and 6.

2.4. Summary

This section introduced the basic concepts and foundations that are relevant for the thesis. First, Section 2.1 introduced Social Clouds as the unifying use case that is applied throughout the thesis. Furthermore, the prototype of a Social Compute Cloud and details of its technical implementation were presented. Section 2.2 described the simulation tool that can be used as complementary methodology in the design of social research exchange platforms. The simulation tool will be used for several evaluations throughout the thesis. Finally, Section 2.3 discussed two relevant coordination challenges in the context of Social Clouds: the incentivization of user participation as well as the allocation of available resources, which are both considered in this thesis.

Based on these foundations, Part II considers the first challenge identified in Section 2.3: the identification of relevant user participation incentives and the design of corresponding incentive schemes. Part III of the thesis concentrates on the second challenge, resource allocation in Social Clouds through preference-based matching.

[13] Exact definitions of the metrics are provided in Section 5.1.2.

Part II.

Incentive Engineering for Social Clouds

Chapter 3.

Incentives in Social Clouds

"The proliferation of online communities may suggest that the design of a community for a particular purpose is straightforward. Unfortunately, this is not the case."

(Cheng and Vassileva, 2006)

ONLINE communities, sharing platforms, and other network-based exchange systems stand and fall by users actively participating on the platform. This seemingly trivial observation has been a valuable, sometimes harsh lesson for many online communities during the past decades. A fitting example is the emergence of various social network platforms and their struggle to achieve a critical mass of users that ensures the platform's sustainability (Westland, 2010). Over the course of several years only few of these platforms survived, with Facebook emerging as the most prominent site. Others disappeared due to a lack of actively participating users.

In the context of Social Clouds, the same important user incentive challenges remain. As with all market platforms, a resource sharing mechanism such as a Social Cloud depends on the active participation of its users in creating a sustainable resource exchange. Hence, providing proper incentives for users throughout their interactions with the platform can be seen as one of the fundamental challenges in the creation and management of sharing platforms.

Whereas the importance of user participation is generally agreed on and incentive issues have been studied for a wide variety of platforms and online communities, the study of user motivation and incentivization in specific scenarios is still an area of active research. User motivation can be quite complex and depends on the specific characteristics of the scenario (see e.g. Ryan and Deci (2000)). For example, the disparity of free-riding behavior in (mostly anonymous) public goods markets (such as P2P platforms) stands in contrast to the considerable quantity of charitable and volunteer activities in other settings (Ariely et al., 2009). Furthermore, different participation activities such as passively consuming information compared to active posting of information, are influenced by different factors and thus require specific stimuli (Koh et al., 2007).

Section 2.3.1 categorized motivation into intrinsic and extrinsic types and discussed that their interplay is far from trivial. In particular, the design of incentives within a particular system might have unexpected consequences on user participation (Frey and Jegen, 2001; Bénabou and Tirole, 2003). It is therefore necessary to consider the motivation and incentive issues in a platform-specific way through the identification and implementation of incentives relevant for the considered scenario. This chapter introduces and analyzes incentive challenges in Social Clouds. Its goal is to address research question 1.1 as stated in Chapter 1.2.

RESEARCH QUESTION 1.1 ≺INCENTIVE ENGINEERING≻ *What are the stages of participation and the corresponding relevant incentives that users exhibit in Social Clouds?*

For the design of an incentive scheme, several steps must be taken. In the general context of online communities, several distinct user participation stages have been previously identified (Jones and Rafaeli, 1999; Iriberri and Leroy, 2009). These stages define how users interact with the community or platform. On social resource sharing platforms such as a Social Cloud, the interaction of users with the platform seems to consist of different stages of participation. Starting with the discovery and registration on the platform, participation can evolve into active contribution and sharing of resources. Hence, the first step is the identification of different stages of participation during which a user interacts with and participates in a Social Cloud. This is the focus of the first part of this chapter. This understanding of participation stages then helps in the identification of relevant incentives for each stage, as the importance of certain incentives may change between stages. For example, from a platform perspective the signing-up stage has a different goal than the active participation stage, and different incentives might be necessary (Fogg and Eckles, 2007).

After identifying the relevant participation stages with their characteristics and challenges, it is necessary to appropriately design and engineer specific incentives to stimulate user participation in each of these stages. Such a process involves two steps: the identification of relevant incentives in the particular stages, as well as the discovery of factors that influence the relative importance of said incentives. This is addressed in the second part of this chapter.

Potential motivations and incentives have been discussed in Section 2.3.1. Among the factors that can have an influence on the perceived relevance of certain incentives for different users are user characteristics (such as personality profiles), the type of resource that is exchanged, and the setting of the exchange (e.g., sharing between friends vs. sharing with acquaintances).

After an introduction of important concepts and related work in Section 3.1, Section 3.2 identifies the different participation stages of user interaction with a Social Cloud and provides a discussion of their respective characteristics and challenges. In Section 3.3, the results of a small-scale web-based survey are presented to demonstrate how relevant user incentives in the different participation stages can be identified. Finally, Section 3.4 concludes this chapter with a discussion of the findings and an outlook on future work in this area.

3.1. Participation Incentives in Resource Sharing Platforms

As the need for proper incentivization is universally agreed upon (see Section 2.3.1) this section extends the incentive concepts introduced in Chapter 2 by providing an overview of the most relevant related work in the field of online and virtual communities, as well as similar resource sharing systems. First, due to its close conceptual background, Section 3.1.1 discusses incentives to participate in online communities in general. Second, Section 3.1.2 summarizes incentivization problems in similar systems, among which P2P sharing networks are a prominent example.

3.1.1. Incentives in Online Communities

Social resource sharing platforms such as Social Clouds are a special form of *online* (virtual) *community*. Starting with the work of Rheingold (1993), online communities have been considered as a type of community that uses and leverages computer technology for communication among members of the community. The original definition is as follows:[1]

Definition 4 (Virtual Community, Rheingold 1993). *Virtual communities are social aggregations that emerge from the Net when enough people carry on those public discussions long enough, with sufficient human feeling, to form webs of personal relationships in cyberspace.*

Once online communities grew larger and more important over the years, researchers became more interested in various concepts revolving around these communities. Hence, a review of related literature is helpful in discussing the concepts that have been discovered and studied since the beginning of online communities. Among the concepts being discussed here are perspectives on participation from different scientific disciplines, aspects such as usability, as well as dependencies between incentives, participation stages, and user types.

Online Communities from Different Research Directions From an economic viewpoint, the emergence of cooperation among community members has been studied using concepts such as public and digital goods. For example, Kollock (1999) applies this approach and further discusses several potential motivations how the cooperation and contribution of members can be explained, mentioning aspects such as reciprocity, effects on reputation, and including the community good in the utility functions of its members. From a business perspective, Williams and Cothrel (2000) argue that the creation and management of virtual communities is paramount for successful online businesses. They present several examples of successful online communities and discuss aspects that have been found to be critical for the studied communities. Two important aspects are reaching a *critical mass* of users and the design of appropriate (communication) tools for the community, which are used to gain feedback of community members and use it for the

[1]The terms online community and virtual community are used interchangeably in this chapter.

development of the community. Another frequently observed aspect is the recognition of different types of user motivation for participation (see Section 2.3.1 for an overview), and the existence of different user types with respect to their contribution (Bishop, 2007; van Dijck, 2009).

Besides economic and business perspectives, in recent years there is an increased effort in trying to understand the social background of online communities. On one hand, researchers are interested in how the ability to interact and socialize with other community members affects the community itself (Preece and Maloney-Krichmar, 2003; Lazar and Preece, 2002). On the other hand, from a viewpoint of social capital theory the effects of underlying social networks on the community (considering interaction between and benefits for members) have also been studied. For example, Ganley and Lampe (2009) find that the structural properties of the social network can impact the perceived benefits for members. This is an interesting implication for Social Clouds, as the position of a user within the social network might affect the decision to join and participate on the platform.

Usability From a technical perspective, usability has also been identified as important concept related to participation in online communities (Preece and Maloney-Krichmar, 2003). Considering the relationship of motivation and usability, Wang et al. (2012) apply a technology acceptance model and structural equation modeling to show that intrinsic motivation significantly influences the perceived usefulness, the perceived ease of use, and the actual use of the online community. Furthermore, guidelines and patterns have been developed that try to encourage user participation and interaction with the platform (see e.g. Porter (2010)). However, Vassileva (2012) argues that these best practices are gained in retrospect from already successful platforms, whereas generalized recipes are not readily available if a platform has to be developed from scratch.

Participation Incentives Considering the lifecycle of online communities and user participation therein, it is also recognized that participation can be structured in separate phases depending on the lifecycle stage in which the community is. Fogg and Eckles (2007) present a model for a "behavior chain" for user participation. They distinguish between three phases: discovery, superficial involvement, and true commitment. They illustrate their model in the context of different web services and discuss implications for the designer of such a service. Users (or user groups) might also require different incentives depending on the participation stage that they are in (Jones and Rafaeli, 1999). In other words, incentives for signing-up and initial participation on a platform might be different than incentives for continued (long-term) participation. Cheng and Vassileva (2006) discuss that incentives are needed to get a critical mass of participants, yet argue that too many low-quality contributions ("information overload") can also be detrimental to the community as some users might be more inclined to leave in such a case. Therefore, they argue for a balance of quality and quantity for participating in a resource-sharing community, and propose an adaptive incentive mechanism that takes into account both the user profile (such as their reputation) as well as the current needs of the community.

Given that literature identifies several different participation incentives, it is generally agreed that different users perceive these incentives differently. Hence, this calls for a personalization of incentives as incentive schemes which do not distinguish between different user types or user behavior lack the capability of addressing this fact. The theory of "User and Group (Community) Modeling" is an example how this can be addressed (Vassileva, 2012). Furthermore, Lampe et al. (2010) apply the "Uses and Gratification" theory as well as "Organizational Commitment" theory, and find that a "feeling of belonging" to an online community is a major motivation factor across user types, and that users might continue participating on the platform for reasons other than the ones they had when they initially joined the community.

Other aspects that have been studied related to participation in online communities are different types of recognition (for users) and their effect on participation (Chan et al., 2004), the effects of social comparison on user contribution in online communities (Harper et al., 2007), and the application of gamification aspects in online communities in order to further foster participation and contribution (Deterding et al., 2011).

3.1.2. Participation Incentives in Similar Sharing Systems

Social Clouds are conceptually close to other sharing platforms, thus it is helpful to consider participation incentives in these similar systems. Examples for systems where the engineering of proper (user) incentives has been studied include file sharing P2P networks (Golle et al., 2001; Feldman et al., 2004; Anagnostakis and

Greenwald, 2004; Antoniadis, 2004; Zhang et al., 2009), Volunteer Computing (Nov et al., 2010), sharing of workflows in social contexts (De Roure et al., 2009), and even in technical areas such as traffic regulation in wireless access networks (Liao et al., 2002).

P2P Networks In contrast to a social scenario where there are direct or indirect relationships between users, P2P systems are mostly anonymous. Certain characteristics of P2P, such as this anonymity and the possibility of whitewashing, i.e. the creation of new identities, make appropriate incentivization techniques necessary. One of the most severe problems in P2P networks is free-riding, i.e. the consumption of resources without providing resources in return. For example, Cuevas et al. (2010) find that only a small fraction of P2P users create most of its content. Various approaches have been proposed in this setting, ranging from micro-payments for contribution (Golle et al., 2001), discriminating server selection and shared history of exchanges/behavior (Feldman et al., 2004), exchange-based incentives through service prioritization (Anagnostakis and Greenwald, 2004), to the use of tokens, reputation and service classes for the exchange of resources (Ranganathan et al., 2004). Novel incentive schemes continue being published, indicating the practical importance of this research.

Interestingly, there is evidence that intrinsic motivations are more important than extrinsic ones which, though sometimes relevant as well, are not considered the dominant motivation (see e.g. Tedjamulia et al. (2005)). Despite this finding, many P2P incentive schemes focus on credit- or payment based systems which can be considered extrinsic incentives. One potential explanation for this is the fact that the P2P networks considered for these schemes are anonymous, which makes it potentially riskier to rely on pro-social behavior or generalized reciprocity.

Other Community-based Networks Conceptually close to the use case Social Cloud are the previously mentioned platforms myExperiment.org and nanoHUB.org. myExperiment.org (De Roure et al., 2009) is an example of workflow sharing within a scientific community. Here, a platform is provided with which researchers can share, adapt and use scientific workflow processes and experiments, therefore enabling collaboration and the spread of common workflows. Due to its target group, the main incentive for scientists to join and participate in the sharing of workflows is the potential improvement of scientific processes through the use of community-fostered workflows and experiments. Similarly, nanoHUB.org (Klimeck et al., 2008) allows for the sharing of teaching and research materials on nanotechnology and aims at fostering collaboration in this field. nanoHUB.org uses virtual credits ("nanos") to reward contributions such as answering questions in forums. The amount of credit indicates the level of contribution of a user, and can also be used to purchase several items in the platform store. Examples of non-scientific communities are online photo-sharing communities, where different motivations such as enjoyment or self-development are found to be important (Nov et al., 2010), and social commerce communities where users are able to open virtual stores and are connected to other sellers via a social network (Stephen and Toubia, 2010). In the latter case, monetary rewards are the primary incentive to participate in such a community.

3.1.3. Discussion

Summarizing the related work, there are two challenges in the design of participation incentives that need to be addressed: 1) the existence of distinct participation stages with potentially different incentivization requirements, and 2) the acknowledgment that not all users react similarly to certain incentives, which has to be considered in the design and evaluation of incentive schemes.

Despite the described literature on similar systems, the effects of incentive schemes on social sharing systems require additional research. For the setting of a Social Cloud (or a general social resource exchange setting), the different participation stages (such as discovery followed by active participation) as well as the relevant incentives therein have to be identified. This is the focus of Section 3.2. In addition, to provide a more general framework for participation stages in social sharing platforms, factors that influence the importance of certain incentives need to be analyzed. For example, resource sharing in a professional setting (i.e., with colleagues, companies, etc.) might emphasize monetary incentives to a higher degree than sharing with close friends. The survey discussed in Section 3.3 aims to address these issues. Finally, considering that user types can have different motivations to participate, the effect of user type distributions on the effectiveness of an incentive scheme needs to be studied as well. This is subject of the case studies in Chapter 4, which aim at taking a first step in this direction.

3.2. Engineering Incentives for Social Clouds

Among the first steps in the design process of incentive schemes is the identification of the different stages of participation that users have with the platform. Only with this insight, and the incorporation of the characteristics of the participation stages, the incentive scheme can be tailored to the specific needs of the exchange platform. This section, therefore, provides a classification of three different participation stages for Social Clouds, as well as a discussion about factors which influence participation within these stages. This section is an extended version of Haas et al. (2011).

3.2.1. Incentives During the Participation Lifecycle

The sustainability of resource sharing mechanisms crucially depends on having a critical mass of active users with continued participation over time. Therefore, in the design of a Social Cloud, providing appropriate incentives for active participation has to be among the most important goals. In order to provide appropriate incentives, different stages of user participation and contribution can be distinguished (Jones and Rafaeli, 1999; Iriberri and Leroy, 2009). The different stages of a community life-cycle have different goals, e.g., starting with aim to get a certain number of registered users and subsequently focusing on encouraging useful contributions. Hence, there is a changing emphasis within these stages on which aspects successful communities and sharing platforms must focus on (Iriberri and Leroy, 2009). An effective incentive scheme has to address these different stages and be adaptable for changing requirements (Vassileva, 2012).

The incentive classification scheme presented in this chapter identifies three participation stages during which users interact with the Social Cloud in different ways. This is similar to related classifications of user participation phases such as (Fogg and Eckles, 2007), yet focuses more on the underlying social connections of users. Each stage can be characterized by unique goals and therefore has specific incentive requirements. Figure 3.1 shows the three stages along with the challenges that have to be met. In the first stage, ***User Discovery and Registration***, potential users of the platform have to be discovered and the value of participating on the platform has to be communicated to them. The next stage, ***User Participation***, addresses the challenge of incentivizing registered users to actually offer resources, while at the same time discouraging free-riding behavior. The last stage, ***Social Behavior in Resource Sharing***, is closely intertwined with the second stage, yet focuses on social aspects. If users actively participate and provide resources, they should have incentives to adhere to certain social behavior. For example, the platform might implement agreements that specify the responsibilities of the sharing partners in the resource exchange. A desired behavior, in this case, could be providing the resources according to the agreement rather than defecting from the offer if a request arrives, or not to engage in malicious behavior such as intentionally providing incorrect feedback about other users (Petri et al., 2012).

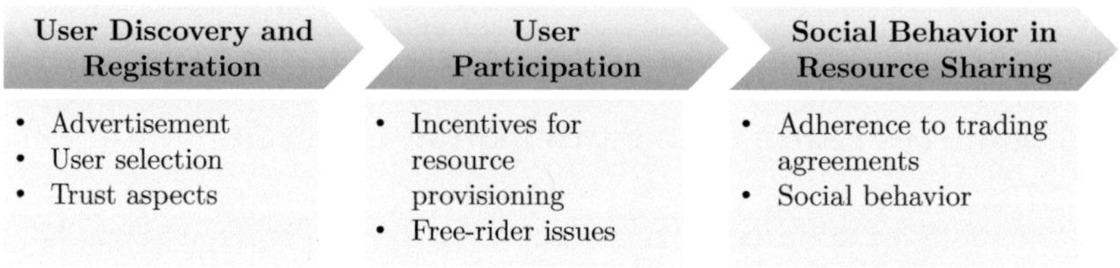

Figure 3.1.: Participation Stages and User Incentivization Problems

Stage 1: User Discovery and Registration

Before users can participate in a resource exchange, they have to be made aware of its existence and be invited to join the corresponding platform. Here, several steps can be distinguished, namely discovery, invitation, and registration of potential users.

For the discovery of users the existing relationships between members of the platform with potential users can be utilized. Both direct discovery through manual invitations as well as automatic discovery, e.g. through automated advertisements or scraping of the social networks of users, are feasible. In case of manual discovery, existing users can be incentivized to find new users by, for example, bonus programs where the user gets a certain amount of credits or other benefits for each invited user that joins the platform. Gamification aspects can also be utilized for this task (Deterding et al., 2011), e.g., by providing badges or trophies for successful user invitations. In case of automatic discovery, mining of available data through the underlying social network platform can be applied to automatically identify and suggest users. Similar to the process of user discovery, invitations can then be sent either manually, or automatically. If potential users are discovered and invited to join the platform, their decision depends on their motivation and the incentives to join the platform. Here, too, several incentivization schemes are possible. For example, invited users who join the platform may receive a sign-up bonus, e.g. credits, or may be awarded priority functionality during a certain time after their subscription. The actual form of incentivization will most likely depend on the specific application scenario.

An important issue that has to be considered is the concept of trust. For example, if the platform (and thereby the social network) gets larger users might not be direct friends of each other, and with such an increase in size and complexity new assumptions about trust may be necessary. The problem of trust transitivity is particularly interesting in this case. Some approaches simply consider the existence of trust transitivity and calculate indirect trust relationships through multiplication of direct relationships (Golbeck, 2005). Transitivity of trust might be, however, highly user-dependent, making such a general assumption problematic. Caton et al. (2012) discuss these and other aspects of trust, specifically in the context of Social Clouds.

Stage 2: Encouraging Active Participation

After the discovery and subscription of new users, they have to be incentivized to actively participate on the platform and offer resources. Only if a certain, critical mass of actively participating users is achieved, will the platform be sustainable (Preece and Maloney-Krichmar, 2003). A lack of participation is considered a danger for such virtual communities (Rafaeli and Ariel, 2008).

Tackling the Free-rider Issue Providing incentives for participation is closely connected to the *free-rider problem*. Naturally, users may perceive the consumption of resources as beneficial whereas the provision of one's resources usually induces costs of some sort, e.g. power consumption. It is a well-known problem in online communities that users may not have adequate incentives to actively participate, which leads to a small number of contributors and a large number of passive consumers. Whereas the contributors actively engage in the community and make up much of the overall participation on the platform, the passive users, sometimes referred to as "lurkers", consume resources without providing resources themselves (Bishop, 2007; van Dijck, 2009). Example communities where this phenomenon can be observed are P2P networks (Adar and Huberman, 2000), open-source communities (Lakhani and von Hippel, 2003), and the platform Wikipedia (Tapscott and Williams, 2007; Priedhorsky et al., 2007). Hence, it is necessary to design the platform in such a way that users profit from contributing. In the long run, this ability will be one of the make-or-break factors of a resource sharing platform.

User Heterogeneity Another issue is the potential heterogeneity of user types with respect to their motivations to participate and contribute. Previous work (see e.g. Andreoni and Miller (2002) for user behavior in social settings) has shown that in exchange scenarios, different user types can be distinguished which have different perceptions and motivations to contribute. This poses a significant challenge in the design of a resource exchange platform such as a Social Cloud. For the design of incentives, this has the crucial implication that incentives have to be provided that address all or most of the potential user types of the community. Ideally, the incentive scheme takes the different user types into account and provides individualized incentives (Vassileva, 2012). One common form of incentive schemes that try to address both free-riding behavior and heterogeneous user types are schemes where users obtain participation points or rewards from contribution, and are only allowed to participate in case they can provide enough points or a high-enough level of previous participation (see e.g. Ranganathan et al. (2004) on P2P systems).

User participation also crucially depends on the chosen economic allocation mechanism. Depending on the type of user and the application scenario, different market mechanisms provide different incentives for active participation. This issue is elaborated in Section 3.2.2. A case study how heterogeneous user types can be addressed in the design of an incentive scheme is provided in Chapter 4.2.

Stage 3: Incentivizing Social Behavior

Even if users share and offer different types of resources, it is not guaranteed that they will adhere to their offers and provide the resources as anticipated. Considering the social setting, *social behavior* in this case can be defined as the adherence to the platform rules and agreements, as well as refraining from malicious behavior. The willingness to provide resources is a necessary first step to get a reasonable amount of offers as well as heterogeneity that increases the attractiveness of the sharing platform, yet it is not a sufficient condition for actual resource sharing.

Only if the providers actually adhere to their offers the sharing makes sense. That is, resource providers should have the incentive to fulfill their (voluntary) obligations and really provide the services. This is also true for resource consumers, as they should be incentivized not to damage other users' resources, e.g., not store illegal of harmful data on other users' machines or use offered VMs to execute malicious code.

Social Service Level Agreements There are several important aspects how a desired social behavior can be induced in platforms such as Social Clouds. One option is through the design of (resource or trading) agreements as well as their enforcement. Unlike the design of these components in other markets for electronic resources or services where agreements are often described by Service Level Agreements (SLAs) and enforcement is achieved through penalties when SLAs are violated, other aspects have to be considered in a socially-oriented scenario such as a Social Cloud. As the sharing of resources is, in its essence, voluntary, standard SLA and penalty approaches are not suitable. This calls for the development of a new type of SLA that considers these issues (see e.g. Michalk and Haas (2011)). One of the premises of a Social Cloud is that real-world relationships should be utilized in the resource sharing mechanism, yet the sharing and trading of resources should have no negative effect on these real-world relationships. Hence, the specification of resources to be shared through hard SLAs may not be an ideal approach as (volunteer) consumption of resources is, in many cases, not business driven. Furthermore, enforcement through monetary or other penalties can be counterproductive. For example, if a friend fails to deliver the agreed-upon resource this is not comparable to when a company fails to deliver business-critical services. Hence, the design of SLAs that are able to address the mentioned specifics of sharing in social contexts is a necessary task, which however is outside the scope of this work.

Trust and Reputation Systems Another attempt at fostering social behavior in online (sharing) communities is the design of a trust or reputation system (see Jøsang et al. (2007) for an overview of related models). By giving users the ability to provide feedback about other users' actions, the trust and reputation schemes aim to discourage malicious behavior through indirect enforcement. In other words, even though users might not have interacted directly beforehand, the trust and reputation system allows them to obtain information about each others' previous behavior. Examples for such trust models are SocialReGreT (Sabater and Sierra, 2002), EigenTrust (Kamvar et al., 2003), PeerTrust (Xiong and Liu, 2004), and PowerTrust (Zhou and Hwang, 2007), all of which are focused on establishing a reliable trust rating for (potentially anonymous) user-based networks. Another example is Petri et al. (2012) who apply a feedback-based trust model to P2P cloud communities, a setting very similar to a Social Cloud.

From the viewpoint of the incentive scheme, the second and third stage are closely intertwined. Incentive schemes usually have the goal to increase participation or encourage certain actions in a system, thereby inherently focusing on the second stage. However, as the incentive scheme prescribes rules in the system (such as which interactions are possible based on the contribution score of a user), these rules might affect the behavior of users in the third stage as they determine the potential action of a user. From a game-theoretic viewpoint on incentive systems, besides the specification of agreement and enforcement structures, the concept of strategically acting users has to be taken into account as well. In this context, users are said to be acting strategically if they pursue some personal goal and take into account the potential actions of other users while trying to achieve this goal. In other words, users try to find the strategy that is most beneficial for themselves, potentially irrespective of the effects of this strategy on other users or the system.

3.2.2. Factors Influencing the Participation Incentives

The importance of certain incentives throughout the user life-cycle depends on the actual characteristic of the specific scenario. On one hand, design characteristics of the platform affect user incentives, namely the relationship types of users given the underlying social network, the applied market mechanism, and the specific application scenario. There are complex dependencies between these factors, which are addressed in this section. On the other hand, users might have personal motivation to participate in a Social Cloud independent of its actual implementation. This issue will be considered in the next section.

Application Scenarios and Market Mechanisms As discussed in Chapter 2.1, there is a wide range of application scenarios for SCs, which are differentiated by the specific types of resources that are shared (e.g., storage or VMs), the use case (sharing among friends vs. sharing for a research project), and the organizational setting of the scenario with respect to the participating users (private users vs. sharing between companies).

Considering these examples it is clear that the choice of proper incentives depends on the actual application scenario, as users' motivation might be quite different in certain domains. In purely social or volunteer scenarios, currently implemented systems such as myExperiment (De Roure et al., 2009) suggest that intrinsic motivations, fostered by Trophy or Reciprocation mechanisms, provide sufficient incentives to share resources. In contrast, extrinsic motivations (e.g., credits such as nanos on nanoHUB.org) might be necessary to incentivize strategically acting users in enterprise scenarios. A universal incentive system, thus, is not promising, and the application scenario and its intricacies have to be taken into account in the design of the system.

Relationship Types Besides the application scenario, other factors influence the choice of an appropriate incentive mechanism. Although Social Clouds build upon the inherent trust relationships between users, the level of trust depends on the type and strength of users' relationships. Ties between users can be different based on the different social groups (family, friends, acquaintances, etc.), or the frequency of interaction. The classification between strong and weak ties is an example for such different strengths of relationships (Granovetter, 1973).

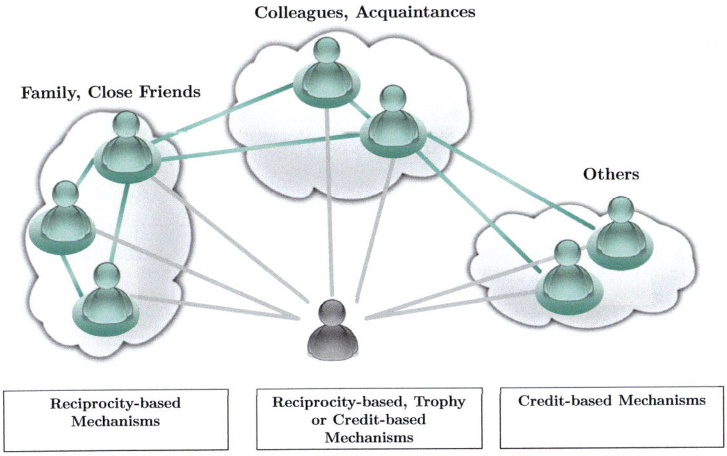

Figure 3.2.: Example of Relationship Types and Resource Sharing Incentives

Consider, for example, the situation shown in Figure 3.2 where a user has different types of relationships with other users of the underlying social network. Suppose that three groups can be identified: Family and close friends, colleagues and acquaintances, and the remaining group of other people which include people where the friendship only exists in digital form. The definition of such groups of friends is already available, for example through relationship lists in Facebook or circles in Google+. As one can imagine, a user might have different incentives to share with users in each of these groups. Intuitively, one would rather share resources with family members than with strangers without direct personal connections. Consider, for example, computation or storage of sensitive data. A user most likely will trust family members or close friends to be reasonably careful with data (given certain technical prerequisites), but this may not be the case with purely online "friends".

Therefore, it is useful to distinguish the incentives to share and the expected rewards with respect to these groups. Whereas users might share altruistically with users from the first group and do not expect direct compensation due to the high level of trust, the weak relationships in the third group might require direct rewards, such as receiving virtual credits, for the sharing of resources between these groups. In practice, however, it is a nontrivial task to infer the relationship type or strength of users based on interaction data within a social network (Xiang et al., 2010). For example, close friends might not use social network platforms to interact frequently as they have other means of communication. Hence, the incentive design of a Social Cloud should offer the users flexibility in the choice of how resources are exchanged and if some form of compensation is required.

Market Mechanisms Another factor that influences user incentives is the choice of market mechanisms, which can also both depend on the application scenario and on the relationship type (and thus the level of trust) between the users. Consider, again, Figure 3.2. Building on the previous reasoning, certain market mechanisms seem to be more appropriate for trading with different types of relationships. For resource sharing with users of the first group, purely volunteer or reciprocal mechanisms may be most appropriate as the closer relationships might infer a sense of reciprocation. In this setting a high level of trust is present and users expect no immediate reward in return or trust other users that they will share resources in the future. On the other hand, for exchanges with users of the second group Trophy, Reputation or Credit mechanisms may be adequate and offer certain advantages.

For example, reputation can compensate the lower levels of trust between the users by providing additional information about other users, and credit systems would allow users to accumulate credits which they can use for resource consumption. Finally, due to the lower trust levels between the user and members of the third group, credit-based systems or other monetary mechanisms might provide the only form of reasonable incentives to engage in trading (see e.g. the multitude of credit- or activity-based incentive schemes in anonymous P2P sharing communities summarized in Section 3.1).

3.2.3. Design Implications for Social Clouds

This section points out several important aspects concerning participation incentives in Social Clouds. First, it is necessary to obtain an understanding of the relevant motivations of potential participants throughout the identified stages of the participation lifecycle. Only with knowledge about different user types and their respective motivations it is possible to design incentive schemes that consider the important, platform-specific intricacies. Second, the relevance of certain incentives is affected by several factors such as the application scenario or the exchange mechanism. The interplay between the different user types as well as their interaction with the incentive scheme and the exchange mechanisms implemented on the platform can be quite complex and hard to predict. This should be acknowledged in the design of incentive schemes, and a design process utilizing sensitivity analyses with respect to user type distributions can provide useful additional insights.

In order to address these aspects and challenges, the next section aims to get an understanding of the relevant user motivations and incentives to participate in a Social Cloud. In addition, Section 4.2 of the next chapter shows how the simulation tool presented in the last chapter is a complimentary methodology in the design of Social Clouds. By simulating the introduction of an incentive scheme, the non-trivial effects of that scheme on the different user types of the system will be studied.

3.3. Identifying Relevant User Incentives

The previous sections introduced the various incentive problems that a market designer for a resource sharing platform needs to consider. Whereas these considerations were mainly driven by theoretical work and empirical observations of similar systems, it is necessary to identify the relevant incentives for users of a particular system and sharing scenario. For this reason, a small-scale web-based survey was conducted as a first step to get a better understanding of incentives for potential users. This survey can be seen as a pre-test of a more in-depth study of incentives relevant for individuals or certain user groups.[2] The focus of this section, therefore, is to describe the web survey and its results, aiming at identifying relevant incentives for sharing platforms such as a Social Cloud.

3.3.1. Goals and Design of Web Survey

Identifying relevant incentives is necessary for all three participation stages as discussed earlier in Section 3.2.1. The survey discussed in this section focuses on the first two stages, as the last stage (incentives for social sharing behavior) is inherently dynamic and requires feedback from participants that have used the system in practice. Being closely related to research question 1.1, the goal of the survey is to answer following questions:

1. What types of resources have users shared previously, with whom did they share them, and what are the relevant motivations for previous sharing?
2. What are relevant incentives to join a sharing platform and actively share resources? How does this depend on the previous experience, the sharing scenario (private vs. professional networks), the use case (sharing of storage) as well as the personality type?

The first goal was to identify the previous experience of the survey participant with other sharing systems. This includes questions about the resources that have been shared, the platforms that have been used as well as the user groups the resources have been shared with. Such information is important for a system designer as the

[2] Ideally, such a survey would be coupled with a prototype of the system in question, and target the users of the prototype. As the technical SC prototype was not ready to deploy at the time of the survey, this was unfortunately not suitable.

(subsequently asked) sharing incentives might be different for users based on their previous experience. The second goal was for users to provide information about their perceived importance of certain incentives, such as monetary compensation or altruism.

Together with the additional data gathered during the survey, which besides the mentioned previous experience also includes demographic data and a short personality test, this allows for an exploratory analysis of the importance of relevant incentives for certain user types. To limit the survey length, the Ten Item Personality Inventory (TIPI, Gosling et al. (2003)) was used instead of the longer standardized questionnaires to assess personality types. Additionally, two sharing scenarios were distinguished, sharing in a private network vs. sharing within a professional network, in order to identify potential differences based on the sharing scenario. In a private network, sharing occurs between friends, whereas the focus of the professional network is to share between colleagues, co-workers and classmates.

Survey Implementation The survey was implemented in English and German using SurveyMonkey[3] and consisted of three main blocks. The first block considered questions about previous sharing behavior. If the survey participant previously shared resources in similar settings, questions about the previously used platforms, shared resources, and the motivations to share these resources are asked. Given that users, independent of their previous sharing experience, are interested in sharing resources in similar settings, the second block studies the motivations to participate and actively provide resources in two hypothetical sharing scenarios. The goal of this block is to identify if there are differences in the importance of certain motivations between the scenarios, which considered sharing in a private (friend) network compared to a professional (business) network. Finally, the last block concluded the survey with the aforementioned personality and demographic questions.

Given that participants of the survey do not necessarily have experience with previous resource sharing, or are not even interested in sharing resources, the survey included two additional questions that acted as filters in the processing logic. The first filter asked participants if they previously have shared resources, and either directed them to the first block of questions, or to the second filter question. This second filter asked survey participants if they are in general interested in sharing

[3] `http://www.surveymonkey.com` – last accessed May 2014

resources. With a positive response, the participant was directed to the second block of questions, otherwise to the demographic questions. Appendix A shows the logical structure of the survey (Figure A.1), as well as the survey questions.

The survey included closed questions with a given set of answers to choose from as well as open questions. For the questions involving assessment or evaluation, a 6-point Likert-scale was used.[4]

3.3.2. Evaluation

Having introduced the survey goals and logic, this section presents the results of the online survey. In particular, the results considering the research questions are addressed. Especially, the following demographic statistics show that the participants reflect the local (student) community to a high degree. Hence, it is not a representative sample of the population, which is why the results and potential implications of the survey have to be interpreted carefully.

General Statistics and Demographics The survey was conducted over a period of two months from December 2012 to February 2013. In total, 172 people participated the survey, whereof 126 fully completed it (73.3%). Of the 126 completed responses, 5 are not considered for the evaluation due to not meeting the data validity criteria. In particular, these five responses contained participants that could not have possibly read all answered questions thoroughly in time (lower time limit 1 minute if all blocks were answered), checking the same item on the Likert-scale for all answers, or being extremely contradictory in their TIPI answers (putting themselves on the opposite extremes for the personality factors). This leaves 121 fully completed and valid responses which are considered for the subsequent evaluation.[5]

[4]There is currently no consensus if a scale with even or odd options should be preferred. On one hand, using a scale with an even number of options cannot represent a truly neutral opinion, and by forcing the participant to choose a non-neutral option might thereby bias the results (Schnell et al., 2011; Garland, 1991). On the other hand, having an odd number of options and using the midpoint can be used to avoid a tendency or to get through the survey as quickly as possible, potentially without reading or thinking about the questions. In such a case it could not represent a truthful statement and hence bias the result as well (Weijters et al., 2010).

[5]Including the not considered 5 responses does not change the presented results significantly.

Considering language, 86.0% of the participants completed the German version of the survey, and 14.0% the English version. This indicates that the main pool of participants was probably sourced locally. Nearly three quarters of respondents were male (73.9%), which also indicates that mostly local people participated as this reflects the local gender distribution at the Karlsruhe Institute of Technology. The majority of participants were in the age groups of either 20-25 (46.2%) or 26-35 (35.3%). Students make up the majority of participants (61.4%), followed by employees (30.3%). 8.3% either list another profession or preferred to not answer this question. In addition, over half of the respondents have a university degree (55.4%), and 36.2% have a high school diploma or "Abitur".

Previous Resource Sharing Experience The first block of the survey asked participants about their previous experience in sharing resources online. This block was answered by 119 out of the 121 participants, meaning that 98.3% of participants had such previous experience.

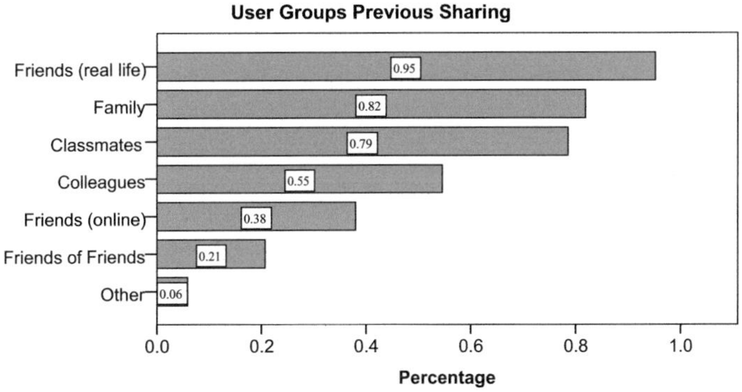

Figure 3.3.: User Groups with which Resources were Previously Shared Online

First, the participants were asked which online platforms they previously used to share resources. For the given sample, the majority of participants used email, DropBox or other (private) social networks to share resources online (see Figure A.2 in Appendix A). Other Cloud- or P2P-based platforms are also frequently used, for example Google Drive, P2P platforms and own servers. Interestingly, professional networks are used much less frequently than private social networks to share resources online (13% vs 74%). Besides the platform for sharing, participants were asked which type of resources they previously shared (Figure A.3 in Appendix A). Whereas resource types such as files, pictures, and music are common as expected, it also shows that both lecture notes and sample solutions are shared frequently, which can be explained by the high number of students in the given sample. Furthermore, storage is shared by approximately 24% of the participants, which is relevant for another question later in the survey.

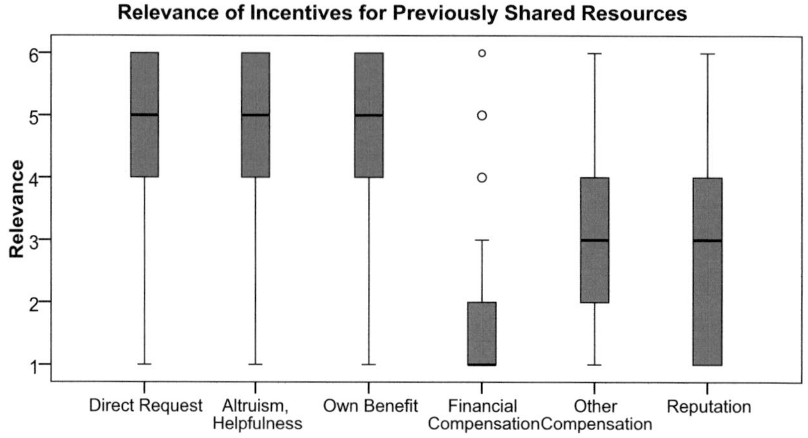

Figure 3.4.: Incentives for Previous Online Resource Sharing

Figure 3.3 shows the user groups with which the participants have shared resources online. Sharing among direct friends, relatives, and classmates is very common, whereas fewer participants share resources with users they only know indirectly or online. This can be an indication that the necessary level of trust to facilitate sharing is higher for these user groups.

Finally, the last set of questions in the first block considered the incentives that were important for participants in their previous online resource sharing experience. The participants were asked to rank the relevance of certain incentives, where 1 on the Likert-scale corresponds to "not important" and 6 is "very important". The results are shown as boxplots in Figure 3.4. The data reveals that direct requests from other users, general altruism and helpfulness, as well as the own benefit of sharing are considered the most important incentives by the majority of users. Social reputation and other forms of compensation are less important for most users, and financial compensation is considered least important. These results indicate that direct compensation is not necessarily a driver in resource sharing, participants rather seem to include strategic considerations such as reciprocity in their decision to share resources online, as shown in the high importance of "own benefit".

Incentives for Registration and Sharing After considering the experiences of previous online resource sharing, the second block of questions in the survey studied the importance of certain incentives in hypothetical resource sharing scenarios. This covered the first two stages of the sharing lifecycle, namely incentives to register as well as incentives to actively participate. Furthermore, the scenarios distinguished between sharing in private social networks (such as Facebook) and professional social networks (primarily used for business and professional networking, such as LinkedIn), to investigate if users have different incentives to participate in resource sharing based on the type of relationships they have with other people in the network.

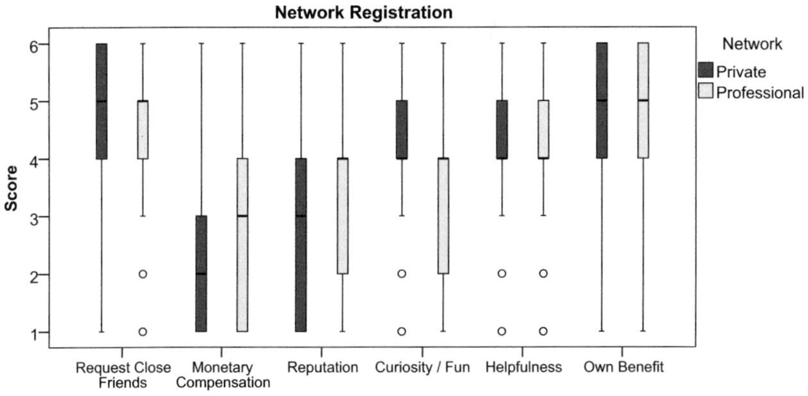

(a) Registration Incentives

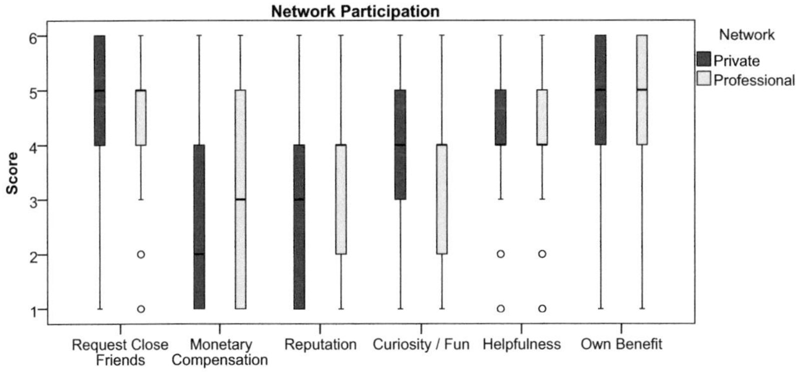

(b) Participation Incentives

Figure 3.5.: Survey Results for Registration and Participation Incentives in Private and Professional Networks

There are several interesting results that can be seen in Figure 3.5. Considering sharing resources with other users in a private network (e.g., non-colleague friends), the relevant incentives for registration and active participation on the platform are quite similar, as shown in Figures 3.5a and 3.5b. The most important incentives are requests from close friends, as well as the own benefit from sharing (e.g., expected reciprocity). Furthermore, curiosity and helpfulness also are important for many participants, yet less important than the previously mentioned incentives. Financial compensation is, similar to the case of previous resource sharing in Figure 3.4, the least important incentive for most participants.

The results were also compared using a Wilcoxon signed-rank test as the data was not normally distributed. The statistical evaluation showed that in private networks, monetary compensation ($p = 0.01$), helpfulness ($p = 0.01$), as well as curiosity/fun ($p = 0.05$) are considered more important for the participation stage. In professional networks, a statistically significant difference in the importance between registration and participation incentives could not be detected.

The Difference of Private and Professional Networks Users might perceive private networks differently to professional networks. Hence, it is interesting to see if the relevance of the considered incentive categories are different for users across these two types of networks. The comparison of incentives in private and professional networks in Figures 3.5a and 3.5b reveals interesting results. In both network types, the personal benefit (expected reciprocity) is the most important incentive for both registration and active participation, even more important than direct requests. Furthermore, curiosity and fun plays a lesser role in case of professional networks, and financial compensation is slightly more important in this context (which is in line with the previous arguments in Section 3.2.2).

As discussed previously, the relative ranking of the incentive categories between the network types is similar, yet there also seem to be differences in the level of importance. Comparing the differences of participating in private networks compared to public networks, a Wilcoxon signed-rank test is used to compare the differences between the two types of networks as the data was not normally distributed. For the different types of incentives to join such a platform, the test detected significant differences in Monetary Compensation (more relevant in professional networks, $p < 0.001$), Reputation (more relevant in professional networks, $p < 0.001$), and Curiosity/Fun (less relevant in professional networks, $p < 0.001$).

Considering the incentives to actively provide resources in private versus professional networks, the Wilcoxon signed-rank test found significant differences in Direct Request (less relevant in professional networks, $p = 0.001$), Monetary Compensation (more relevant in professional networks, $p = 0.012$), Reputation (more relevant in professional networks, $p < 0.001$), Curiosity/Fun (less relevant in professional networks, $p < 0.001$), and Helpfulness (less relevant in professional networks, $p = 0.029$).

As the sample size is rather small, these results are merely a tendency, yet confirm some of the expectations and reveal several interesting facts. The results show that in general, ones own expected benefit as well as direct requests are the most important incentives for both private and professional resource sharing networks. However, there seem to be subtle differences originating from the different context of sharing, where sharing with friends tends to place a higher emphasis on curiosity and helpfulness, and sharing with colleagues leads to a slightly higher emphasis on monetary compensation.

Sharing of Storage Space The last set of questions in the second block considered a scenario in which storage space is shared between users, allowing other users to store data on the participant's machines. The questions were framed in a way that indicated that such storage would be completely safe for the storage providers due to security and encrypting techniques. As storage sharing is a relevant use case and already implemented on certain platforms, the aim of this question set was to identify the necessary user groups and relationship types for which participants might be willing to share storage resources.

Considering the user groups that participants are willing to share storage with, the results show that besides a small minority that either is not willing to share storage at all or willing to share with everybody, most participants would be willing to share with family, relatives and close friends (see Figure A.4 in Appendix A). About 30% are also willing to share with classmates and colleagues, yet only a small subset of participants would be willing to share storage with friends of their friends. This also indicates that most participants require a certain level of trust towards the other user in order to allow sharing of storage space. In particular, assumptions about trust transitivity have to be handled carefully as the results for friend-of-friend relationships indicate that the perceived level of trust considerably decreases for indirect connections. This is confirmed in Figure A.5, which indicates that users specifically require close relationships for sharing of electronic storage space.

The Influence of Personality Type on Sharing Incentives After the previously discussed questions about incentives for online resource sharing, the survey closed with some short demographic questions as well as the TIPI. The aim of including the TIPI questions was to potentially identify if certain incentives are more relevant for certain personality traits. Figure 3.6 presents an overview of the participants' personality profiles based on the ten TIPI questions. The correlation tables with the extended results can be found in Appendix A.

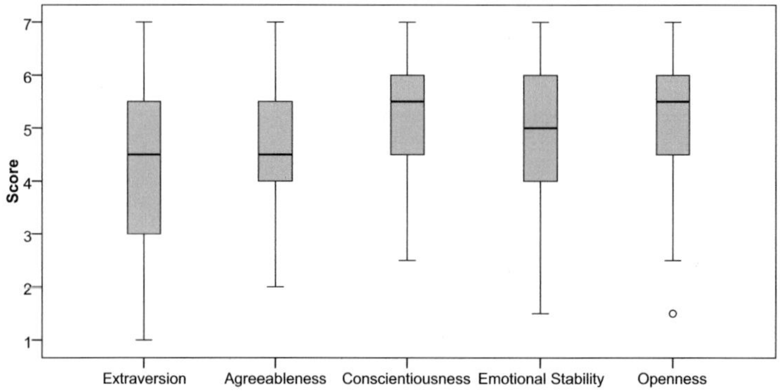

Figure 3.6.: Survey Results for Ten Item Personality Inventory (TIPI)

Table 3.1.: Comparison of Survey TIPI Scores with original TIPI scores (Gosling et al., 2003) and TIPI-G (Muck et al., 2007)

Data	Sample Size	Extrav.	Agreeabl.	Consc.	Emotional Stab.	Openness
Survey	121	4.30 (1.38)	4.72 (1.05)	5.23 (1.16)	5.01 (1.14)	5.17 (1.03)
TIPI	1126	4.56 (1.48)	5.26 (1.12)	5.47 (1.13)	4.85 (1.45)	5.43 (1.06)
TIPI-G	175	4.87 (1.21)	5.20 (0.95)	5.85 (0.93)	5.10 (1.20)	5.49 (0.97)

As the sample size is rather small, and the TIPI cannot provide as thorough a personality trait classification as the longer Big Five Inventory can (John et al., 1991), the results of the correlation analysis have to be interpreted with care. Table 3.1 compares the mean and standard deviation of the answers to two other data sets, the original TIPI data set (Gosling et al., 2003) as well as a German adaption of the TIPI questionnaire (TIPI-G, Muck et al. (2007)). Although there are small differences, overall the values are similar to the other data sets. Unfortunately, even if there are tendencies in the data, the sample size is also too small to conclusively identify significant correlations between personality traits and the importance of certain incentives except for some cases.

Despite these issues, there are some results that are noteworthy to discuss. First of all, there is an expected significant positive correlation between 'Extraversion' and 'Openness'. Further positive correlations are between 'Extraversion' and 'Conscientiousness' as well as 'Emotional Stability', and between 'Conscientiousness' and 'Emotional Stability' (see e.g. Tables A.1 and A.2).

Considering TIPI and relevant previous sharing incentives, there is a significant positive correlation between 'Conscientiousness' and direct requests as well as general helpfulness (see Tables A.1 and A.2). For sharing in private networks, both in case of registration and participation incentives 'Extraversion' is significantly positively correlated with monetary compensation, reputation, own benefit and curiosity/fun, yet only in the participation scenario there is a significant correlation between 'Extraversion' and requests of close friends. Additionally, 'Agreeableness' is positively correlated with helpfulness (see Table A.3). In professional networks, also both for registration and participation incentives, 'Extraversion' is significantly positively correlated with requests from friends, own benefit, curiosity/fun, and reputation. Furthermore, in these cases 'Openness' is also significantly positively correlated with curiosity/fun and helpfulness, indicating that these incentives are more relevant for people considering themselves more open (see Table A.4).

In summary, these results provide a good basis for further investigation of relevant incentives, especially targeted at more specific scenarios. The insights gained by this short survey are helpful in getting an overview of participants' attitudes towards sharing, their potential willingness to share with indirectly connected network users, and different relative importance of incentives based on the type of relationships between the users.

3.3.3. Discussion

The survey results shed light on the relevance of certain incentives for sharing in a Social Cloud. In particular, for the registration and participation on such a platform, non-monetary incentives (such as helpfulness, curiosity, fun, and reputation) have a higher relevance than monetary compensation, which is similar to findings from literature. Considering relationship types, the sharing of resources with close friends is more prevalent than the sharing with acquaintances or indirect friends.

Table 3.2.: Relevance of Incentives for Private and Professional Networks, Mean and Standard Deviation

Incentive	Private	Professional	Stat. Difference (p=0.05)
Registration			
Request Close Friends	4.69 (1.26)	4.45 (1.27)	
Monetary Compensation	2.34 (1.39)	2.88 (1.64)	✓
Reputation	2.66 (1.40)	3.35 (1.55)	✓
Curiosity/Fun	4.13 (1.28)	3.43 (1.44)	✓
Helpfulness	3.99 (1.25)	3.98 (1.29)	
Own Benefit	4.76 (1.15)	4.81 (1.24)	
Participation			
Request Close Friends	4.85 (1.24)	4.50 (1.29)	✓
Monetary Compensation	2.67 (1.61)	3.04 (1.73)	✓
Reputation	2.83 (1.49)	3.31 (1.52)	✓
Curiosity/Fun	3.92 (1.37)	3.46 (1.46)	✓
Helpfulness	4.31 (1.06)	4.07 (1.20)	✓
Own Benefit	4.74 (1.17)	4.70 (1.25)	

The results also show differences in the relative importance of certain incentives with respect to the sharing scenario. Table 3.2 provides an overview of the difference in said relevance. Monetary compensation overall is of lesser relevance than other incentives, yet more important in professional settings. In contrast, curiosity/fun is of higher importance in private settings.

The identified relevant incentives also have to be considered in the design of a Social Cloud. For example, the relevance of direct requests implies that corresponding interaction capabilities between users should facilitate such direct requests. Considering resource sharing in social contexts, the findings show that the specific sharing scenario has to be taken into account for the incentivization of users. In particular, the importance of non-monetary incentives emphasizes the necessity to implement allocation mechanisms that are not based on monetary transactions or compensations.

3.4. Summary

This chapter identified and discussed the explicit need to address user participation incentives in Social Clouds. Its aim was to address research question 1.1. Section 3.2 proposed a model in which three participation stages are distinguished, namely User Discovery and Registration, User Participation, and Social Behavior in Resource Sharing. Additionally, factors that influence the importance of incentives, such as the application scenario, relationship types and the applied market mechanisms, were identified. An online survey was conducted to identify potential differences in the importance of incentives within different stages, and its results discussed in Section 3.3. The results show that non-monetary incentives such as altruism, fun, or expected reciprocity are more important then monetary compensation, which is in line with the Social Cloud assumptions. Regarding factors that influence the importance of incentives, the results indicate that for the given scenario and participation pool, the setting of the network (private vs. professional) influences the importance of certain incentives such as monetary compensation. Furthermore, users prefer to share resources along stronger relationship types, i.e., favor sharing with friends over sharing with colleagues or friends of friends. In contrast, for the given scenario the importance of the considered incentives was similar in both the registration and participation stage.

As discussed before, the identification of user participation stages as well as the relevant incentives in these stages are a necessary first step in the design of an incentive scheme. As a next step, this knowledge can then be applied in the design of an incentive scheme tailored to the given scenario. Before adapting and implementing the incentive scheme on the platform itself, a simulation-based approach can be leveraged to study the sensitivity of said scheme on changes in the system, e.g., a change in user type distributions. Therefore, the next chapter presents two case studies that show how incentive and contribution schemes can be evaluated with respect to different user characteristics.

Chapter 4.

Designing Incentive Schemes and Co-operative Infrastructures

"It is well known in the public goods literature that in the absence of outside incentives the individually rational allocation of resources in such an environment will, in general, be less than the socially optimal outcome."

(Krishnan et al., 2006)

THE identification of participation stages and the relevant incentives therein is the necessary first step in the development of an incentive scheme tailored to the specific needs of a Social Cloud. Based on these insights, incentive schemes can be developed that incorporate the findings. In practice, the impact of such incentive schemes needs to be studied to assure that the goals of the incentive scheme are met and that the incentives are set correctly.

As mentioned before, there are several ways how incentive schemes can be designed and evaluated, such as implementing the proposed incentive scheme and test it through a prototype system with a test user group, or deriving predictions based on analytical models. Complementary to these approaches, a simulation-based study can be particularly helpful when evaluating through a prototype is not possible or feasible, e.g., in the early development stages of a system or when changes to the system are expensive and the effects need to be predicted beforehand. An example for such an application is the prediction of the effects of changing user groups and user behavior, and their impact on the efficiency of the incentive scheme. Simulation-based approaches have been advocated before for use in the design process of incentive systems in online communities, see e.g. Mao et al. (2007) and Ren and Kraut (2011). Hence, such a simulation-based approach in the engineering of incentive schemes is the focus of this chapter.

This chapter illustrates how incentive schemes can be designed and studied using a simulation-based approach by presenting two case studies. Specifically, this chapter aims to answer research questions 1.2 and 1.3. Section 4.1 describes the user model that is used in both case studies. In Section 4.2, the first case study develops an incentive scheme with the aim to encourage resource contribution from users. During the case study, the (dynamic) effects of the incentive scheme on the overall system, as well as on different user types, are evaluated. The second case study, which is presented in Section 4.3, models a platform for which the necessary resources are co-operatively provided by the platform users themselves. Specifically, it aims to study the suitability of different contribution schemes (i.e., how users contribute to the co-operative infrastructure) for the considered platform. The chapter concludes with a discussion of the case studies.

4.1. User Model

Users in the case studies are described by several characteristics, which include:

- *Resources*: Users have a resource endowment, which can be of several resource types. They can offer parts of their resources and may request resources from other users. The resources are generally described by amount and type.
- *Objective*: The goal of the users, in general, is assumed to be the maximization of their utility function. In this case, the objective is generally to maximize the (positive) difference of benefits (e.g., through consumption of resources) and costs (e.g., for offering resources).
- *Availability*: As users are probably not available all the time, their availability can be described by respective distributions. For example, Javadi et al. (2011) identify several user groups for the Volunteer Computing project SETI@home with distinctive distributions for availability and unavailability intervals.

For ease of reference, Table 4.1 provides an overview of the parameters that are used in the case studies.

Table 4.1.: Model Parameters

Parameter	Description
β	Convexity parameter
λ	Degree of altruism
p	Relative price of providing or sharing resources
$\omega_{i,r}$	Resource endowment of user i and resource type r
r	Resource type
$\rho_{i,r}$	Percentage of resources of type r that user i shares
$s_{i,t}$	Contribution score of user i at time t
$\sigma_{i,r}$	Percentage of resources of type r that user i reserves for own purposes
$\sigma_{i,min}$	Minimum amount of resources that user i reserves for own resources
$\Pi_{i,o}$	Amount of resources that user i reserves for own purposes
$\Pi_{i,s}$	Amount of resources that user i shares
$\tau_{i,r}$	Utility parameter from consuming resources from other users

Resources In the case study model, each user i has an endowment of (computing) resources $\omega_{i,r}$ available, where $r \in R$ indicates the resource type. They can use them either for (self-) consumption or provision them to other users or the infrastructure. The percentage of resource type r that the user consumes or reserves for their own purposes is denoted by $\sigma_{i,r}$ (this includes not using the resources at all, i.e., idle resources). Similarly, $\delta_{i,r}$ is the percentage of resource type r that user i shares with other users (or the infrastructure in the second case study).

The cost for resource provisioning is indirectly determined through the parameter p: the higher p, the higher the relative cost of providing resources compared to consuming them or leaving them idle. As users only have a limited amount of resources available, for each user i the following endowment constraint has to be fulfilled:

$$\sigma_{i,r} + p\rho_{i,r} = 1 \quad (4.1)$$

This indirect approach of modeling costs was chosen for following reasons: first, modeling an explicit cost function requires assumptions about its components and their relation. For example, although there are studies that model energy costs for computer systems, their exact form (especially for different resource types) is hard to determine (see e.g. Elnozahy et al. (2003)). In addition, the detailed measuring of energy consumption and costs requires additional equipment such as smart meters, which might not be available to all users. Second, one might question if explicit cost considerations have a major influence on the decisions of users in social contexts. While this might be true for anonymous systems such as P2P, it is not clear if users explicitly take into account the costs for supporting a resource request of a (potentially indirect) friend.

Objective Using the standard economic approach, users are assumed to optimize a certain utility function. In contrast to classic economic theory, however, the utility function is not modeled as being purely dependent on the consumption and costs of resources. As the concept of *social* or *other-regarding preferences* and a multitude of studies have shown, for their decision making users might take other users' behavior and consumption into account (see e.g. Fehr and Schmidt (2000); Bolton and Ockenfels (2000); Andreoni and Miller (2002); Falk and Fischbacher (2006); Fehr and Schmidt (2006)). Hence, the case studies model a user's decision through a utility function that incorporates these aspects.

Specifically, the user model makes use of utility functions studied by Andreoni and Miller (2002). They provide general utility functions that can explain findings from economic experiments in which a significant amount of subjects exhibit altruistic behavior, which is in contrast to the traditional economic principle of self-interest and rational utility maximization.[1] More specifically, altruistic behavior in this case means that a user "is willing to sacrifice own resources in order to improve the well being of others" (Fehr and Schmidt, 2006, p.620). This is the case when users provide resources for others or the platform infrastructure, as they incur costs (not being able to use the resources themselves) but their contribution increases the performance of the system. Andreoni and Miller (2002) show that through correct parametrization of the following utility function (Equation 4.2), altruism can be included in economic decision making. Their approach is used for two reasons: 1) the given setting closely resembles a public goods game where users incur costs for providing resources to the public (other users or the co-operative infrastructure), and in this case self-interest and altruism are often used as the most relevant parameters that characterize the behavior of users (see e.g. Fehr and Fischbacher (2003)). 2) Their utility function is able to capture various forms of utility functions,

[1]Based on certain assumptions, it is common in economics to describe the preferences that users have with respect to an outcome (such as resource allocation) with a utility function that implements these preferences (Andreoni and Miller, 2002). Andreoni and Miller (2002) also showed that this utility function is able to explain empirical data of several laboratory games which are conceptually very similar to the considered scenario, specifically that a user's actions affect the utility of other users.

from classic substitutive and Leontief[2] to convex utility functions, making it very flexible.

$$U_i(\sigma_i, \rho_i) = \sum_r \left(\Pi_{i,s} \left(\sigma_{i,r}, \tau_{i,r}\right)^{\beta} + \lambda \Pi_{i,o} \left(\rho_{i,r}\right)^{\beta} \right)^{1/\beta} \tag{4.2}$$

Here, $\Pi_{i,s}$ denotes the self-consumption of resources of user i, and $\Pi_{i,o}$ denotes the provisioning of resources. As mentioned before, $\sigma_{i,r}$ is the percentage of resource type r that the user reserves for own purposes, and $\rho_{i,r}$ the percentage of resource type r that they share with other users. β is a parameter that defines the convexity of the preferences, and λ defines the degree of altruism.

Besides consuming their own resources and giving their resources to other users, users gain a certain utility from successfully served resource requests, denoted by $\tau_{i,r}$. For simplicity, this is assumed to be linear in the percentage which is served by other users, with limits $[0,1]$. In other words, the more of their resource requests are fulfilled by other users, the higher the respective utility. $\tau_{i,r}$ is included in the utility function as shown in Equation (4.2) because, in some sense, the utility from consuming other resources can be considered similar to consuming one's own resources. Furthermore, note that $\tau_{i,r}$ does not directly depend on (and hence cannot be directly influenced by) the decisions of user i, as it depends on the number of resources that the other users provide.

Furthermore, each user belongs to a certain utility type as identified by Andreoni and Miller (2002). The different types and the parameters of the utility function are summarized in Table 4.2. Besides three types with different values for β and λ (types 4-6), types 1-3 describe special shapes of the utility function. Type 1 models selfish users who only receive utility from resource consumption, having no inherent incentive to provide resources. Type 2 models a classic Leontief utility function, and type 3 models the case when self-consumption and provisioning are perfect substitutes.

Using the individual contribution to the system as the altruistic parameter is not the only possible way of modeling "social" behavior; alternatives can be studied as well. For example, instead of individual contributions, the average utility of other users could be used. Other possibilities are to use the average contribution

[2] In a Leontief utility function, the utility depends on the minimum value of the given components: $U(x_1, x_2) = min\{x_1, x_2\}$. See e.g. (Mas-Colell et al., 1995, p. 49).

Table 4.2.: List of Potential Utility Function Types based on Andreoni and Miller (2002)

Type	Function	Size	λ	β	Description
1	$U_i = \sum_\lambda \Pi_{i,s,\lambda}$	0.227	-	-	Selfish
2	$U_i = \sum_\lambda min\{\Pi_{i,s,\lambda}, \Pi_{i,o,\lambda}\}$	0.142	-	-	Leontief
3	$U_i = \sum_\lambda \Pi_{i,s,\lambda} + \Pi_{i,o,\lambda}$	0.062	-	-	Perfect Substitutes
4	see equation (4.2)	0.245	0.319	0.621	Weak Selfish
5	see equation (4.2)	0.162	0.529	-0.350	Weak Leontief
6	see equation (4.2)	0.162	0.736	0.669	Weak Perfect Substitute

and/or consumption amount in the system, or the average amount of successfully satisfied requests.[3] While undoubtedly interesting, these aspects are left for future case studies.

Based on their utility function, each user will choose their individual optimal values for $\rho_{i,r}$ and $\sigma_{i,r}$ depending on their level of altruism and the convexity of their preferences. Note, however, that a user might wish to reserve a minimum level of their endowment, $\sigma_{i,min}$, for other usage (such as private use or sharing with friends). In the model, this would be equivalent to reserving a certain percentage of ω_i, and only have $(1 - \sigma_{i,min})\,\omega_i$ potentially available for usage. As this is equivalent to an adjustment of user i's available resource endowment, in order to avoid making the model unnecessarily complex this aspect is omitted in the remaining model.

4.2. Case Study: Designing Incentive Schemes

Having identified the participation stages of users as well as relevant incentives for resource sharing in Chapter 3, the next step is the application of this knowledge in the design of an incentive scheme for Social Clouds. To achieve this, the findings have to be transformed into a suitable incentive scheme, which is the focus of this case study. It investigates the effects of an incentive scheme on the considered sharing platform and its users to encourage the contribution of resources to fulfill on-demand computing requests of users. The case study is an example how a simulation-based approach as described in Section 2.2 can be used in combination

[3] Consider the following simple example to explain why such an approach can make sense: a user contributes a data set to a community or colleague and consequently a new discovery is made which benefits that user or the community as a whole. In that case, the benefits for the other users might influence the individual contribution of resources.

with the previously gained insights in the design and engineering of an incentive scheme. The section is an extended version of Haas et al. (2012). It starts with an outline of the scenario in Section 4.2.1, and describes the simulation model in Section 4.2.2. The case study is evaluated in Section 4.2.3 and the findings discussed in Section 4.2.4.

4.2.1. Scenario

The case study builds on the work of John et al. (2011), and Thaufeeg et al. (2011) who analyzed how the Social Cloud concept can be used to augment traditional Volunteer Computing by leveraging social networks to encourage participation. It builds upon the basic premises of volunteer computing that users contribute to "worthy" projects, retaining the argument that if user communities leveraged their social relationships as sources of resources, their accessible compute power would exceed that of existing volunteer computing projects (John et al., 2011).[4]

In the given scenario, a user can request certain technical entities/resources that are needed, e.g. for a specific scientific project. Examples could be a BOINC-like project (Anderson, 2004) that mainly requires computing cycles as resources, or more complex projects that require more than one resource type, e.g. databases, memory, and so on. An exchange of virtual machines as presented in Chapter 6 is also possible. The request of the user is then advertised to other users in their Social Cloud. These users decide whether or not to supply the required resources. In general, the more links to other members a user has in the system, the higher the potential supply of resources and thus the likelier it is that a request can be entirely fulfilled. The main objective of this case study is to evaluate the effects of a trading constraint (TC) on the system, specifically the effects on different user types.

[4]This is based upon the number of users in Facebook (1.19 billion monthly active users in 11.2013, see `http://tinyurl.com/fb-size`), that an average user havs 190 friends see `http://tinyurl.com/fb-anatomy` (last accessed May 2014), and the assumption that sharing also occurs between friends of friends.

4.2.2. Modeling an Incentive Scheme

User Behavior

The user model builds on the utility function presented in Section 4.1. Without loss of generality, $\Pi_{i,s}$ and $\Pi_{i,o}$ can be general functions that describe how a user's utility depends on the consumption and provisioning of resources. This case study, for simplicity, only considers Equation (4.2) with $\Pi_{i,s}(\sigma_{i,r}, \tau_{i,r}) = \sigma_{i,r} + \tau_{i,r}$ and $\Pi_{i,o}(\rho_{i,r}) = \rho_{i,r}$, i.e., the users' utility is linearly dependent on the consumption and provisioning percentage, respectively. Note that the components $\sigma_{i,r}$, $\rho_{i,r}$ and $\tau_{i,r}$ are normalized to the range $[0,1]$. This is done to make different resource types comparable in the utility function, assuming an equal importance of resource types for the users.[5]

The optimal level of resource consumption and (through the endowment constraint) also for provisioning can be calculated through the derivative. Depending on the relative price for resource provisioning, users select a certain percentage of their resources that they contribute to other users. Assuming that the utility function can be segmented into a sum of functions (one for each resource type), and the types are independent of each other, the optimal percentage can then be calculated as:

$$\frac{\partial U_i(\sigma_i, \rho_i)}{\partial \sigma_i} = 0$$

$$\sigma_{i,r} = \frac{\lambda^{\frac{-1}{1-\beta}} p_r^{\frac{-\beta}{\beta-1}} - \tau_{i,r}}{1 + \lambda^{\frac{-1}{1-\beta}} p_r^{\frac{-\beta}{\beta-1}}} \quad \forall r \in R \tag{4.3}$$

Note that the maximization is only meaningful for either $\sigma_{i,r}$ or $\rho_{i,r}$, as one determines the other, and $\tau_{i,r}$ only depends on the amount of resources that other users provide and cannot be directly influenced by user i.[6]

While the percentage of provided resources as in Equation (4.3) might be individually optimal when utility maximization is considered to be the goal of the users,

[5] The model can be augmented to capture user-specific preferences for different resource types, which is, for ease of understanding, omitted in this case study.

[6] Note further that for utility type 5, restricting the range to $[0,1]$ would yield a theoretical optimum of $\sigma = 1$, due to asymptotic conditions. However, as this is unrealistic, 1 is excluded from the optimization, in which case equation 4.3 applies again.

one might ask if there are other, system-centric goals that are more in line with the philosophy of the system. One such example could be the percentage of resource requests that can be fulfilled.

Incentive Scheme

While a utility function only models the willingness to contribute, given assumptions or data on the distribution of user types and the respective parameters, a sharing platform without additional rules might not induce the proper incentives for each user group to participate in resource sharing. Hence, an additional trading constraint is introduced as a type of incentive scheme in order to limit the effects of free-riding and incentivize users to increase their resource contributions.

The trading constraint is similar to the incentive scheme described by Ranganathan et al. (2004) and other contribution-based schemes. The main idea of the incentive scheme is that each user receives a contribution score based on its contribution to the Social Cloud, and each user can only trade with other users that have a lesser or equal contribution score. In other words, if $s_i(t)$ is the score of user i at time t, a trade can only occur with users j for which $s_j(t) \leq s_i(t)$. Increasing one's score allows the user to select from a broader base of other users to satisfy resource requests, which affects the probability that resource requests are fulfilled (and thus has an influence on the utility).

Ranganathan et al. (2004) argue that this is an effective incentive scheme in P2P networks, leaving free riders with little options but to increase their participation if they want to continue using the network. However, they did not study the effect of the incentive scheme on the system itself, e.g., considering performance metrics such as number of different files (resources) shared in the system. Different user types, which might be adversely affected by the constraint, were also not considered.

For the evaluation this case study looks at two system performance measures:

1. The average utility of users
2. The number of satisfied requests

Intuitively, one might suspect that introducing a trading constraint reduces both average utility (due to the utility of free riders being lowered) and successful allocations (as the supply for a request is shortened for users with lower contribution scores). However, as users gain utility also from successful requests in the system, increasing their contribution could increase the number of successful allocations (more supply), and thus in turn increase their utility again. This case study evaluates which of these effects prevail.

Contribution Score The contribution score consists of two weighted components as given in Equation (4.4).[7] As a baseline, $\kappa_1 = \kappa_2 = 0.5$, is used, i.e., an equal weighting between the contribution components. This can be changed in order to shift the emphasis for different scenarios.

$$s_i(t) = \frac{\kappa_1 s_{quantity,i}(t) + \kappa_2 s_{scarcity,i}(t)}{\kappa_1 + \kappa_2} \tag{4.4}$$

The first component, $s_{quantity,i}$, is calculated based on the *quantity of resources* that a user provides, giving an incentive to provide more resources to increase the contribution score. While this is, for itself, not necessarily beneficial for the system, as a user can provide huge amounts of resources that are not needed by other users at all, quality and relevance of resources can also be included. The quantity score of a resource is determined through Equation (4.5). Over a certain time period (T_c), the maximum contribution of all users is determined, and the contribution of every user is normalized by that maximum such that the range of the score is in $[0, 1]$.

$$s_{quantity,i}(t) = \frac{\int_{t-T_c}^{t} \sum_{r \in R} \rho_{i,r}(\tau)\, d\tau}{\max_j \int_{t-T_c}^{t} \sum_{r \in R} \rho_{j,r}(\tau)\, d\tau} \tag{4.5}$$

The second component of the contribution score, $s_{scarcity,i}$, is the *scarcity of a resource*, which is determined through Equation (4.6) as the relative amount of requests vs. offers. The higher the ratio, the scarcer a resource is, and providing scarcer resources yields higher contribution scores (with $|\mathcal{O}_i|$ being the number of resources the user offers).

$$s_{scarcity,i}(t) = \frac{\sum_{o_{i,r} \in \mathcal{O}_i} \psi_r(t)}{|\mathcal{O}_i|} \tag{4.6}$$

[7] More components can be easily integrated. Examples are quality, relevance to the system, and diversity of resources.

The relative scarcity of a resource can be determined by Equation (4.7), where $r_{i,r}$ are the requests for resource r by user i, and $o_{i,r}$ are the offers of resource r by user i.

$$\eta_r = \frac{\sum_i r_{i,r}}{\sum_i o_{i,r}} \tag{4.7}$$

An s-shaped scarcity function is used to normalize the scarcity value to the interval $[0,1]$. Equation (4.8) defines this function, where κ_T is a threshold value that can be set to specify the amount from which a resource is considered is scarce. This approach allows for modeling flexibility by allowing to set different thresholds for different types of resources.

$$\psi_r = \begin{cases} 0 & \text{for } \eta_r < 1 \\ \frac{1}{2} \cdot \sin(\frac{\pi}{\kappa_T} \cdot \eta_r - \frac{\pi}{2\kappa_T}(\kappa_T + 2)) + \frac{1}{2} & \text{for } 1 \leq \eta_r \leq \kappa_T \\ 1 & \text{for } \eta_r > \kappa_T \end{cases} \tag{4.8}$$

Trust-based Allocation Matching

Given the resource requests from other users, the selection process of a user has to be modeled. In this case, trust-based resource allocation is used. Each user has a certain (resource-specific) trust value with every other user, which depends on previous experiences between the users (granted and fulfilled resource requests leading to higher trust).

Initially, in a real-world Social Cloud users can categorize their friends with respect to trust values. In the simulation, the initial assignment of trust values is based on the network structure. Directly connected users are randomly assigned to trust scores according to $\vartheta \in [0.5, 1.0]$. For not directly connected users the initial assignment is based on trust transitivity. As argued by Golbeck (2005), trust is to some degree transitive, meaning that the direct trust scores on the path of an indirect relationship can be used as a proxy for indirect trust. However, the exact degree of transitivity is not clear, and the survey results in Section 3.3 indicate that trust to a friend-of-friend is considerably lower than trust for users with a direct social connection. For this reason, and as repeated multiplication for indirect relationships of a higher degree quickly decreases the corresponding trust value, the case study assumes that trust is transitive for friend-of-friend relationships, and that the initial trust value for connections involving more than one friend in between the users is set to zero.

The trust score dynamically changes based on the rating that each user gets from other users for the provisioning of resources or services. Similar to the trust-based recommendation system described in (Walter et al., 2008), users are able to provide feedback about the quality of resource provision, where $\chi_{r,j,i}(t)$ denotes the feedback of user j about user i for resource type r.

The update of trust values is done through following formula:

$$\vartheta_{i,j,r}(t+1) = \begin{cases} w_t \cdot \vartheta_{i,j,r}(t) + (1-w_t) \cdot \chi_{r,j,i}(t) & \text{for } \chi_{r,j,i}(t) \geq 0.5 \\ (1-w_t) \cdot \vartheta_{i,j,r}(t) + w_t \cdot \chi_{r,j,i}(t) & \text{for } \chi_{r,j,i}(t) < 0.5 \end{cases} \tag{4.9}$$

In this formula, w_t is the weighting factor that determines the smoothness of the moving average, i.e., how fast new information (positive or negative feedback) $\chi_{r,j,i}(t) \in [0,1]$ is taken into account (where user j rates user i). For values $w_t \in [0.5,1]$, this update scheme propagates negative effects fast and positive effects slow, which is representative for the property of trust (Walter et al., 2008), and is also aligned with trust aspects in Social Clouds (Caton et al., 2012). In the simulation, $w_t = 0.75$ is used as baseline value for this reason. To study the sensitivity of the system with respect to this update rule, an alternative trust update scenario (ATU) with $w_t = 0.25$ is studied as well, in which case positive feedback effects are incorporated fast whereas negative effects slowly.

For every resource r, the potential matches are shown to user i in a list sorted according to the trust values. The probability of selecting one of the requests of the list is simulated through the Click through rates of Google (Hearne, 2006), as a proxy for real choice behavior. In other words, this probability function assigns a higher probability for matches on top of the list, as these are chosen more likely than lower-ranked matches. Additionally, users are modeled to have a certain minimum trust threshold for sharing, ϑ_{min}, that indicates the minimum trust score that has to exist between users. In the simulation, $\vartheta_{min} = 0.3$ is chosen to reflect that even in case of transitive trust, users might not be willing to share with users they do not know (e.g. friends of friends) or have low trust ratings.[8]

[8] Due to the other assumptions and the relatively low level, the simulation results do not seem to be sensitive towards the chosen value.

4.2.3. Evaluation of Dynamic Effects

The evaluation of the incentive scheme consists of two parts. First, the effect of the participation constraints on certain performance indicators of the Social Cloud is studied. In addition, the dependency of underlying user type distributions on the results is investigated. Hence, the evaluation aims at addressing following questions considering the usefulness of a trading constraint for the resource exchange platform:

- **Effects of trading constraint:** What is the effect of introducing the trading constraint on the average users' utility? How does the trading constraint change the number of successfully shared resources?
- **Consequence for different user types:** To what degree are different user types affected by the trading constraint?

Simulation Specifics

For the case study, a social network with small-world properties is used as network topology (using a connection rewiring probability of 40%, see Watts and Strogatz (1998)). To study the effect of network size, networks of 20, 50, 100, 200 and 500 users are compared. Depending on the size, each user has a direct connection to roughly one quarter of the other users, which also reflects certain small-world network properties.[9] As a baseline, $\kappa_1 = \kappa_2 = 0.5$ is used in the simulation. For the trust calculation, the average feedback given by users is $\chi_{r,j,i}(t) = 0.7$ with a standard deviation of 0.3 to account for changing quality in the requests. The scenario considered 3 resource types, a maximum resource amount of 10, as well as a scarcity value of $\kappa_T = 5$. All users are initialized with the same contribution score, which changes over time according to the individual contributions of the users.

In all scenarios, 10 repetitions of the setting were made to minimize the potential effects of initialization and random number effects. Results were averaged over the 10 repetitions. Each scenario was implemented as a discrete event simulation with 1000 simulation periods. In each period, the users decided on the amount of resources they offer (based on the utility function in Section 4.2.2), and the matching is performed. In order to avoid the start-up problem and potentially skewed

[9] For example, in a network with 500 users, each user is directly connected to 100 other users.

results due to initialization effects (Law, 2007, 508ff.), only the last 900 periods are used for the evaluation.

Effects of the Trading Constraint on the System

While the introduction of a trading constraint as shown in the Section 4.2.2 was proven to increase participation and reduce free-riding in P2P systems (see Ranganathan et al. (2004)), its usefulness in social collaborative scenarios is not clear. Therefore, the effects of the trading constraint on the system are studied first. This is followed by a more detailed analysis of the trading constraint on the different user types.

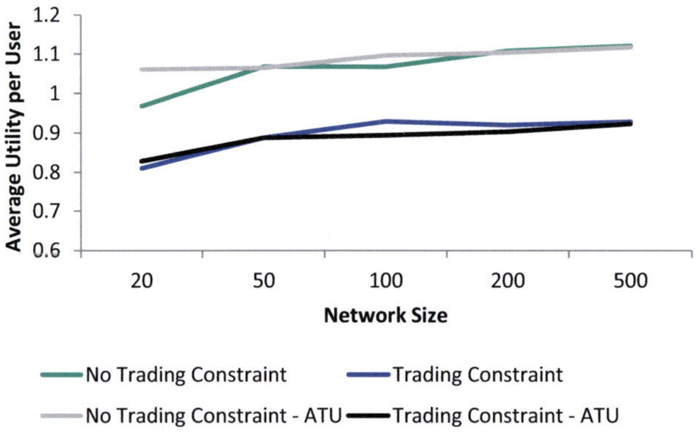

Figure 4.1.: Average User Utility

Figure 4.1 shows the average utility per user for different network sizes for the baseline trust update as well as the alternative scenario where negative feedback propagates slowly (ATU). Two effects can be observed. First, the average utility increases with the network size. This is intuitive, as a larger network (and more connections to other users) provides each user with more possibilities to share resources. That is, the larger a network and the more connections a user has, the higher the likelihood of an accepted request. Second, the average utility per user is lower in the scenario with the active trading constraint. This could also be expected, as the trading constraint yields lower contribution scores for free-riders, thus indirectly lowering their utility. As the trading constraint limits the number of users each user can share resources with[10], less requests are accepted, which lowers the utility of users. Additionally, both effects are not sensitive to the trust update mechanism, i.e., whether negative effects are propagated slowly in the trust score or not. This can be seen by the qualitatively similar average user utilities for the two different trust update mechanisms in Figure 4.1. This is an indication that the qualitative effects are related to other factors such as the user types and their behavior, rather than the trust calculation.

Looking at additional simulation results also yields interesting observations. Figure 4.2a shows the effect of the trading constraint on the probability that a resource requests is successfully granted (i.e., matched with a suitable offer). Clearly, due to similar reasons as for the decrease in average utility, the percentage of granted resource requests is decreased if the trading constraint is introduced. As users, on average, have a smaller set of other users they can potentially share resources with, the probability that a request is successfully matched is decreased, on average.

Considering the trust update, Figure 4.2a shows that especially smaller networks are affected by the trust update mechanism. If negative feedback affects the trust score to a high degree, it is likelier that users affected by this fall below the necessary trust threshold needed for a successful transaction. This leads to the lower percentage of successful requests compared to the alternative scenario (ATU) with slow negative propagation.

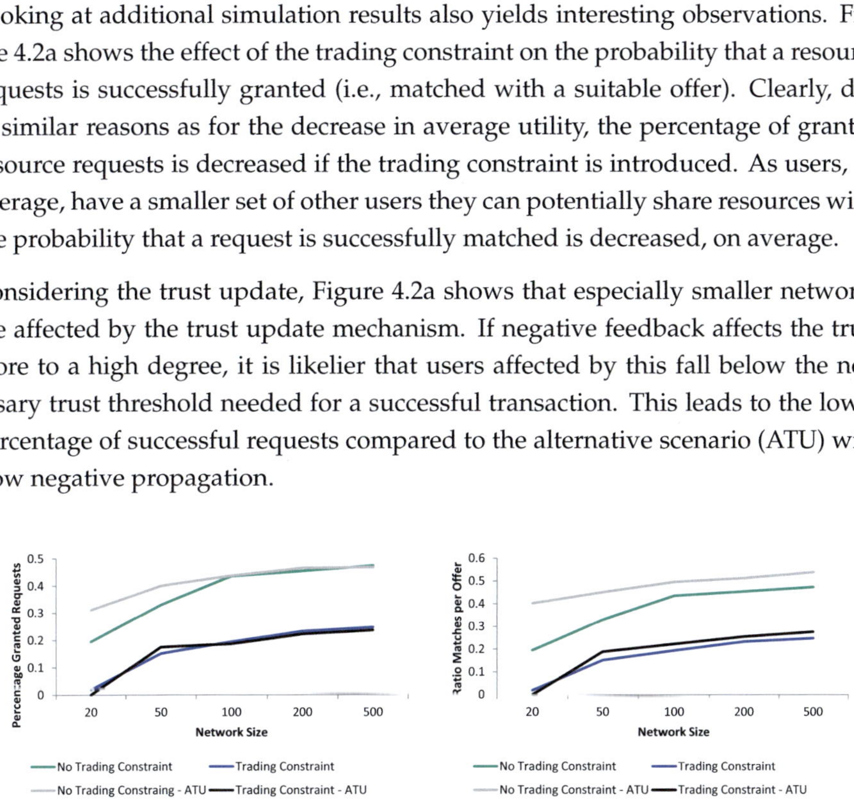

(a) Percentage of Granted Resource Requests

(b) Ratio Matches per Offer

Figure 4.2.: Average Offers and Matches per Offer

Furthermore, while the simulation results reveal that the average amount of offers per user does not significantly change with the network size, the ratio of successful

[10] I.e., the subset of users each user can share with is strictly included in the set of users in the setting without the trading constraint.

matches per offer significantly increases with the network size (see Figure 4.2b). This can be explained by the fact that the more connections each user has, the higher the potential number of other users that could be interested in a specific offer. Again, due to the contribution score which reduces the potential set of sharing users, the scenario with the active trading constraint yields a lower match per offer ratio. Similarly, the scenario with fast negative trust propagation yields lower ratios as well.

Effect of Trading Constraint on User Types

The previous results are expected, due to the design of the trading constraint. However, it is at first not clear how different user types are affected by the trading constraint. The contribution score aims to provide incentives to share resources, as selfish users with a low contribution score will not be able to request resources from users with a higher contribution score. To study the second question stated at the beginning of this case study, the ratio of utility per user in the active trading constraint scenario is compared with the baseline scenario without trading constraint. Figure 4.3 shows the baseline trust update scenario, which yields several interesting results.[11]

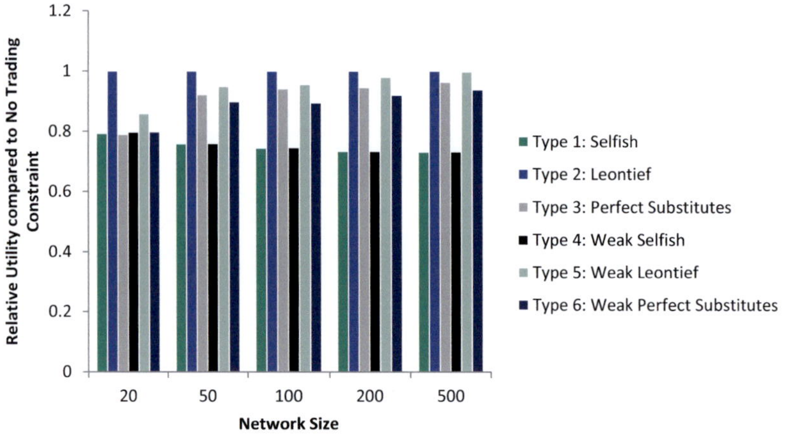

Figure 4.3.: Relative Change in User Utility through the Trading Constraint

[11] The alternative trust update scenario yields very similar results and is therefore omitted.

First, as observed earlier, the average utility of some user types increases with the network size, due to the larger pool of potential resource sharing partners. Second, the trading constraint discriminates users of different utility types. Having a closer look, it can be seen that user types 1 (selfish) and 4 (weak selfish) are particularly vulnerable to the trading constraint, and their utility even decreases with the network size. Indeed, these two user types represent selfish users who are only interested in their own resource consumption. Due to the contribution score, their set of potential sharing partners is reduced, which leads to less granted requests in the scenario with active trading constraint. Hence, the simulation confirms that selfish users (free-riders) are punished by the incentive scheme.

In contrast to the selfish users, other utility types perform better, especially with increasing network sizes. The utility of user types 3 (perfect substitutes), 5 (weak Leontief) and 6 (weak perfect substitutes, see Table 4.2) is close to the utility in the scenario without trading constraint, especially with increasing network sizes. This confirms that non-selfish users have less negative effects due to the contribution score. In particular, user type 5 performs as well as in the baseline scenario for larger network sizes, which means they are not affected at all by the trading constraint. In addition, the utility of user type 2 (Leontief) is not affected by the trading constraint.[12]

Effect of User Type Distribution

The previous results are based on the distribution of utility types as given in (Andreoni and Miller, 2002). As this is a rather specific assumption which potentially influences the results considerably, this section studies two different types of utility distributions in order to compare the validity of the previous findings. The first user type distribution considers a larger percentage of social user types, which is modeled as 70% of type 6 and only 30% selfish users of type 1. The second distribution considers the opposite, 70% selfish users (type 1) and only 30% of more social users (type 6), based on empirical findings that many online and P2P networks exhibit a large number of non-contributing users (e.g., Adar and Huberman (2000)).

[12]This specific result, however, should not be overemphasized, as this is a very specific utility function and in this simple scenario, users only apply a simple optimization function which ultimately determines their utility (in fact, the minimum in the Leontief utility function is responsible for the unchanged utility).

Table 4.3.: Incentive scheme with different user type distributions. Numbers in brackets are average utilities without and with active trading constraint.

Users	Social Scenario			Freerider Scenario		
	Average Offers	Relative Utility Type 1	Relative Utility Type 6	Average Offers	Relative Utility Type 1	Relative Utility Type 6
20	1.38	0.87 (1.15,1.00)	0.87 (1.36,1.18)	0.65	0.92 (1.09,1.00)	0.92 (1.28,1.18)
50	1.39	0.80 (1.25,1.00)	0.94 (1.46,1.37)	0.73	0.86 (1.16,1.00)	0.93 (1.36,1.26)
100	1.42	0.77 (1.29,1.00)	0.96 (1.51,1.44)	0.66	0.84 (1.19,1.00)	1.01 (1.40,1.42)
200	1.40	0.76 (1.31,1.00)	0.97 (1.53,1.48)	0.59	0.82 (1.21,1.00)	1.04 (1.42,1.47)
500	1.46	0.75 (1.33,1.00)	0.98 (1.55,1.52)	0.65	0.82 (1.22,1.00)	1.06 (1.43,1.52)

Table 4.3 shows the relative utilities of the user types as well as the average number of offers per user for the two scenarios. The more social scenario with the larger number of sharing users yields almost twice the average number of offered resources per user, and also a higher average utility than the baseline scenario. In addition, the relative decrease in utility for selfish users is higher in the social scenario and lower in the free-rider scenario. This is due to the higher utility for selfish users in the social scenario without trading constraint, as they are able to benefit from the higher number of offered resources by altruistic users and thus have a higher utility in that case. Once the trading constraint is active, though, the average utilities of both types are same for both scenarios (based on the fact that in neither scenario their resource requests are fulfilled).

For the type 6 users, an additional interesting effect can be observed. In the free-riding scenario, the relative utility is sometimes even higher with the trading constraint than without, whereas for the social scenario the relative utility is smaller with the trading constraint. This can be explained by the observation that in the free-riding scenario without trading constraints, users of type 6 have to compete with selfish users, hence potentially lowering their chance of getting a resource request granted. With the trading constraint and with a higher number of users in the system, they only have to compete with other users of the same type, thus increasing their chances to receive resources.

Overall, the results for the different user type distributions show that, in general, the effect of the trading constraint is qualitatively the same (punishing free-riders). In certain scenarios it can even be beneficial for more altruistic users to introduce the trading constraint.

4.2.4. Summary

Summarizing the findings, the incentive scheme with the trading constraint discriminates between different user types. While selfish types are punished by the constraint and their utility is significantly lowered, non-selfish users often perform almost as well as, and sometimes even better, as the baseline scenario. Hence, this simple case study outlines the usefulness of using simulation as tool in the design process for Social Clouds. It both confirms the expected behavior of the incentive scheme, and at the same time discovers interesting relationships concerning different user type distributions.

The case study can be augmented by a more detailed analysis to determine the sensitivity of the results on the simulation assumptions. Further sensitivity analyses include the effect of different network structures (random, small-world, etc.), additional parameters in the contribution score (e.g., quality of the provided resources), and different values for a trust threshold, below which resources are not granted to a requesting user.

4.3. Case Study: Co-operative Infrastructures

Computational social resource sharing platforms such as Social Clouds aim at facilitating the exchange of resources among users by providing means to register as a user, advertise or request resources, user lookup queries, communication utilities, allocation algorithms, and so on. All these tasks require infrastructure resources to store and use data, and the platform owner/provider has to decide how to acquire these infrastructure resources. Two of the most common means are to either invest in dedicated computational infrastructure resources on which the platform runs, or to use third-party Cloud resources to host the platform. Both approaches incur costs for the infrastructure and its maintenance.

Yet, a currently underrepresented approach to provide infrastructure resources to host a platform is to make use of the computational resources available to the platform users in a co-operative resource provisioning model. Especially when users are willing to share and exchange computational resources between other users, they might be willing to share a certain part of these resources with the platform itself. Such platforms already exist, for example cloud storage solutions that use storage space provided by users, which can increase their allowed space by contributing to the platform.[13]

Such an approach is perfectly suitable for Social Clouds. As the platform requires coordination mechanisms to facilitate their basic functionality (user management, resource allocation, etc.), an underlying computational infrastructure must be provided. Supporting a distributed computing platform requires an initial investment, advertising, or the introduction of fees. In a social context, this might be undesirable or counterproductive. For example, Shampanier et al. (2007) showed that users will not even pay negligible fees when free alternatives are available.

Following this reasoning, the second case study proposes a novel co-operative infrastructure on which socially oriented exchange platforms, such as a Social Cloud and potentially even social network platforms, can be supported, without incurring the overhead or costs of provisioning dedicated infrastructure resources. Instead of using dedicated, out-sourced, or third-party infrastructure, the platform is hosted upon the computational resources it manages.

Such a co-operative scenario is particularly fitting for social and volunteer computing, as users are providers as well as beneficiaries of the platform. In this setting, resources are defined as the computational capabilities needed by the collaborative platform to function, which in the simplest case includes: computational power and storage. This can also be extended to services like (distributed) databases and P2P overlay networks. Although aspects like reliability, redundancy, and technical instrumentation are important, these are not focus of this section. Instead, this section focuses on the economic methods to address system availability, redundancy, and scalability.

The section is an extended version of Haas et al. (2013) and is structured as follows. Section 4.3.1 defines the notion of co-operative infrastructures and gives an overview on related work and similar concepts. Section 4.3.2 introduces and describes the economic model behind co-operative infrastructures, and Section 4.3.3 evaluates the economic model with respect to certain performance metrics. Section 4.3.4 concludes with a summary and outlook on model extensions.

[13]See `http://www.symform.com` – last accessed May 2014

4.3.1. Definition of Co-operative Infrastructures and Related Work

Before the case study can consider the effects of contribution schemes for co-operative infrastructures, a general definition of this concept is needed to provide a basis for the subsequent model. The unifying characteristic of practically all types of co-operative organizations, such as credit unions, grocery shops, or infrastructures, is the fact that it is owned by a group of people. Depending on the type of co-operative, not only the ownership but also the management of the organization is shared by its users. These characteristics are the basis of the following definition of co-operatively provided infrastructures:

Definition 5 (**Co-operative Infrastructure**). *A co-operative infrastructure is a scalable computing platform where all (computational) resources constituting the platform's infrastructure, as well as those made available over the platform, are owned and/or managed by its users.*

Co-operatives can provide specific advantages over other methods, especially over third party solutions. For example, it is difficult to quantify the platform's required quality of service. Consequently, commercial entities may be incentivized to act opportunistically, i.e., maximize profit, which might not be in the users' best interest (Spear, 2000). Therefore, trust in the platform is critical, and inherent in the concept of collaboration and co-ownership in a co-operative.

User View on Co-operative Infrastructures

From the viewpoint of a user within a Social Cloud which utilizes co-operative infrastructures, the decision to share resources involves two levels as shown in Figure 4.4. Given that the user has resources available for sharing or exchange, they can either share them directly with other users, or contribute the resources to the co-operative infrastructure. These decisions are naturally intertwined, as making the resources available to either the infrastructure or to other users implies that the resources are not available for other purposes anymore. In other words, the contribution of a user to the sharing platform depends on the contribution to the co-op infrastructure, and vice versa.

An important implication of this viewpoint is that models for sharing resources within the resource exchange environment should incorporate the possibility to

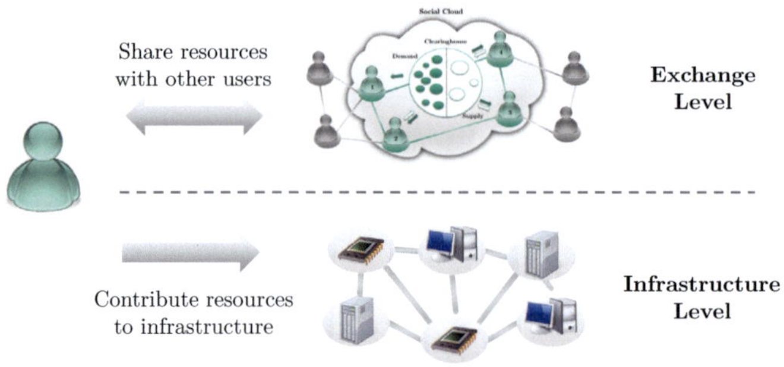

Figure 4.4.: Levels of Sharing for Platforms with Co-operative Infrastructures

provide resource to the infrastructure, thus blocking these resources from sharing with other users. However, this is not an easy task for several reasons. On one hand, the decision of users to either use their available resources for sharing with other users or for the infrastructure might be highly dynamic, and might depend on factors such as current requests of certain friends or the overall contribution to the co-op platform. On the other hand, the individual motivations to contribute to the infrastructure might be different compared to sharing the resources with friends (e.g., reciprocity considerations), and depend on the respective incentive scheme. Hence, an integrated model is likely to be too complex for the given case and the two levels are considered independently. Yet, the independent models can include parameters that approximate the contribution to the other level. For example, in the co-op model presented in this chapter, the parameter σ_i represents the percentage of resources blocked for other uses, such as own consumption or sharing with other users.

Related Work

Co-operative (co-op) business models are prevalent in a range of domains including grocery stores, credit/banking unions, health care and even housing. The core premise of a co-op model is distributing ownership, management and profit-sharing across its members. Depending on the scenario, co-ops can be formed between different groups of individuals and for many different reasons. Consumers, employees, producers, and residents are all motivated in different scenarios to form a co-op business. From an economic point of view, Porter and Scully (1987) investigate the formation of co-ops by comparing their efficiency to other organization forms. They compared different efficiency metrics (price, scale and managerial efficiency) and found that non-cooperative firms tend to be more efficient than co-ops. These metrics are, however, not applicable in this scenario as they are price-based, which implies that other metrics are needed in case of non-monetary Social Clouds.

In computer science, a co-op metacomputer was first introduced by Cime and Marzullo (1999). In this system, contribution is voluntary but intended to be mutually beneficial for users. More recently, in Grid and Cloud computing, federations have been created that span multiple institutions allowing resources to be shared amongst members of a virtual organization (VO). In these domains, novel co-op approaches to resource management and task allocation such as the Community Scheduler Framework (CSF) (Xiaohui et al., 2006) and the DRIVE metascheduler (Chard and Bubendorfer, 2008) have been proposed. Both CSF and DRIVE utilize community contributed resources for core metascheduling tasks such as resource allocation. Considering the feasibility of that approach, Xu and Yung (2010) showed that secure and privacy preserving auction protocols can be used in a co-operative metascheduling architecture to conduct trustworthy resource allocations on potentially untrusted resources. Unlike the Social Cloud model, these metaschedulers are designed to support job submission on a large scale, comparably static, Grid environment where providers have huge resource pools and can provide explicit availability guarantees.

The concept of a co-op is implicit in the definition of a Social Cloud, as members benefit directly from resource sharing with one another. A Social Cloud differs from many other resource sharing architectures as it leverages the relationships defined in a social network. However, Social Clouds and therefore the co-op infrastructure are not free from risk, as relationships can change over time. The implications for security in dynamic Social Cloud environments have been investigated by Xu and Yung (2010). Socially based systems are also becoming increasingly common in both academic and commercial applications. For example, social networking principles are commonly employed for coordinating ad hoc research communities such as the previously mentioned myExperiment.org (Roure et al., 2009), nanoHUB.org (Klimeck et al., 2008), and GlobusOnline[14] (Foster, 2011). Commercial applications such as FriendStore[15] (Tran et al., 2008) offer distributed file storage provided by a

[14]https://www.globus.org/ – last accessed May 2014
[15]http://friendstore.news.cs.nyu.edu/ – last accessed May 2014

user's friends. Diaspora[16] is a first step towards creating a Facebook-like social network platform relying on content resources (e.g., images) provided by its members (rather than dedicated resources). The model proposed in this case study builds upon this idea, by also capturing the computational resources needed to run the system, providing a platform free of dedicated centralized servers.

The concept of co-operative infrastructures is conceptually similar to several other sharing scenarios. For example, in public goods scenarios users contribute parts of their resources to a public good which is accessible to other users (e.g., paying taxes where the projects funded by tax money can be subsumed as public goods). Another example is the sharing of knowledge in related communities. In both cases, the contribution of each user affects the other users as they are able to consume the public good. As mentioned in Section 3.2, the "Tragedy of the Commons" problem can be observed in many related systems, which states that in public goods scenarios a single user's incentives to contribute might be inversely affected by the contributions of other users. Hence, this issue also has to be addressed in a co-operative setting. In the following case study, this is done through certain contribution schemes by which the users contribute to the infrastructure.

Whereas this case study focuses on the economic model of contribution schemes, similar systems have been studied from a conceptual and technical perspective. Babaoglu et al. (2012) consider the creation of P2P Infrastructure Clouds in which the (potentially unreliable) cloud resources are provided by the participants of the cloud. Their prototype implementation focuses on aspects such as self-organization and robustness to failures. In another model, Khan et al. (2013) study infrastructure clouds based on community networks. Their evaluation focuses on technical aspects such as response time and its dependency on the heterogeneity of provided resources. Both approaches, however, focus on technical issues and do not consider resource contribution schemes.

4.3.2. Economic Model

Previous literature on co-operative models focuses either on the organizational level (Porter and Scully, 1987; Spear, 2000), or the individual member level (Sexton, 1986). As no existing organizational data is available for this study, the approach of Sexton (1986) is applied which looks at individuals incentives to participate in

[16] `https://joindiaspora.com/` – last accessed May 2014

the co-op.[17] To do this, the following aspects need to be specified: 1) the users and their characteristics (e.g., endowment, utility function, etc.) (Sexton, 1986); 2) the resource requirements of the distributed system (Cime and Marzullo, 1999), in this case the Social Cloud platform; and 3) the contribution schemes through which users are encouraged to join the co-op and provide resources (Sexton, 1986). Each of these aspects are elaborated on in the following subsections to create a co-op model that is adequate for the considered scenario. As discussed, only computational infrastructure resources are considered in the co-op model, not software requirements such as databases.

User Model

The basic user model was presented in Section 4.1. In particular, the six different utility functions as given in Table 4.2 are used to model six different types of users. For this case study, the availability of users is additionally considered. Users are modeled as having a rate of availability α_i, in which their resources are available to the Social Cloud. This aspect constitutes the notion of quality of (a contributed) service (QoS), as availability is a standard QoS measure.

As Social Cloud implementations are still in their prototype phase, no traces of user behavior within the context of a Social Cloud exist. Consequently, the performance of a Social Cloud cannot be analyzed based upon production user data. However, to develop a co-op model it is assumed that user behavior within a Social Cloud is similar to behavior patterns in Volunteer Computing, as both rely on ad-hoc user communities donating spare computing capacity. Therefore, to model users the SETI@home (Anderson, 2004) host availability traces for the years 2007-09 is selected, which contain information for over 220,000 hosts.[18] These traces have been the subject of many analytical studies (e.g., Anderson and Fedak (2006); Javadi et al. (2009, 2011)), motivating their selection, as they provide a solid foundation to base a Social Cloud context upon. Statistical analysis of the data in (Javadi et al., 2011) reveals that 21% of the monitored hosts exhibit statistical independence in

[17] It should be noted that this is only one possible approach. The fact that economic actions are influenced by the social relations of a user has long been recognized (see e.g. Granovetter (1985)). Yet, it can be argued that these approaches (taking social embeddedness into account) are especially helpful when applied to (economic) network analysis based on observed data. However, as the actions of individual users are simulated without existing data, the model relies on specific behaviors instrumented through theoretically grounded and context fitting utility functions.

[18] Available: `http://fta.inria.fr` – last accessed May 2014

their availability. The authors also provide probability distributions for these hosts as well as for several clusters that can be distinguished within these 21% of hosts. These clusters are used to define different user types in the co-op model. Based on these results, Javadi et al. (2011) deduced a distribution of the length of availability intervals, which is used to simulate the availability of users. Table 4.4 summarizes the statistics of the six clusters, providing their relative size, average availability and the distribution functions of the interval lengths.[19]

Table 4.4.: List of User Cluster based on Javadi et al. (2011)

Cluster	Relative Size	Avg. Availability	Avail. Interval Dist.	Unavail. Interval Dist.
1	0.042	83.9%	Gamma(0.289,311.711)	Hyper-Exponential
2	0.108	82.2%	Gamma(0.340,152.216)	Hyper-Exponential
3	0.658	26.0%	Weibull(0.431,1.682)	Hyper-Exponential
4	0.004	91.7%	Gamma(0.347,371.622)	Hyper-Exponential
5	0.094	72.3%	Gamma(0.342,89.223)	Hyper-Exponential
6	0.094	56.7%	Gamma(0.357,43.652)	Hyper-Exponential

While the user types in Table 4.2 are found in experimental games, one might ask if this is a realistic setting for the case of co-operative infrastructures. Hence, this setting is also compared with another user type distribution which considers sharing in P2P networks. The basis for this distribution is obtained from Adar and Huberman (2000), who present a study on free-riding in Gnutella, a then-popular P2P platform, and shows that in this platform approximately 70% of the users do not share at all. Therefore, another scenario is introduced which captures this user type distribution in which 70% of users have a selfish utility function of type 1, and the remaining 30% share to some degree (according to utility function type 6). The second scenario is used to study the effects of different user type contributions on the applicability of the considered contribution schemes.

Modeling System Requirements

Determining the feasibility of users providing the computational infrastructure of a platform requires knowledge of the platform's resource requirements (i.e., the resources required to guarantee the functionality of the platform). In general, system requirements $R(n)$ can be modeled as $R(n) = l_1 f(n) + l_2$ where $l_1 f(n)$ specifies the increase in resources based on the number of users (n) and l_2 is the minimum

[19]The specifics of the unavailability interval distributions can be found in Javadi et al. (2011).

amount of infrastructure resources needed for the platform. This is a reasonable base model as the computational requirements for necessary platform tasks generally increases with the number of users (and transactions), while some base functionality must also be provided at all times (e.g., database services).

A realistic model of required resources is essential for the co-op model and the evaluation results. Hence, the system requirements function is modeled based on certain assumptions as well as empirical observations from the Social Cloud prototype presented and evaluated in Chard et al. (2010). They studied several aspects of the deployed prototype, such as resource (CPU, memory) usage, on which the requirements function is based. In abstract terms, the system requirements are calculated for one time period. In this time period, each of the n users participates in y transactions which are typical for the platform. For example, this could be the computation of an auction or preference-based allocation for a particular resource. The reverse second-price-sealed-bid auction as implemented in Chard et al. (2010) is considered as a proxy for the transaction. This mechanism is known to be resource-demanding and has high resource requirements, thus representing the necessary computational power needed to host a Social Cloud and ensure its functionality.

Every transaction requires a certain amount of resources for execution. From Chard et al. (2010) it can be empirically derived that an average computer (represented as the average resource amount, $\bar{\omega}$) requires $f(n) = \bar{\omega}\frac{\sqrt[3]{n^2}}{\gamma}$ resources for one transaction.[20] As it is unrealistic that all transactions in one time period have to run simultaneously, the parameter δ denotes the percentage of transactions that require resources at the same time. If ω_{min} denotes the minimum number of resources that have to be provided regardless of supporting basic functionality, then the system requirements function (SR_1) can be expressed as:

$$SR_1 : R(n) = \delta * y * n * \bar{\omega}\frac{\sqrt[3]{n^2}}{\gamma} + \omega_{min} \tag{4.10}$$

Equation (4.10) assumes that all users participate in every transaction. If for example, only half of the users, on average, participate in transactions then the system

[20]The exact function was found using curve fitting in Matlab, which yields $\gamma = 933$ and a goodness of fit of 0.97. Note that Chard et al. (2010) provides values for up to 50 users, but the findings strongly suggest that the general trend of the curve can be extrapolated for more users.

requirements function (SR_2) will be:

$$SR_2 : R(n) = \delta * y * n * \bar{\omega} \frac{\sqrt[3]{(n/2)^2}}{\gamma} + \omega_{min} \tag{4.11}$$

Contribution Schemes

Considering the social context of the Social Cloud paradigm, it can be argued that the goal of such a system should be to provide sufficient resources to run the platform, but at the same time not burden users with too much effort or high costs. If r_i is the resource contribution of user i to the co-op infrastructure, the following optimization problem has to be solved from a system-wide perspective:

$$\begin{aligned}
& max_{\rho_i} \sum_i U_i(\rho_i, \sigma_i) \\
& s.t. \sum_{i=1}^{n} r_i \geq R(n) \\
& r_i = \rho_i * \omega_i && \forall i \in 1, ..., n \\
& \sigma_i + p\rho_i = 1 && \forall i \in 1, ..., n \\
& \sigma_i, \rho_i \geq 0, && \forall i \in 1, ..., n
\end{aligned} \tag{4.12}$$

In order to acquire the required infrastructure resources by the co-op's members, the following contribution schemes are considered:

- **Enforced fixed contribution (EFC)**: Users are required to provide a certain quantity of resources to the infrastructure as a membership requirement.
- **Voluntary fixed contribution (VFC)**: Users choose to contribute a predefined percentage of their own resources.
- **Voluntary variable contribution (VVC)**: Users may freely choose what percentage of their endowment they are willing to contribute, i.e., no minimum is prescribed.

Enforced Fixed Contribution For fixed contribution schemes, two alternatives are possible: either the contribution can be fixed independent of the user's resource endowment, or the contribution can be proportional to the user's endowment. The first alternative is used by some popular file sharing systems, where a minimum amount of resource sharing is required. However, such a scheme might exclude users from the system which do not have the required resources available, or would force some users to allocate most of their resources for the infrastructure. Hence, the latter case is used to calculate the fixed percentages, because it is more considerate of users with low resource endowments.

In the proportional contribution scenario, let ρ_i^* denote the percentage of user i's resource endowment that needs to be allocated to the co-op infrastructure. The minimum necessary percentage per user, taking their average availabilities into account, can then be calculated as:

$$\rho_i^* = \rho_{min}^* * (1 - \sigma_i) \tag{4.13}$$

$$\rho_{min}^* = \frac{R(n)}{\sum_i (1 - \sigma_i) * \omega_i * \alpha_i} \tag{4.14}$$

The calculation of the expected contributed resources depends on the assumptions about the users, specifically σ_i and ω_i. Without information about user types an assumption has to be made, otherwise the expected or observed user type distributions can be used to estimate σ_i and ω_i. Clearly, if the estimate of user types does not reflect the true distribution, it will affect the overall amount of resources that are contributed, and thus impact the availability of the system.

This calculation represents a static view of the system, as only average availabilities are taken into account. Dynamic effects such as the distribution of availability and unavailability intervals might affect the overall performance of the system, however, especially if these intervals are correlated between users (e.g., availability patterns during the week compared to during the weekend). Hence, the feasibility of such a contribution scheme has to be studied via simulations to capture the dynamic properties.

Voluntary Fixed Contribution In this scenario, the percentage ρ is prescribed by the system according to some criteria, and users voluntarily contribute if ρ is smaller than their individual optimum ρ^*, otherwise they choose to not contribute resources. This differentiates this scheme from EFC, as in the latter case a certain contribution is mandatory.

Hence, the contribution of user i can be described as follows:

$$\rho_i = \begin{cases} \rho & \text{if } \rho^* \geq \rho \\ 0 & \text{else} \end{cases} \tag{4.15}$$

Although this scheme does not enforce contribution of users, it also significantly depends on the choice of ρ. If it is set too low, more people will contribute, yet the overall amount of contributed resources might not be high enough. On the other hand, setting ρ too high potentially leads to less contributing users.

Voluntary Variable Contribution In this contribution scheme, users choose their level of contribution based on their individual preferences for resource usage, considering for example altruistic motivation. This scheme addresses the key motivation of a Social Cloud, that is, users voluntarily choose to provide resources to the platform.

Using the utility function described earlier (Eq. 4.2) and the resource constraint (Eq. 4.1), the optimization problem can be solved for user i. With the basic assumption that $U_i \geq 0$, the following result can be obtained:

$$\frac{\partial \mathcal{U}_i(\sigma_i, \rho_i)}{\partial \sigma_i} = 0 \tag{4.16}$$

$$\frac{1}{\beta}(U_i)^{\frac{1}{\beta}-1}\left(\beta \Pi_{i,s}^{\beta-1} - \beta \lambda p^{-\beta}(\omega_i - \Pi_{i,s})^{\beta-1}\right) = 0 \tag{4.17}$$

$$\left(\beta \Pi_{i,s}^{\beta-1} - \beta \lambda p^{-\beta}(\omega_i - \Pi_{i,s})^{\beta-1}\right) = 0 \tag{4.18}$$

$$\Pi_{i,s} = \frac{\lambda^{\frac{-1}{1-\beta}}}{p^{\frac{-\beta}{1-\beta}} + \lambda^{\frac{-1}{1-\beta}}}\omega_i \tag{4.19}$$

Hence, the relative contribution to the infrastructure depends on several factors: 1) the importance of donating resources to the infrastructure (λ, the level of altruism), 2) the convexity of the utility function (β), and 3) the relative price p for giving resources to the infrastructure. In particular, the more expensive it is to allocate resources to the infrastructure, compared to consuming them (i.e., $p > 1$), the lower the users' contribution to the infrastructure.

4.3.3. Evaluation of Contribution Schemes

Having developed a comprehensive economic co-op model, the focus of this evaluation is to investigate the following aspects of a co-op infrastructure for a Social Cloud: 1) the average utility of users between the contribution schemes, and 2) the effects of specific parameters, especially the relative price p to provide resources, in the proposed contribution schemes. Additionally, two QoS factors of the platform are studied: system availability (as the percentage of time periods in which the resource requirements are met) and the ratio of provided to required resources (as a measure of redundancy). To study the effects of the number of users on the results and the scalability of each approach, Social Clouds of different sizes (10 to 400 users) are considered. Note that these numbers are much smaller than the hundreds of millions of users that are registered on Facebook, however individual Social Clouds represent individual social network islands, and not the entire social graph.

Simulation Specifics

The general simulation framework is implemented as follows. In total 100 simulation runs per scenario are performed and the results averaged, in order to account for possible simulation bias with respect to the initialization of users. At the beginning of a simulation run, users are created according to the clusters in Table 4.4. Users might have different resource endowments available, hence their respective resource endowments are drawn uniformly from the interval $[5, 15]$, and the average resource endowment is given by $\bar{\omega} = 10$. As a baseline, the minimum amount of resources required to host the Social Cloud is assumed to be half of an average user's resource endowment (i.e., 50% computation power of an average computer). For the enforced fixed contribution scenario, ρ_i^* is calculated according to the equations in Section 4.3.2, and σ_i is calculated based on the type of user i.

All scenarios include 10,000 simulated time periods. In the first period, it is determined whether users are initially available (or not) based on the average availability of the cluster, and the length of the first (un)availability interval is drawn according to the respective distribution. In every following time period, the amount of resources provided for the infrastructure is calculated, and if an (un)availability interval ends, the availability of a user is switched and the next interval is determined. Considering the startup problem (Law, 2007), the simulation requires approximately 50-500 time periods to reach a steady state, so only the results of the time periods 500-10,000 are considered for the evaluation.

Two different system resource requirements functions, SR, are considered for each contribution scheme in order to study the robustness of the findings. First, the worst case requirements SR_1 where $R(n)$ is set according to Equation (4.10) with $\delta = 1$, $y = 1$, $\bar{\omega} = 10$ and $\omega_{min} = 5$. In this case, every user participates in every transaction and all transactions have to be computed simultaneously, which reflects a peak scenario with very high system load. The values for $\bar{\omega}$ and ω_{min} are determined because users' endowments are drawn from $[5, 15]$. Second, the second system requirements function SR_2 represents an off-peak scenario with lower requirements, and is determined by Equation (4.11). For SR_2, only half of the users participate in each transaction, and δ is set to 0.5. This is still a high average load, yet acknowledges that the co-op infrastructure might be set up to capture average requirements instead of peak loads.

Enforced Fixed Contribution

In this contribution scheme, each user has to provide a certain percentage of their endowment to the system. For the evaluation, the actual resource contributions are simulated when users provide exactly the minimum percentage (as calculated in Equation 4.14), and also when they must provide 10%, 20% and 50% more than the minimum percentage.

Figure 4.5 shows that the results of this contribution scheme depend on several factors: first, the minimum contribution percentage initially decreases with the number of users, but if the system size surpasses 50 users ρ^*_{min} begins to increase again (Figures 4.5c and 4.5d). Second, the number of provided resources is higher than the amount of required resources (i.e., there is some level of redundancy, see Figures 4.5e and 4.5f). Third, the average availability of the system ranges from 80% to 100%, for the optimal contribution ρ^*_{min} (Figures 4.5a and 4.5b). This is mainly due to the fact that the calculation of ρ^*_{min} only considers average values of user availability, which does not account for the dynamics of the system (such as multiple users being unavailable simultaneously). Furthermore, for worst case resource requirements it begins to slightly decrease for larger systems. For average resource requirements, the availability is slightly better for larger systems and remains constantly at 100%.

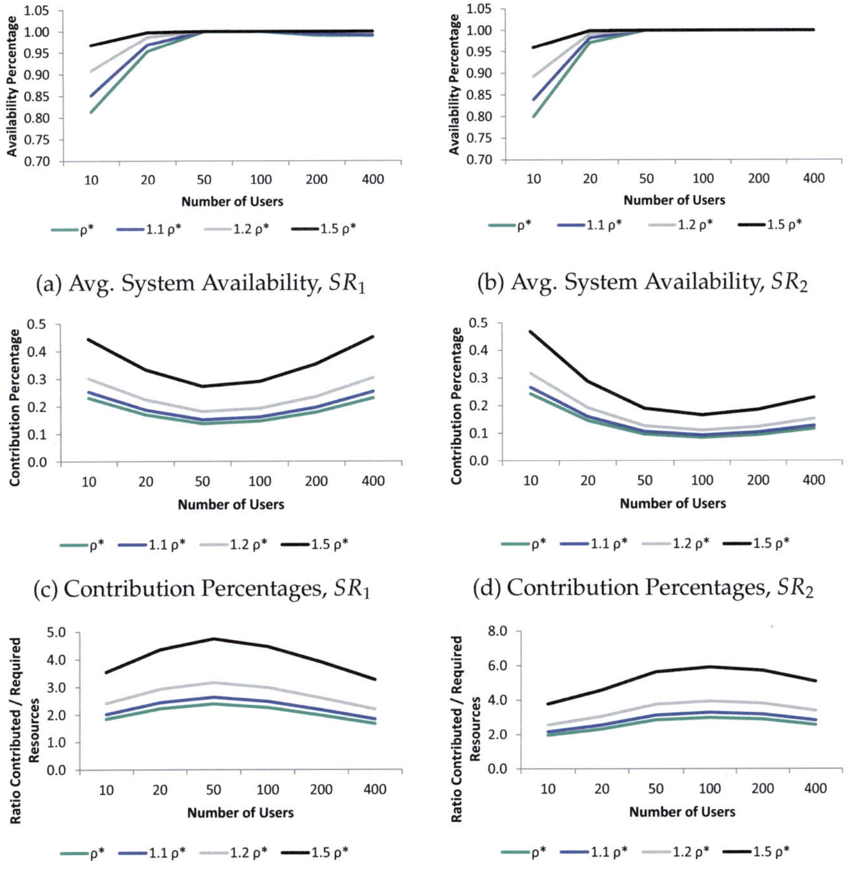

(a) Avg. System Availability, SR_1 (b) Avg. System Availability, SR_2

(c) Contribution Percentages, SR_1 (d) Contribution Percentages, SR_2

(e) Provided vs. Required Resources, SR_1 (f) Provided vs. Required Resources, SR_2

Figure 4.5.: Simulation Results for Enforced Fixed Contribution

Two issues can be observed with this contribution scheme. On one hand, if the minimum contribution percentage is increased to account for dynamic (un)availability, the average availability of the system increases, reaching values very close or equal to 1 (Figures 4.5a and 4.5b). On the other hand, the system is also scalable as the average system availability increases with the number of users. This can be explained by the fact that the more users contribute, the larger the pooling effects of (un)available users, which leads to a "smoothing" of provided resources and a higher probability that the system resource requirements are met at any point in time. Furthermore, the percentage of time periods where the system resource requirements are actually met does not seem to depend on the specific resource function as a comparison of Figures 4.5a and 4.5b shows. This is mainly due to the fact that the (un)availability interval distributions determine the number of contributing users, and the requirements function mainly affects ρ^*_{min}.

Overall, the results show that if an enforced fixed contribution scheme is used, it is better to set the required ρ higher than the minimum ρ^*_{min}. This leads to higher system availability even for small increases of ρ because the larger individual user contributions alleviate the unavailability of other users.

Voluntary Fixed Contribution

In this scenario certain users contribute a fixed percentage of resources if this percentage is lower or equal to their optimal percentage. The decision criterion can be found in Equation 4.15 in Section 4.3.2. This scheme does not force users to contribute resources, as EFC does, yet the usability depends on the choice of the fixed contribution percentage ρ as well as the user type distribution.

Figure 4.6 displays the simulation results where not all users have to contribute to the co-op infrastructure. Several interesting findings can be observed. First, as expected the percentage of users who contribute to the infrastructure decreases as the required contribution amount increases (Figures 4.6c and 4.6d). Second, especially for high resource requirements the provided resources are lower than the required amount, therefore leading to a lower system availability as in EFC (Figures 4.6a, 4.6e as well as 4.6b and 4.6d). This indicates that the worst-case system requirements (SR_1) increase disproportionally to the contributed resources for larger system sizes (in this case, more then 50 users). For average resource requirements (SR_2), system availability is better and even can reach 100%, and the scalability behavior improves as well.

In particular, the results also show that the system performance crucially depends on the required contribution that is selected. Contribution levels between $\rho = 0.2$ and $\rho = 0.3$ seem to be most promising for the given scenario.

Voluntary Variable Contribution

The variable voluntary scheme in Section 4.3.2 allows each user to calculate their optimal individual contribution for infrastructure resources, based on individual

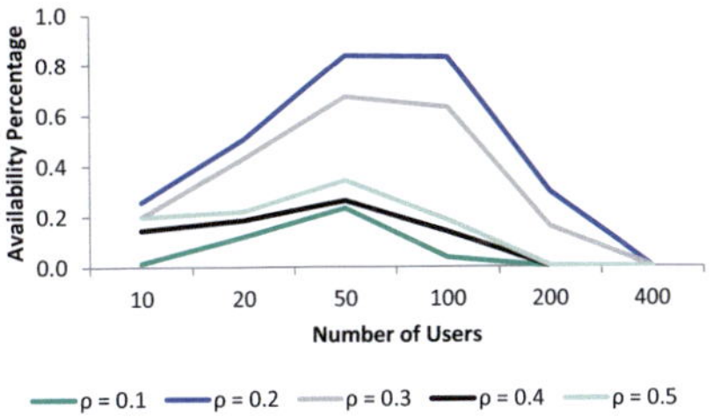

(a) Avg. System Availability, SR_1

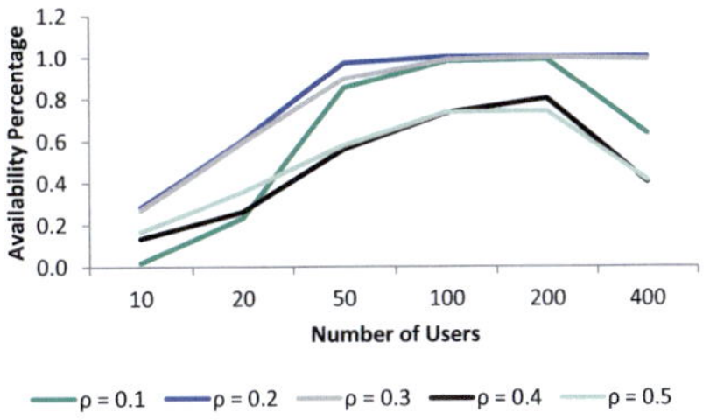

(b) Avg. System Availability, SR_2

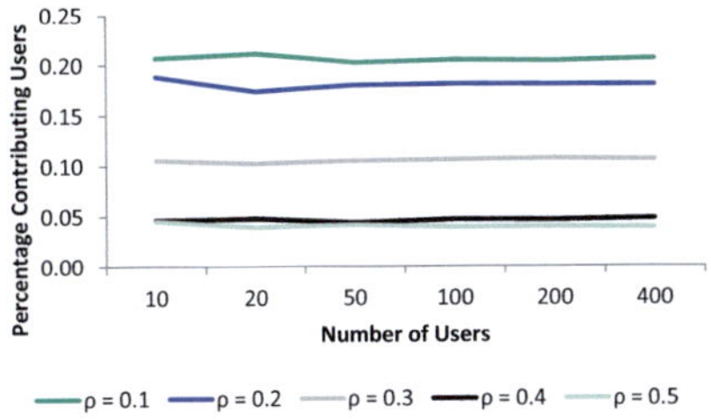

(c) Contribution Percentages, SR_1

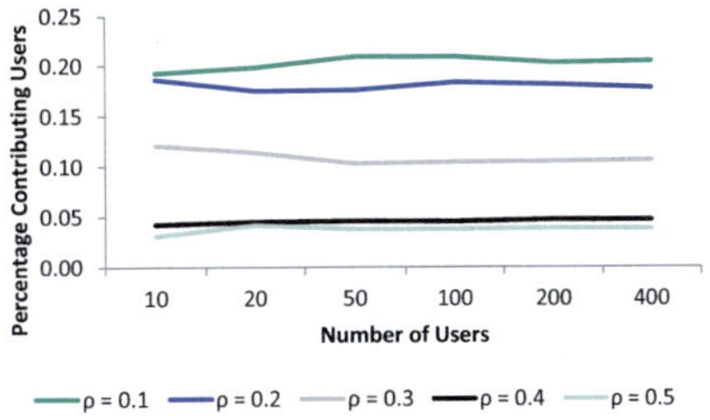

(d) Contribution Percentages, SR_2

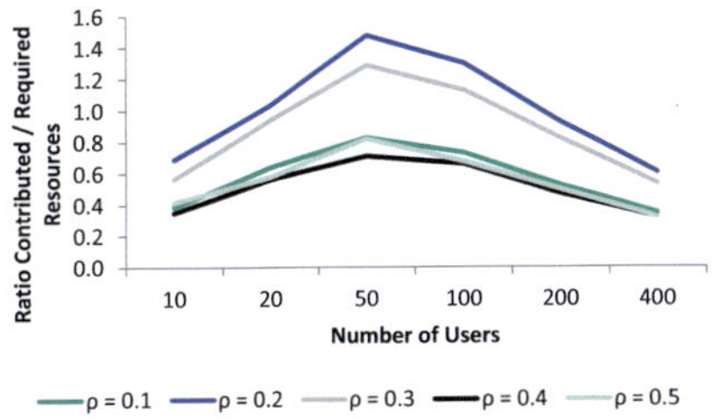

(e) Provided vs. Required Resources, SR_1

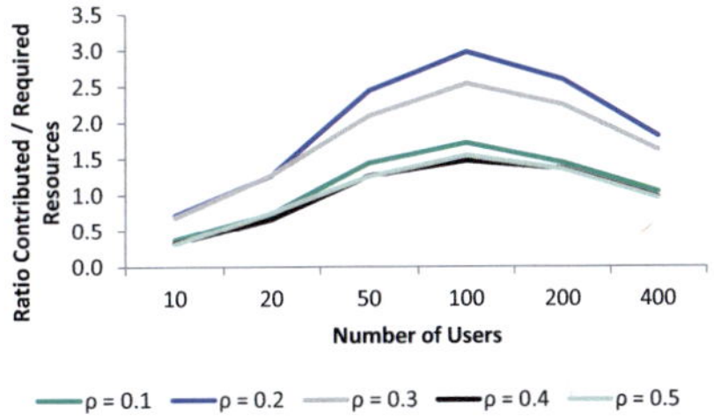

(f) Provided vs. Required Resources, SR_2

Figure 4.6.: Simulation Results for Voluntary Fixed Contribution

preferences, according to Equation (4.19). In the following simulations the relative price of resource contribution p was also varied between 1.0 and 3.0 to capture that providing resources might be comparably more expensive than using them or leaving them idle.[21] In order to study system behavior in a more realistic setting, each user is assigned to a certain availability cluster and is given a particular type of utility function, according to Table 4.2. The type of utility function also determines

[21] Prices $p < 1$ would mean resource provisioning is less expensive then leaving them idle, which can be, e.g., achieved through subsidization. Although this might be an option to encourage contribution to the co-op, it has to be determined where such subsidies would come from. This is not the focus of this case study, hence the case $p < 1$ will not be considered in this evaluation.

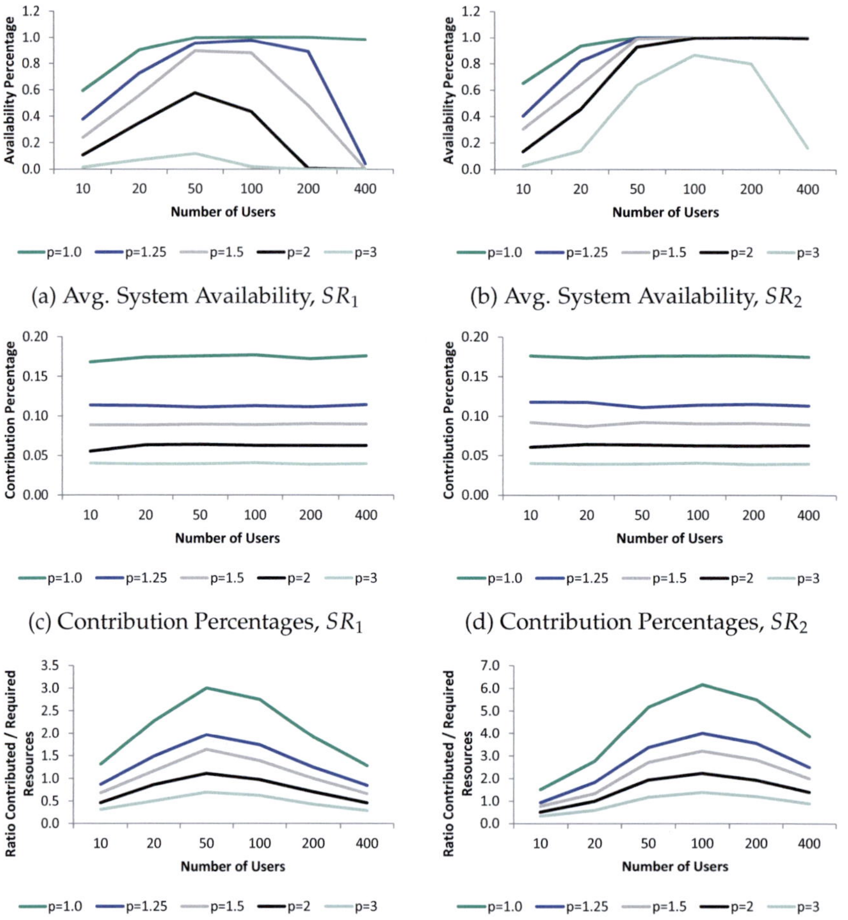

(a) Avg. System Availability, SR_1

(b) Avg. System Availability, SR_2

(c) Contribution Percentages, SR_1

(d) Contribution Percentages, SR_2

(e) Provided vs. Required Resources, SR_1

(f) Provided vs. Required Resources, SR_2

Figure 4.7.: Simulation Results for Voluntary Variable Contribution

the optimal contribution level, given the optimal condition based on the resource endowment constraint.

Using the user type distribution from Andreoni and Miller (2002), the results shown in Figure 4.7 are obtained. The simulation shows several interesting results. On one hand, the intuition that higher relative contribution prices leads to fewer contributions is confirmed in Figures 4.7c and 4.7d. The average contribution decreases with increasing relative prices for provisioning, a result which is independent of the system resource requirements. On the other hand, system availability as well as the average amount of contributed resources strongly depend on the relative prices that users bear for providing resources. If relative prices are too high users choose to provide only a small number of resources, which leads to the decrease in system availability as shown in Figures 4.7a and 4.7b. This also affects the scalability of the system; if prices for contribution are roughly similar to prices for self-consumption, the contribution scheme is scalable with the number of users.

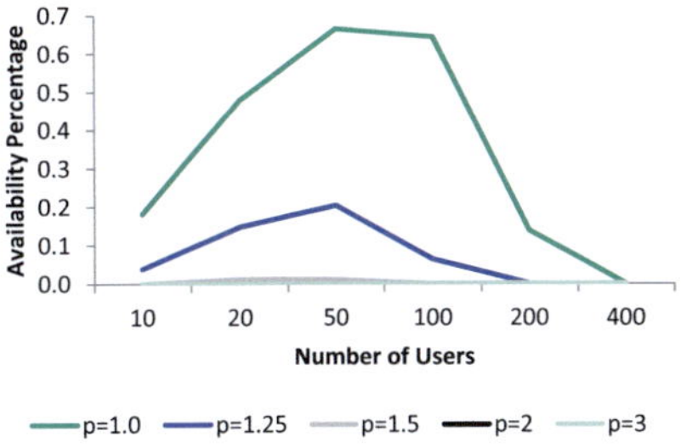

(a) Avg. System Availability, SR_1

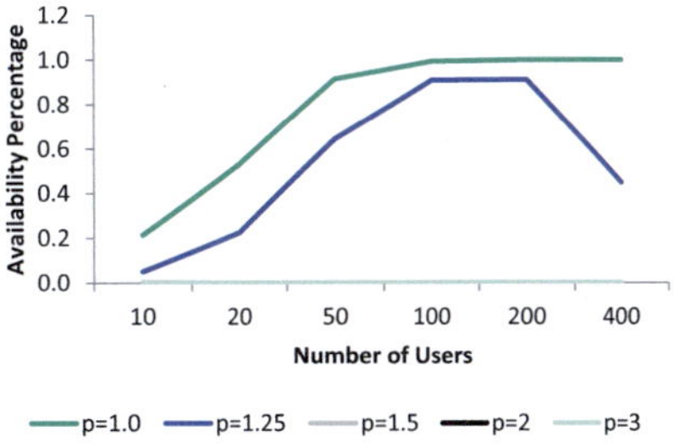

(b) Avg. System Availability, SR_2

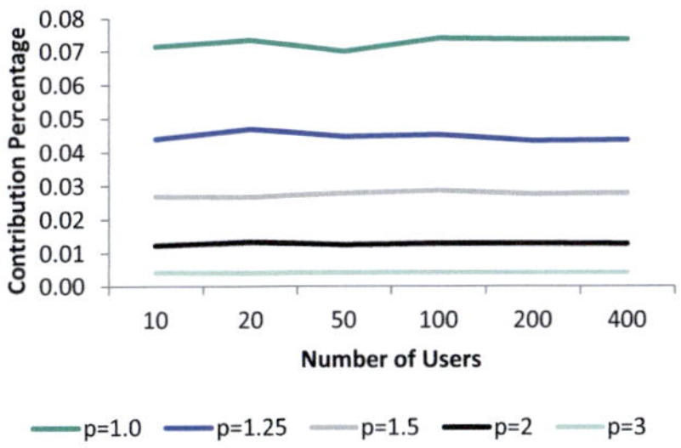

(c) Contribution Percentages, SR_1

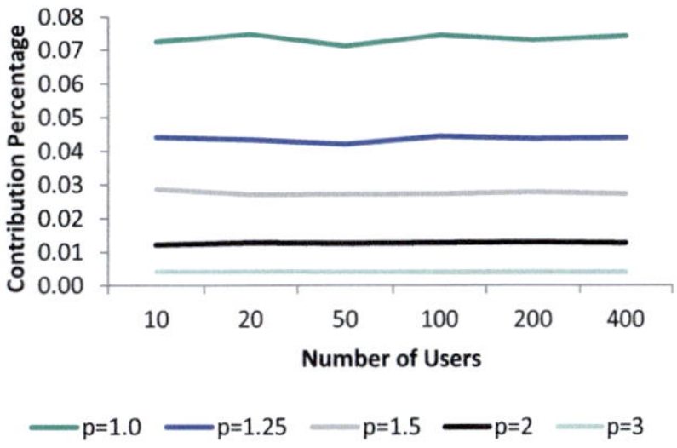

(d) Contribution Percentages, SR_2

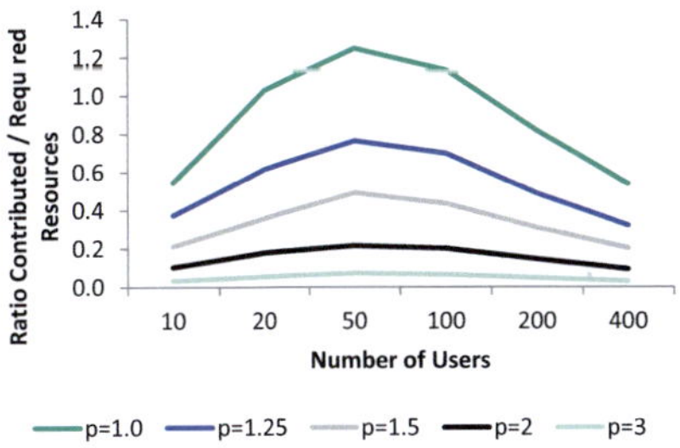

(e) Provided vs. Required Resources, SR_1

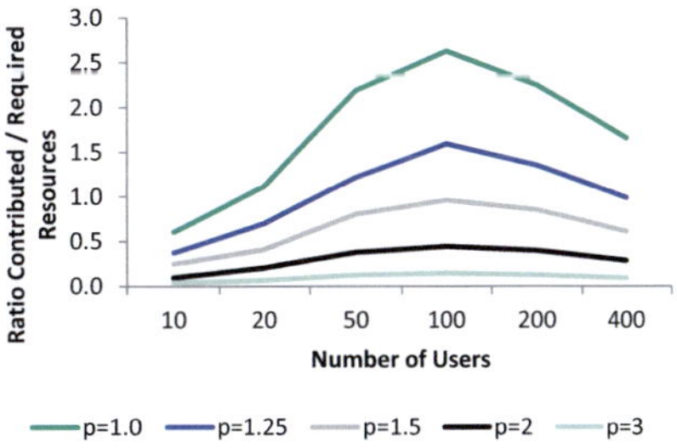

(f) Provided vs. Required Resources, SR_2

Figure 4.8.: Simulation Results for Voluntary Variable Contribution, mostly Selfish User Types

Furthermore, on average, significantly more resources are provided than required, leading to higher redundancy levels (Figures 4.7e and 4.7f). Along with the previous finding this indicates that the incentive-based scenario would be especially vulnerable when only a few users contribute to the system. Although individually they might contribute a significant amount of resources, the system is more dependent on these few contributors. In case of their unavailability the resource requirements might not be met.

To study the dependency of the simulation results on the underlying distributions of user types (and hence, utility functions), the previous results are now compared with a more conservative distribution, as shown in Figure 4.8. As stated in Section 4.3.2, this distribution is obtained from observed P2P systems, where 70% of users are purely selfish free-riders, and only 30% are willing to give resources to the infrastructure (types 1 and 6 in Table 4.2, respectively).

In this scenario, based on the high number of free-riders, the general level of system availability is much worse than in the previous case (Figures 4.8a and 4.8b). This is especially evident at peak times where resource requirements are high, as the high number of selfish users leads to a significant decrease in resource contribution. In the case of moderate resource requirements, the system performs well when contribution is not expensive ($p \approx 1$) and for larger numbers of users. Moreover, both the proportion of provided to required resources (Figures 4.8e and 4.8f), and the average contribution per user (Figures 4.8c and 4.8d), are lower compared to the results in Figure 4.7, which explains the reduced system availability. It is noteworthy that despite the conservative distribution of user types, the system performs surprisingly well for moderate resource requirements and lower relative prices.

4.3.4. Discussion

Figure 4.9 shows a comparison between the average utility per user in the enforced fixed, voluntary fixed and voluntary variable schemes and for both resource functions. As predicted, the average utility is higher when users are allowed to choose their individual optimal level of contribution (rather than being forced into potentially suboptimal levels of contribution, as in the case of EFC and VFC).

Based on the previous evaluation results, there are some further observations through which the feasibility and scalability of a co-op infrastructure can be evaluated. First, if a fixed contribution is enforced by the system, the (un)availability

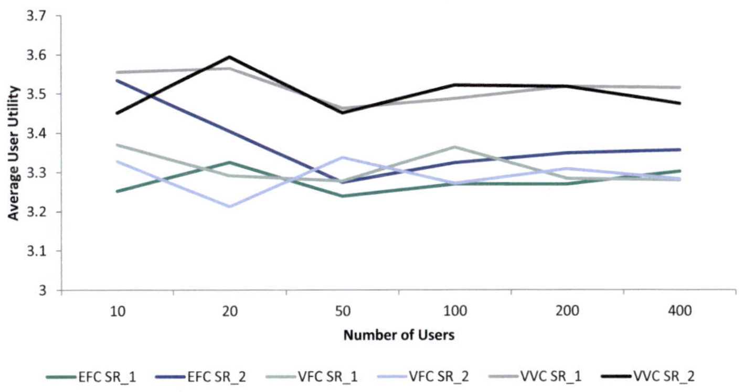

Figure 4.9.: Utility per User for Different Scenarios

characteristics of the users have to be taken into account when the necessary contribution percentage is calculated. In this case there is an inherent trade-off between increasing the individual contribution ρ_i^* and making the entire system perform better or more reliably. That is, the QoS factor availability is directly dependent on the chosen level of parameter ρ_i^*. For example, an increase in ρ_i^* significantly increases the system availability, but in this case individual contributions can be very high for large system sizes (up to 47% of the endowment). Second, the results from the voluntary variable contribution scheme indicate that even under worst case requirements, allowing users to select their contribution level the system resource requirements are met in many time periods when relative contribution prices are low (corresponding to high availability, as well as a rather high redundancy factor as shown in Figures 4.7e and 4.7f). Furthermore, the average individual utility is higher than in the fixed scheme. However, based on the underlying distributions of user types, the system performance is much more dependent on the voluntary contribution of single users.

Hence, the system designer has to address the following trade-off: either force users to give a certain, fixed percentage of their endowment to the co-op infrastructure, e.g. as a condition for participation, or let users freely choose their contribution. In the latter case, the average utility of users as well as system availability/redundancy tends to be higher, but one must carefully study the user type distribution to ensure that there are enough users willing to contribute. For practical settings, it might be beneficial to monitor the resource contributions and/or determine the distribution of user types, and adjust the used contribution scheme if the system availability level falls below a certain threshold.

There are several potential extensions of the co-operative infrastructure model that can be pursued. First, the model can be augmented to account for additional resource types. Instead of only considering one resource type, real co-operative systems require several different types of resources to run, e.g., computational power to calculate transactions, bandwidth to accommodate large file transfers, and storage to save databases and other information. In this case, the co-op infrastructure requires a certain amount of each resource type to be successfully deployed, and over-provisioning of one resource cannot compensate underprovisioning of another resource, leading to a combinatorial problem.

Another extension of the presented model is to analyze how specific incentives (e.g., reputation mechanisms, compensation for resource provisioning, etc.) alter the willingness of users to contribute. This is particularly interesting when combined with an integrated model that considers both sharing resources with other users and contributing to the co-op infrastructure. Such a unified model would allow the design of tailored incentive schemes that take both aspects of contribution into account.

Furthermore, as a co-op infrastructure induces both positive and negative external/network effects with a growing number of (contributing) users, another question is if there is an optimal size of a co-op infrastructure depending on the interplay of negative and positive effects. While this has been studied in context of P2P music sharing networks (Asvanund et al., 2004), the adaption to co-op infrastructures remains an open issue. For example, the previous results show that for EFC, the system availability level increases with a higher number of users which indicates that the co-op is more robust for larger number of users, whereas for VVC the results depend on the relative price of resource provisioning. Finally, the ultimate goal of a co-op model is to provide a sustainable infrastructure for its users. To guarantee sustainability, concepts such as Key Performance Indicators (KPIs) can be investigated and applied to the co-op model. Through the management of these KPIs, the administrators of the co-op infrastructure could monitor, analyze, and steer the system to ensure that the minimum service quality levels are fulfilled.

4.4. Summary

This chapter presented two case studies how a simulation-based approach can be leveraged in the design of incentive schemes for exchange and sharing platforms such as Social Clouds. The focus of the first case study (Section 4.2) was the introduction of an incentive scheme in resource sharing networks, and its effects on user participation and utilities. The evaluation showed interesting dependencies between the effects of the scheme, the user type, and the user type distribution. The second case study (Section 4.3) introduced the concept of co-operative infrastructures. It studied several contribution schemes for the provision of infrastructure resources needed to run the platform by the users themselves.

Considering research question 1.2, these exemplary case studies show that the use of a simulation-based approach to evaluate certain aspects of a sharing system, such as an incentive scheme, can provide useful additional information about potential effects on the system. The first case study exemplified that dynamic effects can be identified through the simulation tool, e.g., the effects of introducing an additional trading constraint on different user types. With such an approach, potential changes to a Social Cloud can be evaluated before their implementation, and can yield useful information about the predicted consequences. Additionally, the second case study showed that entirely new scenarios can also be studied through the simulation tool. For example, if a co-operative infrastructure should be introduced for a Social Cloud, the simulation approach can help to determine the most effective contribution scheme to ensure a certain level of system availability.

Addressing research question 1.3, the second case study showed that the decision for a certain contribution scheme depends on the user type distribution of the respective Social Cloud. If resource provisioning to the Social Cloud does not incur considerable additional costs and the Social Cloud does not mainly consist of selfish users unwilling to participate in the co-op, a voluntary contribution scheme is feasible. In contrast, if users are less willing to provide resources on their own, an enforced contribution scheme can be necessary to ensure the applicability of a co-op approach to host the platform infrastructure. Hence, in practical scenarios, the identification of user type distributions is important to select the appropriate contribution scheme. In addition, the importance of non-monetary incentives for participation in a Social Cloud (in particular general helpfulness and reciprocity aspects, see Section 3.3) indicates the general feasibility of such a co-operative infrastructure approach.

It is important to emphasize that such an approach is complimentary to other methodologies such as prototyping or live experiments. Ideally, these methodologies complement each other and yield valuable insights which together lead to a more holistic design process. To augment the case studies shown in this chapter, two prototypical implementations, a Social Storage Cloud (Chard et al., 2012) as well as a Social Compute Cloud for sharing virtualized resources (Caton et al., 2014), have already been implemented. These prototypes are particularly helpful in observing actual user acceptance, behavior and feedback with respect to the general idea, system usability as well as specific implementation details. For example, user interaction can be observed and analyzed with respect to demographics and other user characteristics. Complementary to the simulation and prototype approaches, lab experiments can capture user behavior in certain market scenarios and determine the motivation of potential users to contribute and share resources in different application scenarios. This can be accompanied by surveys and questionnaires which are specifically suited to study the motivation of users, their incentives as well as determine the reason of their observed behavior.

Overall, Chapters 3 and 4 showed the relevance of non-monetary incentives for Social Cloud settings, and how the identified relevant incentives can be implemented in incentive and contribution schemes that encourage user participation. A web-based survey showed that non-monetary motivations and incentives such as helpfulness and reciprocity considerations are more important for users than monetary compensation. Additionally, the survey revealed that the setting of a Social Cloud (e.g., sharing in a private compared to a professional setting) influences the relative importance of certain incentives.

The findings are also relevant for the design of allocation mechanisms. Once users of a sharing platform offer resources while others request these resources, the question arises how an allocation can be derived in this setting. Due to the low relevance of monetary incentives, the use of non-monetary allocation mechanisms is a promising approach to retain the benefits of a centralized market allocation while focusing on preferences rather than (monetary) valuations for resources. This is the focus of the next part of the thesis. Chapters 5 and 6, thus, take a market view of the system and consider resource sharing where users have preferences with whom they want to share. Specifically, several allocation mechanisms, their relative performance, as well as strategic implications will be the focus of these chapters.

Part III.

Two-Sided Matching in Social Clouds

Chapter 5.

Resource Allocation in Social Clouds

"Two properties of key importance for market design are stability, which encourages groups to voluntarily participate in the market, and incentive compatibility, which discourages strategic manipulation of the market."

(Nobel Prize Committee, 2012)

IN social settings, the exchange of resources is often driven by non-monetary factors. This can be observed empirically by considering the various platforms which use non-monetary incentives and mechanisms (such as trophies or reciprocity, see Section 3.1). The results of Chapter 3 also indicated that these types of incentives are considered most important for users participating in a Social Cloud. As identified in Section 2.3.2, two-sided matching provides the means to allocate resources with a market-based approach that allows for the optimization of desirable criteria, such as fairness of welfare of an allocation, while at the same time does not involve monetary transactions. Instead of (monetary) valuations for resources, participating users specify a preference ranking that reflects their willingness to share and exchange resources with other users. This chapter, therefore, considers the application of preference-based matching algorithms in the context of Social Clouds.

To introduce the relevant concepts, Section 5.1 provides the definitions and notation needed to study preference-based resource allocation. In particular, different types of preference structures and performance metrics as well as their impact on problem complexity are discussed. Section 5.2 provides an overview of the two-sided matching literature and discusses several aspects that are commonly studied in preference-based matching.

Using this terminology, Section 5.3 describes existing algorithms for preference-based matching. Most of these algorithms are specialized for specific scenarios, i.e., focus on a certain combination of preference structures. While there are efficient (approximation) algorithms for certain scenarios, there are cases for which no approximation algorithm exists.[1] Additionally, only certain standard combinations of optimization metrics are considered in the literature. However, there are cases in which the flexible combination of optimization metrics might be useful. For example, in a Social Cloud the desired goals of an allocation might change over time. In the beginning, the platform might focus on the benefits for the individuals to provide incentives for participation, whereas in later stages aspects such as fairness with respect to different users might be of higher importance. Existing algorithms are not able to provide such a flexibility and can only focus on a small combination of metrics. Heuristic algorithms, on the other hand, allow for a flexible optimization of metrics and are suitable for different preference structures. Therefore, the focus of this part of the thesis is the development and evaluation of heuristics for two-sided matching. In particular, Genetic Algorithms (GA) (Goldberg, 1989) and Threshold Accepting Algorithms (TA) (Dueck and Scheuer, 1990) are considered for this case.

The sole existence of heuristics does not guarantee their usefulness, especially considering the quality of allocations calculated by the heuristics. Therefore, it is necessary to compare the performance of these heuristics with existing algorithms, which is the goal of this chapter. Thus, the performance of the currently best-known algorithms is compared to the heuristics in Section 5.4, which considers several scenarios with different types of preferences. With the corresponding evaluation, research question 2.1 can be addressed:

RESEARCH QUESTION 2.2 $\prec$ **PERFORMANCE OF HEURISTICS** $\succ$ *What is the performance of heuristics for preference-based matching compared to existing matching mechanisms?*

The contribution of this chapter is twofold. On the one hand, GA and TA heuristics are defined for general two-sided matching scenarios and different optimization goals. On the other hand, the chapter provides a performance comparison of these

[1] In fact, for some scenarios non-trivial approximation guarantees cannot exist (Manlove et al., 2002; Halldórsson et al., 2003), which means that no algorithm can guarantee to always find better than worst-case lower bounds on approximation.

flexible heuristics compared to existing algorithms as well as the study of these algorithms in various settings. For example, the performance of the algorithms in the case of correlated preferences is a relevant problem that has not been examined extensively before.

5.1. Preference-based Resource Matching

This section formalizes two-sided matching problems. Section 5.1.1 starts by introducing notation, definitions, and fundamental theorems on preference-based matching, following standard literature. Building on this, Section 5.1.2 presents the commonly considered performance metrics used to determine the quality of a solution. Finally, Section 5.1.3 categorizes different problem types according to the structure of the preference rankings, and discusses the computational complexity of these problem types.

5.1.1. Definitions and Relevant Theorems

A two-sided matching model considers scenarios where users i are participants in a market and want to share and exchange resources. It is assumed that a user i cannot concurrently supply and demand the same resource type r. Therefore, it is possible to split the users into the set of n_X requesting users, X_r, and n_Y providing users, Y_r. Note that in this model matching is considered only within the same resource type, i.e., the index r is omitted from all subsequent formulas. In total, there are $n_X + n_Y$ users participating in the market. For easier notation, *requesters* will denote users of side X and *providers* of side Y. Without loss of generality, the index j will denote users of the opposite side.

Each user i has a **preference profile** $P_i = (P_{i,j_1}, \ldots, P_{i,j_n})$ over users j of the other market side with whom they want to share resources, where $P_{i,j}$ denotes the (ordinal) preference rank that user i has towards user j. The preference towards $\emptyset$ indicates the preference for being unmatched. Preference profiles are transitive and can be asymmetric. The preference profiles represent transitive priority structures $\succsim = (\succsim_i)$ where each user of the opposite side is ranked according to its priority. The asymmetric part $\succ_i$ indicates a strict priority, whereas the symmetric part indicates an indifference. All users j with $j \succ_i \emptyset$ are said to be **acceptable** for user i

(and vice versa). A common representation of preferences is through ranked order lists. For example, if user i has preferences $j_2 \succ j_1 \sim j_3 \succ j_4$, the most preferred alternative is j_2, which is preferred to both j_1 and j_3, which are in turn preferred to j_4. The corresponding preference ranks in this case would be $P_{i,j_1} = 2$, $P_{i,j_2} = 1$, $P_{i,j_3} = 2$, and $P_{i,j_4} = 4$.[2]

A preference profile of user i is said to be **complete** if $j \succ \emptyset$ for all users j. If $\emptyset \succ j$ for some users j, the preference profile is said to be **incomplete**. This indicates that user i prefers to remain unmatched rather than be matched to user j. A preference profile is **strict** if for all users j,k of the opposite side $j \succsim_i k$ is asymmetric. If $j \sim k$ for some users j and k, then the preference profile is said to have **indifferences**, or ties.

Given the representation of users' preferences and the supply and demand in the market, the goal of two-sided matching is to find a **match** $\mu = \langle X, Y \rangle$ that defines which users are matched. $\langle X, Y \rangle$ consists of pairs $\langle x,y \rangle$ with $x \in X$ and $y \in Y$. In this work, only one-to-one matches are considered, i.e., one requesting user is matched to one providing user, and vice versa.[3]

A **matching** is a function $\mu : X \to \{Y \cup \emptyset\}$ that allocates one requesting user from X (or $\emptyset$) to one providing user from Y (or $\emptyset$) and fulfills the constraints $\forall i \in X : \mu(i) \in \{Y \cup \emptyset\}$, $\forall i \in Y : \mu{-}1(i) \in \{X \cup \emptyset\}$, and $\forall i,j \neq \emptyset$ with $\mu(i) = j$: $\neg \exists k$ such that $\mu(k) = j$ or $\mu^{-1}(k) = i$. In other words, each user is either matched to another user or remains unmatched, and users can only be part of one matching (i.e., no user can be matched to more than one other user). A **mechanism** implements μ for the given preference profiles.

The quality of a match μ is characterized by certain criteria. Fundamental to the theory of two-sided matching is the question of whether users have the incentive to deviate from a given match. If no two users have the bilateral incentive to deviate, a match is called *stable*. For the definition of stability, the definition of blocking pairs is necessary:

Definition 6 (**Blocking Pair**). *A* ***blocking pair*** *is defined as a pair $\langle x,y \rangle$, $x \in X$, $y \in Y$, such that*

1. *$\mu(x) = \emptyset$ or $y \succ_x \mu(x)$, AND*

[2] An alternative ranking would be $P_{i,j_4} = 3$, in case only strict priorities increase the ranking.
[3] A discussion of many-to-one and many-to-many markets is provided in Section 5.2.

2. $\mu^{-1}(y) = \emptyset$ *is single or* $x \succ_y \mu^{-1}(y)$, *AND*

3. x *and* y *are mutually acceptable.*

Blocking pairs are essential in characterizing the notion of stability in two-sided matching. Throughout the chapter, following definition for stability will be used:

Definition 7 (**Stability**). *A match is said to be* ***stable*** *if it contains no blocking pairs.*

Stability infers that no user can find another user of the opposite side who prefers it to its current partner, and both mutually benefit from the change of matched partners. This is an important concept for theoretical and empirical reasons, and the implications are discussed in the next section.

It is important to note that in case of preference profiles with indifferences, there are other concepts of stability that can be used. Irving (1994) introduced the concepts of *strong stability* and *super stability*. Both build on a slightly adjusted notion of a blocking pair. In the case of weak stability (as used in this thesis), both partners in the blocking pair have to strictly prefer each other to their current partner. For strong stability, only one of the users has to strictly prefer the other user while the second user can be indifferent between the options. In case of super stability, both can be indifferent between their current match and the potential new match. It was shown that while there always exists a weakly stable solution, this need not be the case for strongly or super stable solutions (Irving, 1994). As weak stability is the most often used in the literature, and strongly stable and super stable solutions do not always exist (see Irving (1994)), this chapter will concentrate on this notion of stability.

Considering the existence of solutions to the two-sided matching problem, the following result provides an optimistic outlook:

Theorem 1 (**Gale and Shapley, 1962, and Irving, 1994**). *For each two-sided matching problem, potentially with incomplete preference lists and/or indifferences, there exists at least one stable solution.*

As mentioned before, stability is usually considered to be the most important characteristic of a match. Therefore, the existence of at least one stable solution to the matching problem as shown in Theorem 1 is a very important and helpful result.

On the other hand, the next definition shows that the number of different stable solutions can be very large:

Theorem 2 (**Irving and Leather, 1986; Gusfield and Irving, 1989; Knuth, 1997**). *Depending on the preference profiles, the number of different stable matches can be exponential.*

Theorem 2 is an important result as it implies two aspects: 1) the number of different stable solutions can be very large, and an enumeration of these solutions might not be feasible; 2) different stable solutions can be further evaluated considering other performance criteria as well. Therefore, the next section introduces the commonly considered criteria which are used alongside stability to measure the quality of a solution.

5.1.2. Performance Metrics for Two-Sided Matching

In standard two-sided matching scenarios, stability is often seen as the most important property. Yet, as seen in the last section the number of stable solutions for a given set of preference profiles can be large, sometimes even exponential in the number of users. For this reason, several other criteria are commonly used in conjunction with stability. For the matching problems considered in this chapter, the following *economic performance criteria* are considered:[4]

Stability Stability is measured by the number of blocking pairs in a solution (see Definition 6).

Welfare As a measure of the total "satisfaction" of users with respect to their preferences, welfare is defined as the average rank of the matched partner for each user.[5] In formal terms:

$$\text{Welfare} = \frac{\sum_{i,j \in \langle X,Y \rangle} P_{i,j} + P_{j,i}}{n_X + n_Y} \tag{5.1}$$

[4]The definitions of welfare and fairness scores are adapted from Gusfield (1987) and Iwama et al. (2010). In addition to the presented metrics, *regret* is sometimes considered as well. It is defined as the lowest preference rank that any user is matched with, and is a measure for how good a solution is for the user with the lowest-ranked matched partner.

[5]Welfare is also sometimes referred to as the most "egalitarian" solution.

Note that lower numbers indicate better solutions, as the most preferred alternative has rank 1.

Fairness Considering the welfare distribution of the two sides, fairness is measured as the difference of the average ranks of the matched partner. A higher fairness score reflects that users of one side are, on average, matched to partners with a better rank than users of the other side, whereas scores around 0 reflect a more equal welfare distribution. Formally:

$$\text{Fairness} = \left| \frac{\sum_{i,j \in \langle X,Y \rangle} P_{i,j}}{n_X} - \frac{\sum_{i,j \in \langle X,Y \rangle} P_{j,i}}{n_Y} \right| \tag{5.2}$$

Number of Matched Pairs For problems with complete preferences, the algorithms considered in this thesis always yield the maximum number of matched pairs. In contrast, this property is lost by introducing incomplete preferences. In such cases, the number of matched pairs is used as a quality metric for the matches:

$$\text{NumPairs} = \sum_{\langle X,Y \rangle} \{ \langle x,y \rangle \, | x \neq \emptyset \wedge y \neq \emptyset \} \tag{5.3}$$

In case of incomplete preferences, finding the stable match with the highest number of matched pairs is the most commonly considered combination of metrics. Even though finding the welfare- and fairness-best stable solution can also be goals in this case, the application of the welfare and fairness metrics to the incomplete preferences case requires the specification how unmatched users are handled for the calculation of metrics. There is no standard in the literature how this case is handled, and most approximation algorithms focus on the mentioned combination of stability and matched pairs. In the subsequent evaluation, the welfare and fairness metrics will consider the matched users only.

For the given definitions, ranks are equally weighted, i.e., weights for different preference rankings are not considered. This follows standard literature on two-sided matching, yet cannot capture the fact that preference rank differences might not be equidistant in real settings. For example, a user might consider the difference between the first and second rank differently than between the tenth and eleventh. Although the subsequently described heuristics are easily adapted to a weighted preference setting, the unweighted setting is evaluated as algorithms for the weighted settings do not exist for each relevant scenario.

5.1.3. Preference Structures and Computational Complexity

The goal of two-sided matching is to find an allocation that optimizes a certain combination of the aforementioned performance criteria. The complexity of finding an optimal solutions depends on two input parameters: 1) the type of user preference profiles, and 2) the combination of metrics that are used in the optimization.

To classify the preference types considered in a given problem, the case of complete and strict preferences is abbreviated as **SM** (stable matching), complete preferences with indifferences as **SMT** (stable matching with ties), and incomplete preferences with indifferences as **SMTI** (stable matching with ties and incompleteness).

Theorem 3 (**Iwama et al. (1999); Manlove et al. (2002); Halldórsson et al. (2003)**). *If preferences are complete and include indifferences, finding a welfare-optimal or fairness-optimal stable match is NP-hard, and also hard to approximate. If preferences are incomplete and include indifferences, finding a maximum size stable match is NP-hard, and finding a welfare-optimal maximum size stable match is NP-hard and hard to approximate.*

There are two noteworthy implications when preference structures with indifferences (SMT) or incompleteness (SMTI) are considered. First, Theorem 3 shows that finding an approximation algorithm for the welfare- of fairness-optimal stable solution is a hard problem itself, meaning that for these problems there is no approximation algorithm that is able to guarantee a non-trivial solution quality. This result exemplifies the importance of studying heuristics for finding solutions in these cases. Second, if only indifferences are allowed in preference structures, yet the preferences themselves are complete, then the adapted algorithms as well as the heuristics guarantee that the maximum number of matched pairs is found. This simply follows the fact that in case of completeness, every user of the other side is acceptable, leading to a matching with maximum size (which is the size of the smaller market side). As soon as incompleteness is introduced, the algorithms are not able to guarantee a maximum size matching anymore. In this case, finding the maximum size stable matching is usually considered the most relevant objective, and finding the welfare- or fairness-optimal stable matching out of the maximum size matching is considered a subordinate goal which further increases problem complexity.

Table 5.1.: Computational Complexity of Two-Sided Matching Problems. SM indicates complete and strict preferences, SMT complete with indifferences, and SMTI incomplete with indifferences. Objectives are Stability (S), Welfare (W), Fairness (F), Number of Matched Pairs (NM), or Multiple Objectives (MO).

Scenario	Objective	Complexity	Authors	Type	Abbreviation
SM	S	$O(n^2)$	Gale and Shapley (1962)	Exact	DA
	S & W	$O(n^4)$	Irving et al. (1987)	Exact	WO
	S & F	NP-hard	Romero-Medina (2001)	Exact	-
	S & F	NP-hard	Iwama et al. (2010)	Approx	FE
	S & F	NP-hard	Nakamura et al. (1995)	Heuristic	-
	MO	NP-hard	Vien and Chung (2006)	Heuristic	-
	S, W, Equity	NP-hard	Kimbrough and Kuo (2010)	Heuristic	-
SMT	S	$O(n^2)$	Gale and Shapley (1962)	Exact	DA
	S & W	NP-hard	Irving et al. (1987)	Exact	WO
	S & F	NP-hard	Halldórsson et al. (2003)	Approx	FE
	S & W, S & F	NP-hard	Haas et al. (2013)	Heuristic	GA
SMTI	S	$O(n^2)$	Gale and Shapley (1962)	Exact	DA
	S & NM	NP-hard	Halldórsson et al. (2007)	Approx	Shift
	S & NM	NP-hard	McDermid (2009)	Approx	McDermid
	S & NM	NP-hard	Paluch (2012)	Approx	GSModified
	S & NM	NP-hard	Király (2011)	Approx	Király
	S & NM	NP-hard	Gelain et al. (2013)	Heuristic	LocalSearch
	MO	NP-hard	This Work	Heuristic	GA, TA

Table 5.1 provides an overview of the computational complexity of the matching problems relevant for this work. For the baseline case of complete and strict preferences (SM), it is possible to find a stable match, as well as the stable match with the best welfare, in polynomial time. Yet even with these rather strict assumptions about preference types, finding the stable match with the best fairness score is NP-hard. Once either the completeness or the strictness assumption is relaxed, the complexity of finding stable solutions that optimize an additional performance criterion increases. In case of complete preferences with indifferences (SMT), finding the welfare-optimal solution becomes NP-hard. The algorithm of Irving et al. (1987) can still be used to calculate a solution, yet as the solution quality depends on the way that the indifferences are broken, it cannot guarantee an optimal solution anymore.[6] Computing the fairness-optimal solution remains NP-hard. In

[6] To guarantee optimality, the algorithm would have to be applied to all possible ways to break the indifferences. In the general case, this number can be exponential in the lengths of ties and number of users.

the general case of incomplete preferences with indifferences (SMTI), the standard goal is to find a stable solution of maximum size. This problem is also NP-hard, and several approximation algorithms have been developed for this case.

Considering preference structures, besides the classification into SM, SMT and SMTI, preferences can be categorized according to their **correlation**, i.e., the degree to which the preferences of multiple users are correlated. On the one hand, preferences are uncorrelated if each user's preferences are independent of other users' preferences, e.g., if preferences are created randomly. On the other hand, Celik and Knoblauch (2007) propose a method to create correlated preferences. Given a certain threshold percentage x, the first x preferences are common among all participants of a side, and the last $n - x$ preferences are common as well (the actual order can be different, of course). This introduces a correlation in the set of preferences which can have an effect on the algorithm performance.[7] In the subsequent evaluation, uncorrelated preferences will be used as a baseline, and preference correlation according to the mentioned method will be applied as well to study its effects on the matching outcome.

5.2. Related Work

The literature on two-sided matching, beginning with the seminal paper of Gale and Shapley (1962), has emphasized *stability* as the design objective for two-sided matching. Under the assumptions that preference rankings are strict and independent (of preferences of other individuals),[8] Gale and Shapley (1962) introduced two of the standard problems in two-sided matching, the College Admissions problem and the Marriage Market. They also provided the first description of the Deferred-Acceptance (DA) algorithm, which under the mentioned assumptions is able to find at least one and at most two stable matches rapidly (in polynomial time).[9]

The literature on two-sided matching has grown considerably since Gale and Shapley (1962), as have the applications of two-sided matching. Roth (2008) and Abdulkadiroglu and Sönmez (2010) provide extensive overviews on the field of two-

[7] Another possibility is to study intercorrelated preferences (see Boudreau and Knoblauch (2010)), however this is left for future work.

[8] In particular, no "two-body problems" in which two or more individuals preferentially interact, such as in spouses preferring to locate near each other, were permitted.

[9] As Roth (2008) notes, certain labor markets had been managed successfully since the 1950's using a version of DA, but Gale and Shapley were unaware of this at the time.

sided matching and related concepts such as one-sided matching. Broadly speaking, there have been several main areas of research:

1. Types of Matching Problems
2. Preference Structures
3. Alternative Design Objectives
4. Computational Complexity.

Types of Matching Problems As mentioned earlier, the focus of this work is $1:1$ resource allocation, i.e., one user of side X is matched to one user of side Y, and vice versa. This model, often termed a "Marriage Market", was first defined by Gale and Shapley (1962) and has received considerable attention. There are, however, other types of models that are noteworthy to discuss. For example, if providing users of side Y have the capacity to serve (or to be matched with) several users of side X, the problem becomes a $1:n$ matching. The standard model in this case is the College Admission Model (see e.g. Gale and Shapley (1962); Roth (1985); Balinski and Sönmez (1999)), where users of side X request one unit of a resource (e.g., a college space), and users of side Y have a certain capacity, $c_y \geq 1$, of resources they can provide. It is noteworthy that some of the algorithms used for $1:1$ matching problems can be used for $1:n$ problems through certain adjustments as well, and that several of the important theorems and implications presented in the previous chapters also hold in this case. For the more general model of $m:n$ matching, Roth and Sotomayor (1992) provide a good overview of algorithms that can be used in this case.

Preference Structures Regarding preferences, the DA and much of the subsequent literature focuses on problems with strict preference orderings. If ties (indifferences) are introduced into the problem, certain characteristics of the algorithms can no longer be guaranteed. For example, in order to use the standard algorithms such as DA, the ties have to be broken first as the DA only allows strict preferences as input. Erdil and Ergin (2006, 2008) introduced an algorithm that can cope with ties in preferences. Their algorithm tries to find potential Pareto-improvement cycles in a given solution which might improve the overall quality of the solution. As Gusfield and Irving (1989, p.219) note, however, many of the strong results for DA and related algorithms depend upon strict preference orderings, and characterizing stable matches under partial ordering remains a largely open problem. Scott (2005) considers several variants of the standard, symmetric matching problem, specifically concentrating on different concepts of stability. Abdulkadiroğlu et al. (2009) study the effect of tie-breaking on the efficiency of the DA mechanism, and also consider the stability-cost of finding an efficient matching which does not have to be stable. They show that in some cases the welfare of participants of one side can be improved, which leads to the introduction of a potentially large number of blocking pairs.

Considering the type of preferences, the previously introduced definitions follow standard literature and specify a qualitative preference ranking, i.e., for every two alternatives the ranking determines whether the first alternative is better, worse, or equal to the second alternative. They do not, however, allow for a quantitative comparison of how much better or worse an alternative is. For example, from the ranking $a_1 > a_2 > a_3$ it cannot be inferred how much better a_1 is compared to a_3. The concept of *weighted preferences* extends the previous qualitative definitions and assigns a weight (or score) to each preference rank. Such a weighting of preferences has been proposed by Irving et al. (1987). They present adapted algorithms for certain matching problems, using the standard performance metrics. However, Pini et al. (2011b) argue that the performance metrics themselves have to be adapted to capture preference weights. Overall, as algorithms for weighted preferences have only been developed for certain preference structures and a quantitative weighting of preferences might not always be necessary, this work focuses on the standard definition of qualitative preferences in two-sided matching.

Objective Functions Regarding design objectives for matching, other than stability, it was shown early on that DA is heavily biased as it finds the optimal stable match for one side, and the pessimal stable match for the other side (Roth and Sotomayor, 1992). This raises the question of finding stable matches (or matches with only a few unstable pairs of pairs) for the sake of other criteria, such as fairness and social welfare. For strict and complete preferences, Irving et al. (1987) efficiently compute the welfare-optimal stable match. Axtell and Kimbrough (2008) discuss trade-offs between stability and welfare, and Klaus and Klijn (2006b) study (procedural) fairness and stability. Iwama et al. (2010) propose an algorithm that approximately yields the fairness-optimal stable matching. Using heuristics such as Genetic Algorithms, Kimbrough and Kuo (2010) show that they can yield superior solutions for welfare and fairness if a certain instability is allowed. Other approaches that look at different or multiple objectives for certain matching problems include Vien and Chung (2006), Klaus and Klijn (2006a), Pais (2008), Pini et al. (2011a), and Boudreau (2011) which also consider economic criteria such as welfare. From the perspective of what metrics are most relevant in practice, Echenique and Yariv (2011) study one-to-one matching in experimental settings where participants have full information about the preferences. They find that, among other things, stable matches are the most prevalent outcome, and that the cardinal representation of the ordinal preferences impacts which of the different matches is selected.

Computational Complexity The issue of computational complexity arises once preferences with incompleteness or indifferences are considered. On one hand, the number of stable matches can be large, sometimes exponential in the size of the problem (Gusfield and Irving, 1989; Knuth, 1997), and it has been shown that the two-sided matching problem in general is #P-complete (Gusfield and Irving, 1989, p.157). Furthermore, for the considered SMT and SMTI preference structures, the respective optimization problem is NP-hard (Halldórsson et al., 2007), and for certain scenarios such as finding the maximum number of matched users Integer Program formulations exist (Iwama et al., 2010). As discussed in Section 5.1.3, for strict and complete preferences there are polynomial-time algorithms to compute the welfare-optimal (Irving et al., 1987) and approximately fairness-optimal solutions (Iwama et al., 2010). However, by introducing indifferences and/or incompleteness, the problem of finding the welfare-optimal, minimum-regret or fairness-optimal stable match becomes NP-hard, and sometimes even hard to approximate (Halldórsson et al., 2007). Due to this complexity, heuristics have been studied to obtain solutions to the matching problem, the GA being a prominent example. For example, Nakamura et al. (1995) study whether a GA can yield stable matches with higher fairness than the DA solutions, yet do not consider indifferences or other objectives. Aldershof and Carducci (1999) describe a GA to compute stable solutions from random initial assignments, with stability as the sole objective. Furthermore, both Kimbrough and Kuo (2010) and Vien and Chung (2006) compare a GA with multiple objectives to the standard algorithms, yet neither of them consider indifferences in preferences.

Summary

The literature review shows that while two-sided matching is a well-studied problem in the literature, there are still some aspects that need further investigation. Table 5.2 provides an overview of the most relevant related work for 1 : 1 resource alloaction. Especially considering the flexibility towards optimizing different or changing objectives, existing algorithms mostly focus on a given set of optimization goals, and for certain combinations of goals no efficient optimization or approximation algorithms exist. As the calculation of the optimal solution is, in general, NP-hard, heuristics are particularly well suited for scenarios with multiple or flexible objective functions and different preference settings as they can be adapted to cover the respective scenario. Previously developed heuristics, however, have either focused on the setting of strict preferences or a certain combination of optimization goals. Hence, the heuristics developed in this thesis bridge this research gap by providing the flexibility to cover different preference structures.

Table 5.2.: Overview of Related Work

Authors	Flexible Preference Structures	Flexible Objective Function	Computational Complexity
Iwama et al. (2010)	●	◑	○
Gale and Shapley (1962)	●	○	●
Irving et al. (1987)	◑	○	●
Iwama et al. (2010)	◑	○	●
McDermid (2009); Király (2011); Paluch (2012)	◑	○	●
Erdil and Ergin (2008)	●	◑	●
Vien and Chung (2006)	○	●	●
Kimbrough and Kuo (2010)	○	●	●
Goal	●	●	●

5.3. Algorithms for Preference-based Matching

Most algorithms found in the literature concentrate on finding stable matches under certain conditions. Depending on the quality guarantees that an algorithm offers, they can be distinguished into exact, approximate and heuristic algorithms. Exact algorithms yield the optimal solution for a given scenario, and approximate algorithms guarantee that the solution quality is within a certain bound of the optimal solution. Heuristic algorithms, in general, do not provide such a quality bound, yet have other advantages such as the flexibility to consider multiple simultaneous objectives. This section introduces the algorithms considered for this chapter. Section 5.3.1 starts with the description of exact algorithms and the scenarios they can be applied in, and Section 5.3.2 continues with an overview of state-of-the-art approximation algorithms. Finally, Section 5.3.3 introduces and describes the heuristic algorithms that are focus of this chapter.

5.3.1. Exact Algorithms

As seen in Section 5.1.3, for certain preference structures the calculation of the optimal solution is possible in polynomial time. For strict preferences the Deferred Acceptance (DA) algorithm by Gale and Shapley (1962) can be used which always yields a stable outcome. Additionally, in this case the welfare-optimal (WO) algorithm by Irving et al. (1987) yields the welfare-optimal (or most egalitarian) stable solution in polynomial time. In the case of indifferences, a tie-breaking rule has to be applied first in order to apply these algorithms. The tie-breaking rule greatly affects the quality of the resulting matching and, in general, applying the algorithms after tie-breaking does not guarantee a good solution. This section describes the respective algorithms. In addition, the matching problem is formulated as a Linear Program for the SM case and as Integer Program for the SMTI case.

Formulation as Optimization Model The two-sided matching problem can be formulated as an optimization problem. For the standard model of strict preferences, Vande Vate (1989), Rothblum (1992), and Roth et al. (1993) introduced a linear programming (LP) formulation to obtain stable matches, which consists of a set of linear constraints:

$$max_{(x,y)} \sum_{i \in X, j \in Y} z_{i,j} \tag{5.4}$$

$$\sum_{i \in X} z_{i,y} \leq 1 \qquad \forall y \in Y \tag{5.5}$$

$$\sum_{j \in Y} z_{x,j} \leq 1 \qquad \forall x \in X \tag{5.6}$$

$$\sum_{j \succ_x y} z_{x,j} + \sum_{i \succ_y x} z_{i,y} + z_{x,y} \geq 1 \qquad \forall \langle x,y \rangle \in A \tag{5.7}$$

$$z_{x,y} \geq 0 \qquad \forall x \in X, y \in Y \tag{5.8}$$

$$z_{x,y} = 0 \qquad \forall (x,y) \in (X \times Y) \setminus A \tag{5.9}$$

In their model, the decision variable $z_{i,j}$ determines whether users i and j are matched $(z_{i,j} = 1)$ or not $(z_{i,j} = 0)$, and A defines the set of acceptable matched pairs. The optimization function (5.4) maximizes the number of matched pairs. Equations (5.5) and (5.6) ensure that each user is only allocated once. Equation (5.9) prohibits matched pairs which are not mutually acceptable, and Equation (5.7) guarantees that the solution is stable. Although Equation (5.8) is formulated as a linear constraint, the properties of the optimization problem ensure that a solution that satisfies constraints (5.5) - (5.9) is in fact an integer solution of the given optimization problem (Rothblum, 1992; Roth et al., 1993).

For the case of indifferences in preferences, the previous formulation has to be adapted. In particular, applying the formulation to a problem with indifferences might not yield valid integer solutions anymore, which makes an adaptation of constraint (5.8) necessary. This also implies that the corresponding optimization problem is an Integer Program (IP), which are, in general, NP-hard to solve.[10] Using a formulation similar to Iwama et al. (2014)[11], the SMTI one-to-one matching problem can be formulated as follows:

[10]This is in accordance with the previous theoretical findings in Table 5.1.

[11]The difference in this formulation is in Equation (5.13), which stems from a slightly different definition of the $\succsim$ relation. Conceptually, however, the two formulations are equivalent.

$$max_{(x,y)} \sum_{i \in X, j \in Y} z_{i,j} \tag{5.10}$$

$$\sum_{i \in X} z_{i,y} \leq 1 \qquad \forall y \in Y \tag{5.11}$$

$$\sum_{j \in Y} z_{x,j} \leq 1 \qquad \forall x \in X \tag{5.12}$$

$$\sum_{j \succsim_x y} z_{x,j} + \sum_{i \succsim_y x} z_{i,y} + z_{x,y} \geq 1 \qquad \forall \langle x,y \rangle \in A \tag{5.13}$$

$$z_{x,y} \in \{0,1\} \qquad \forall x \in X, y \in Y \tag{5.14}$$

$$z_{x,y} = 0 \qquad \forall (x,y) \in (X \times Y) \setminus A \tag{5.15}$$

As before, the optimization goal is to maximize the number of matched pairs (Equation 5.10). Other optimization functions can be used as well, provided they are linear. For example, for complete preferences with indifferences the welfare-optimal solution can be obtained by using the optimization function $\sum_{i \in X, j \in Y} \left(P_{i,j} + P_{j,i}\right) z_{i,j}$. Constraints (5.11), (5.12), and (5.15) are unchanged, and constraint (5.13) ensures a (weakly) stable solution.

Deferred Acceptance Algorithm

Being introduced in the seminal article by Gale and Shapley (1962), the Deferred Acceptance (DA) algorithm has been widely used and adapted for applications in research and practice. It was first introduced for the simple Marriage Market (symmetric matching instances with $n_X = n_Y$), and subsequently adapted for other matching problems such as College Admission problems. The strengths of the DA are its fast runtime, applicability for different preference structures, and simplicity.

Considering complexity, the DA runs in $O(n^2)$ where n is the size of a (symmetric) market side, which makes it the fastest deterministic algorithm among the described algorithms to solve the matching problem. It can be easily adapted to cope with incomplete preferences, and indifferences are usually handled by breaking the ties first before applying the DA in its standard formulation. The pseudocode of the DA is given in Algorithm 1.

Algorithm 1: Pseudocode of Deferred Acceptance Algorithm (Gale and Shapley, 1962)

```
Data: Preference Profiles
Result: Stable match μ
begin
    If some preference profiles are not strict, break the ties to get a strict ranking;
    while Unmatched users of side 1 who have not proposed to all acceptable users in their
    preference list do
        select a user of side 1 that is unmatched and has acceptable partners to which
        they didn't propose yet;
        user proposed to partner that is highest on their list;
        if partner is unmatched and finds user acceptable then
            partner temporarily accepts proposal;
        else if partner is matched and prefers user to current match then
            partner temporarily accepts proposal;
            formerly matched user becomes unmatched and removes partner from
            preference list;
        else
            user removes partner from preference list;
        end
    end
    All users are matched to their current partner
end
```

Despite these advantages, the DA has several limitations as well. Firstly, although it always yields a stable solution, for a given set of strict preferences it can only find at most two different stable solutions by switching the side that starts the algorithm. As there are up to exponentially many stable solutions (Knuth, 1997), the solution quality of the DA with respect to other performance metrics such as welfare is not immediately clear. Secondly, the DA yields particularly unfair solutions in the sense that it calculates the best stable solution for the starting side and the pessimal stable solution for the second side. This has to be considered especially when fairness aspects between the two market sides are of importance. Lastly, in case of incomplete preferences the DA does not guarantee a matching of maximum size. Albeit an undoubtedly useful algorithm, for these reasons other algorithms have been developed over time to address these issues.

Welfare-Optimal Algorithm

For the problem of finding a welfare-optimal stable solution in case of strict and complete preferences, Irving et al. (1987) present an algorithm that yields a solution in polynomial time (henceforth called Welfare-Optimal algorithm, WO). If n is the size of one side in a symmetric setting, the runtime of their algorithm is $O(n^4)$. The pseudocode of WO is shown in Algorithm 2. The algorithm uses the concept of *rotations*, which were studied in the context of a symmetric 1:1 market by Irving and Leather (1986). They showed that all stable solutions of a given matching problem can be identified by the use of these rotations. Essentially, the algorithm by Irving et al. (1987) uses this rotation concept in combination with graph-theoretic algorithms in order to find the sequence of rotations that yield the welfare-optimal stable solution. Similar to the DA, WO can be used in case of strict preferences with or without indifferences by breaking the ties before the start of the algorithm. However, in case of indifferences WO only guarantees the welfare-optimal stable solution for a given tie breaking; the global welfare-optimal matching cannot be guaranteed.

Algorithm 2: Pseudocode of Welfare-Optimal Algorithm (Irving et al., 1987)

Data: Preference Profiles
Result: Welfare-optimal stable match μ

```
begin
    Calculate shortlists for each user;
    Calculate all rotations given the shortlists;
    Create graph from weighted rotation poset P;
    Compute maximum-weight closed subset;
    Eliminate all rotations in maximum-weight closed subset;
end
```

The $O(n^4)$ algorithm by Irving and Leather (1986) was later improved to a $O(n^{2.5} log\ n)$ algorithm by Feder (1992). As the focus of the subsequent evaluation is the solution quality rather than the runtime (the quality is the same as both are optimal algorithms), only WO is considered in the evaluation.

5.3.2. Approximation Algorithms

As it is not possible to calculate optimal solutions through polynomial-time algorithms for all matching problems, in certain cases approximation algorithms can be used to calculate a solution with a specified quality bound. Examples of the problem types where an exact solution cannot be computed in polynomial-time is finding the fairness-optimal stable solution (even for strict and complete preferences), and finding the maximum size stable matching in case of incomplete preferences (see the overview in Table 5.1). For these problems, approximation algorithms have been developed.

Fairness Approximation

Finding the fairness-optimal stable solution is NP-hard even for strict and complete preferences. Hence, Iwama et al. (2010) propose an approximation algorithm (henceforth called Fairness-Equal, FE) that yields stable solutions with a certain quality bound on the fairness score. The FE algorithm works with a parameter ϵ that specifies the fairness bounds within which the near-optimal fair solution is intended to be found. Without loss of generality, the implementation of FE used for the evaluation assumes $\epsilon = 0.1$. Clearly, the specification of this bound involves a certain trade-off. On one hand, if the bound is too tight, it is possible that no solutions will be found within the bound. On the other hand, if the bound is too large, the solution quality with respect to the fairness score might be worse, as solutions are accepted which might be further away from a perfectly fair solution.

MaxPairs Approximation

As described earlier, in case of incomplete preferences it is NP-hard to find the stable match of maximum size. Several approximation algorithms have been suggested for this case. As the trivial approximation ratio in this case is 2, i.e., the worst case size of a solution is half the size of the optimal solution, any approximation ratio smaller than 2 is desirable.

- *Shift*: Halldórsson et al. (2007) describe an approximation algorithm for this case, in the following abbreviated as *Shift*. For certain preference structures, this algorithm provides non-trivial quality bounds for finding the stable match of maximum size. Shift operates through breaking indifferences in a systematic manner and applying the DA on the resulting set of strict preferences. In particular, if indifferences occur on both sides of the market, Shift guarantees non-trivial quality bounds if the length of indifferences is at most 2.
- *McDermid*: McDermid (2009) presents an algorithm with a 3/2 approximation ratio, which is the best known approximation ratio for the general case without restrictions on tie lengths.

- *Király*: Similarly, Király (2011) presents an algorithm with a 5/3 approximation ratio, which has a slightly better runtime than that of McDermid (2009).
- *GSModified*: Paluch (2012) presents another algorithm with the same runtime and approximation ratio as the algorithm by Király (2011).

These algorithms are used in the subsequent comparison. If ties are only one-sided, (Iwama et al., 2014) provide an algorithm that guarantees an approximation ratio of 25/17. Irving and Manlove (2008) present algorithms to approximate stable marriage and hospital/residents problems. As the former puts a considerable restriction on the preferences, and the latter has a worse approximation ratio than McDermid, Király and GSModified, they are not considered in the evaluation.

5.3.3. Heuristics

In addition to the mentioned algorithms, the use of heuristics to find solutions to the matching problem is investigated. In this chapter, besides improvement cycles as suggested in the literature (Erdil and Ergin, 2008), two different heuristics are used: a Genetic Algorithm (GA) (Goldberg, 1989) as an example of a evolutionary (meta)heuristic, and a Threshold Accepting algorithm as an example of a local search heuristic. In general, heuristics can be used to find (stable) solutions from random initial assignments (see Aldershof and Carducci (1999); Kimbrough and Kuo (2010)), or to improve an initial stable matching by trying to retain stability and increasing other performance criteria (see Haas et al. (2013)).

Improvement Cycles

In the case of (potentially incomplete) preferences with indifferences, Erdil and Ergin (2008) suggest an algorithm that computes *improvement cycles* for a given stable solution. This algorithm, called Requester-Optimal-Stable-Matching (RSMA) throughout the chapter, looks for ordered sequences of matched pairs, such that each requester (weakly) prefers to be matched to the provider of the next pair. If such a sequence of matched pairs exists, switching each requester to the next provider on the respective sequence element yields another stable match that is Pareto-superior for the requesting users (though not necessarily for the providers). In case the sequence of pairs contains a pair with an unmatched requester and a pair with an unmatched provider, the sequence is called an improvement cycle, otherwise an improvement chain. It is easy to see that an improvement cycle increases the number of matched users, whereas an improvement chain yields a match with the same number of matched users.

While RSMA guarantees that users of one side are not worse of from the improvement, this is not necessarily true for users of the second side. For such cases, Erdil and Ergin (2006) suggest an alternative algorithm, the Efficient-and-Stable-Matching-Algorithm (ESMA), which focuses on improvements in which both sides are (weakly) better off. As this restricts the potential chains and cycles that can be found, the subsequent evaluation only considers RSMA, as initial results have shown that applying ESMA does not significantly improve the solution in but a small number of cases.

MaxPairs Heuristic

Gelain et al. (2013) present local search heuristics to solve the generalized stable matching. They start with solving the relaxed version of the problem (assuming complete preferences), thereby potentially introducing instability, and then deleting unstable pairs through an iterative process until stable solutions are found. Initial tests showed that its performance with respect to solution quality is worse than the heuristics proposed in this chapter, which is why it has not been considered for further evaluation.

Genetic Algorithms

Starting with the groundbreaking works of Goldberg (1989) and Holland (1992), Genetic Algorithms (GA) have been widely used for and successfully applied to many optimization problems. Specifically, they have been found to perform well in case of large search spaces (Duffy, 2006; Kimbrough and Kuo, 2010; Haas et al., 2013).

GAs start with a (usually randomly created) initial set of potential solutions (the *population*) and evolve this solution set by applying certain mathematical operations on them. The quality of a potential solution is determined by its *fitness*, i.e., how well it performs with respect to the given objective function. The aim of this type of evolutionary algorithm is to create new solutions which are better than the initial population. Each potential solution, a *chromosome*, consists of several *genes*, where each gene represents the value of an attribute of the solution. Traditionally, chromosomes and genes are encoded as bit-strings, although integer- or real-valued genes are also commonly used in practice. In order to find solutions with high fitness values, the GA evolves the population by applying the mentioned operations, yielding a new population of potential solutions.[12] Usually, there are three main genetic operators used to obtain the new population, which are specified as follows (see Goldberg (1989)):

Selection Through the selection operator, a certain number of chromosomes of the old population are selected into an intermediate population, and the subsequent operations are performed only on this intermediate population. Intuitively, this means that only a certain number of solutions are allowed to reproduce, and usually only the fittest solutions are selected in this step. The selection itself can be implemented in various ways. In practice, many GA implementations use either a tournament or a roulette-selector. A tournament selector of size k randomly selects k solutions out of the population and selects the fittest of these k solutions. In contrast, a roulette-selector assigns probabilities to individual solutions, where the probability of being selected is proportional to the solution's fitness.

Crossover The crossover operator was developed as an analogy to biological reproduction. Usually, crossover is only applied to a certain percentage of solutions of the intermediate population. The crossover itself is performed in two steps. First, two solutions of the intermediate population are selected. Second, certain parts of the two selected solutions are swapped. There are several commonly used crossover operators that determine which parts of the chromosomes are swapped. As some crossover operators might create invalid solutions depending on the specific encoding of the chromosomes, the right crossover operator has to be chosen for the given problem. The newly created solutions, called offspring, then usually replace the parent solutions.

Mutation After crossover, the mutation operator randomly changes the values of some genes according to a specified mutation probability. The rate of mutation is essential for the performance of the genetic algorithm. If the mutation rate is too

[12] An important theoretical result on the efficiency of a GA is the schema-theorem, also referred to as the *building block hypothesis*. The theorem states that schemas, defined as a subset of genes which are inherent to fit chromosomes and that are found across several chromosomes, are exponentially more often propagated in successive generations (Goldberg, 1989). In other words, inherent characteristics of successful solutions are exponentially more often found in next generations of the population. This is important for the matching problem, as it states that successful matched pairs are propagated to the new solutions.

low, the chance of getting stuck in local optima increases. In contrast, setting the mutation rate too high does not allow the algorithm to settle and converge to a solution due to the continuous adjustments through mutations. Hence, care must be taken in selecting a mutation rate, as this fundamentally affects the outcome of the genetic algorithm.

For the matching problem, each chromosome represents a solution $\langle X, Y \rangle$. A chromosome consists of several genes, where each gene encodes a provider-requester match $\langle x, y \rangle$ of the solution. In other words, when a solution has m matches, the chromosome has m genes, and each gene consists of two identifiers, one for the provider, one for the requester.[13] As fitness functions for two-sided matching, the maximization of stability, welfare, fairness, number of pairs, or a combination thereof are used. As each chromosome only encodes a set of matched pairs, the preferences of the users are needed to evaluate its fitness.

In order to improve the fitness of the solutions, the two described genetic operators are applied after the fitness evaluation in order to derive new, potentially better-performing solutions. For crossover, the *cycle crossover* operator (Goldberg, 1989) creates new potential solutions by combining two parent solutions. This type of crossover operator ensures valid solutions for the given encoding by exchanging the same set of IDs for the two chromosomes.[14] The mutation operator, given a certain mutation probability, depends on the type of preferences and optimization objective. In case of complete preferences with indifferences, it randomly selects two genes (matched pairs) of a given chromosome and exchanges either the requester or provider identifiers to create a new chromosome. In case of incomplete preferences, it randomly selects a gene with an unmatched requester, a randomly chosen amount of genes representing matched pairs, and a gene with an unmatched provider. This is done for a similar reason as the RSMA algorithm by Erdil and Ergin (2008): to potentially find an improvement cycle that, when each requester is matched to the provider of the next pair in the cycle, increases the number of matched pairs. This specification of crossover and mutation operators ensure valid solutions which are not necessarily stable. As the subsequent evaluation focuses on stable matching algorithms, blocking pairs are discounted in the objective function

[13]Note that the maximum number of genes is $n_X + n_Y$, which represents the case that each user is unmatched.

[14]The use of standard crossover operations might yield solutions where users are matched multiple times. Hence, only the class of crossover operations that are applicable for enumeration settings are of interest.

of the GA, which ensures that newly created, unstable solutions are not likely to be propagated through the evolution rounds. The population is evolved using these operators over a given number of rounds. For the selection of solutions that form the new population in the next evolution round, a tournament selector of size 2 is used. Additionally, through an *elitist selection* the 5 best solutions are guaranteed to be transferred to the next population. Algorithm 3 shows the pseudocode for the GA.[15]

Algorithm 3: Pseudocode of Genetic Algorithm based on (Goldberg, 1989; Holland, 1992)

Data: Preference Profiles
Data: Crossover and mutation probabilities
Data: Number of evolution rounds and size of population
Data: Number of best solutions retained: n_{best}
Data: Optional: Starting Solutions
Result: Match μ

```
begin
    Create initial population: solution set ← initial population;
    for i ← 1to number evolution rounds do
        temporary solution set ← perform crossover operation;
        for solution ∈ temporary solution set do
            mutate solution according to mutation probability;
        end
        solution set ← ∅;
        solution set ← n_best solutions;
        while size of solution set < size of population do
            run tournament selection and include winner in solution set;
        end
    end
    μ ← best solution of population;
end
```

To show the actual encoding and how the genetic operators work, an example for the encoding, the cycle crossover, and the mutation operator are provided in Appendix C.

Threshold Accepting Algorithms

The second class of heuristics studied in this thesis are Threshold Accepting (TA) al-

[15]The number of evolution rounds can be dynamically adjusted if the available computation time is limited, e.g., in settings where a solution has to be calculated in short time. If the calculation of a solution is not time-critical, the solution quality can be potentially increased by evolving the population over more rounds.

gorithms (Dueck and Scheuer, 1990). TAs are an example of local search heuristics, where a given starting solution is improved by sequentially adjusting the solution and accepting adjustments within a certain threshold. TAs are conceptually similar to Simulated Annealing approaches and have been successfully applied in many optimization problems. Depending on the definition of the solution adjustment per step, TAs try to improve a given solution and hence are suitable for finding (especially local) improvements. Compared to GAs which work on a population of different solutions in the solution space, the performance of a TA depends on the quality of the starting solution. However, it is more flexible on incrementally improving this solution than the GA which has to rely on mutations to find improvements once it settled on a local or global optimum. The subsequent evaluation studies its applicability in the case of two-sided matching.

The general procedure is shown in Algorithm 4. Given a starting solution, a set of thresholds is defined. For each of these thresholds, a certain number of adjustments are sequentially performed on the solution. For the matching problem, the adjustment is similar to the mutation operator of the GA. For complete preferences, it selects two matched pairs and switches either the requesting or providing users. For incomplete preferences, it selects an unmatched user of side X, a randomly drawn number of matched pairs, and an unmatched user of side Y (thus forming a cycle of matched pairs), and replaces the users of side X with the respective user of the previous matched pair in the cycle. An adjustment is accepted as new (temporary) solution if it does not decrease the solution quality by more than the threshold (compared to the current solution). Thresholds are reduced over time such that convergence to a (local) optimum becomes more likely, whereas the initial thresholds are set to avoid being stuck in a local optimum too soon.

Genetic Algorithm with Subsequent Threshold Accepting

GAs tend to sample (especially large) search spaces better than local search heuristics as they start with a potentially diverse set of solutions. However, as mentioned before the incremental improvement of a given solution depends on mutations. This might not be as efficient as using local search heuristics that aim at improving a given solution. Hence, the combination of the two approaches is also studied, where the GA is used to find a good starting solution for the TA, which then tries to further improve this solution. For the purpose of evaluation, this combination of heuristics, which represents a *memetic algorithm*, is abbreviated as GATA.

Algorithm 4: Pseudocode of Threshold Accepting Algorithm based on (Dueck and Scheuer, 1990)

```
Data: Preference Profiles
Data: Number of thresholds
Data: Number of repetitions per thresholds
Data: Optional: Starting Solution μ_start
Result: Match μ
begin
    if μ_start = ∅ then
        μ_current ← create starting solution;
    else
        μ_current = μ_start;
    end
    for i ← 1to number of thresholds do
        for j ← 1 to number of repetitions per threshold do
            μ_adj ← apply adjustment to μ_current;
            if score μ_adj ≤ μ_current + current threshold then
                μ_current ← μ_adj;
            end
        end
    end
    μ ← μ_current;
end
```

5.4. Performance of Matching Algorithms

Algorithms such as GA and TA have an inherent flexibility to be adjustable to many different optimization functions and combinations of metrics that need to be optimized. This stands in contrast to specialized algorithms, such as the approximation algorithms for calculating the solution with the maximum number of matched pairs, which focus on one specific scenario or set of goals. The aim of this section, therefore, is to provide a comparison of the performance of the different algorithms in specific settings.

For the evaluation, a simulation-based approach is used. This provides the flexibility to test the performance of the algorithms in various different settings and perform sensitivity analyses. Section 5.4.1 presents the specifications of the simulations, including the scenarios, the varied input parameters, and the process to create preference profiles. Afterwards, Section 5.4.2 shows the runtimes of the studied algorithms in different settings. Considering algorithm performance, for the case of SMT instances, i.e. preference profiles which are complete and have indifferences, Section 5.4.3 compares the solution quality of the relevant algorithms and evaluates how sensitive the results are with respect to certain input parameters. Section 5.4.4 considers the same issues for SMTI instances, i.e., if preferences are both incomplete and have indifferences.

5.4.1. Simulation Specifics

To obtain robust results and study their dependency on certain input parameters, a systematic simulation plan is used which specifies the simulation scenarios with the respective input parameter settings. Table 5.3 shows an overview of the most important input parameters and the ranges of values that are used.

Table 5.3.: Simulation Input Parameters

Parameter	Range	Description
n_X	$\{10,20,50,100,200,500\}$	Number of requesting users
n_Y	$\{10,20,50,100,200,500\}$	Number of providing users
l	$\{0.5,0.3,0.1,0.05\}$	Relative length of preference lists
ψ	$\{2,5,10\}$	Maximum length of ties
ξ	$\{25,100\}$	Percentage of users j that are correlated in the preferences of users i

The numbers of users per side, n_X and n_Y, determine the size of the problem instance. Usually, symmetric problems with $n_X = n_Y$ are considered in the literature. The evaluation, however, also considers unequally sized problem instances. The remaining parameters are concerned with the structure of the preferences. l determines the average expected number of ranked users in the preference lists and is used during preference creation (see parameter p_D in Algorithm 5). ψ specifies the maximum length of the ties in the preference lists. Furthermore, ξ defines if and to what degree the preferences are correlated. For a given value of ξ, the users of the respective other side are split into two groups, and ξ determines what percentage of users are in the first group. This grouping of users is the same for all users of the side, yet the subsequent randomization leads to randomized rankings within the two groups.

For the creation of preferences, an approach similar to (Gent and Prosser, 2002; Gelain et al., 2013) is used. The general procedure is shown in Algorithm 5. The probability of deletion, p_D, is varied between 0.5 and 0.95 to account for a decrease in ranked users (this corresponds to the input values for parameter l). Together with the 3 different values for the maximum length of ties, this parametrization represents a full factorial 3x4 design for the variables tie-length and probability of deletion, and allows for a study of the respective effects on the matching outcome. For all considered scenarios, 100 randomly created independent repetitions are made.

Algorithm 5: Pseudocode of Preference Generation

```
Data: Deletion Probability p_D = (1 − l)
Data: Max Length of Ties ψ
Data: Size of X and Y
Data: Correlation Parameter ξ
Result: Preference Profiles
begin
    for user in set of requester or provider do
        if ξ!=100 then
            split users of other side into two groups of relative size ξ and 1 − ξ;
        end
        create random preference list;
    end
    for preference list of users i ∈ X do
        iterate over the users in the preference list;
        for user j ∈ Y do
            delete j from i's list with probability p_D;
            if j is deleted, also delete i from j's list;
        end
    end
    for preference list do
        for user in preference list do
            randomly determine size of next tie length ∈ {1,...,ψ};
            set ranking of all users in the tie to the same value;
        end
    end
end
```

In case of complete preferences with indifferences (Section 5.4.3), the algorithms DA, WO, FE, GA, TA, and GATA are considered. Finding a stable solution is trivial by using DA, hence the goal is to find a stable solution with good welfare or fairness scores. For GA, TA, and GATA, several different objective functions are compared. In case of welfare optimization, the main objective was to decrease the previously introduced welfare metric. Additionally, the objective function adds a penalty for each blocking pair, thereby discouraging unstable solutions. Similarly, for fairness optimization the fairness metric is the main objective, and the penalty on blocking pairs is used as well. To show a multiple objective function, the suffix $'' - EW''$ indicates an objective function that puts equal weight on the welfare and fairness score, while also having a penalty on blocking pairs. Furthermore, as the performance of DA, WO and FE depends on the way that ties are broken, these algorithms are run 50 times per preference setting to study the variability in solution quality with respect to tie breaking. For evaluation purposes, the average, best, and worst performance of these 50 repetitions is presented to show the variability of results due to the tie-breaking.

For incomplete preferences with indifferences (Section 5.4.4), the considered algorithms are DA, RSMA, Király, Shift, McDermid and GSModified, as well as GA, TA and GATA.

For the parametrization of the GA, several different parameter combination for mutation rate, crossover rate, crossover type and population size were compared. Similar to suggestions in the literature (see De Jong and Spears (1991)), and due to the best performance of this combination during initial pre-tests, a population size of 50 was chosen, along with a mutation rate of 0.2, and a crossover probability of 0.6 using a cycle crossover operator. Additionally, the best 5 solutions of a given population were always guaranteed to be ported into the next generation. The GA was evolved for 100 evolution rounds. This is a smaller value than usually found in the literature, yet with the trade-off between computation time and solution quality, initial experiments had shown that this is a suitable value. As mentioned before, increasing the number of evolution rounds, if the expected runtime permits, can help to further improve the quality of GA and GATA. In other words, the presented results can be considered a conservative view on GA and GATA performance. For the TA, the threshold values of $\{0.04 * min\{n_X, n_Y\}, 0.02 * min\{n_X, n_Y\}, 0.01 * min\{n_X, n_Y\}, 0\}$ are used with 10,000 repetitions per threshold.

5.4.2. Algorithm Runtime

Table 5.1 showed that introducing indifferences or incompleteness yields NP-hard optimization problems. The computation of an optimal solution for these problems cannot be expected in polynomial time, which is the reason why approximation and heuristic algorithms are necessary. This section gives an overview of the runtimes of the considered algorithms in different scenarios.

Finding Optimal Solutions The integer program as shown in Section 5.3.1 solves the matching problem (with indifferences) optimally for certain cases, for example finding a welfare-best or a maximum-size stable match. However, the calculation of the solution to the integer program might not always be feasible in reasonable time. In order to test the feasibility of calculating the optimal solution, the integer program was implemented for the welfare-optimal (for the SMT case) as well as maximum-size stable match (for the SMTI case) using ILOG CPLEX 12.1[16] and the corresponding Java integration to make it callable from within the simulation tool. The solution was calculated for various problem instances, using up to 16 parallel threads on 2 Quad-Core Xeon processor with 2.53 GHz and 24-48 GB main memory.

The runtime experiments yield the following interesting results. First, for random uncorrelated preferences the solver is able to calculate an optimal solution for the given problems up to problem sizes of 200x200 users in a matter of minutes. For larger problem instances the solver usually runs out of memory. Second, correlated preferences significantly increase the runtime of the solver. For example, for $\xi = 25$ the runtime of the solver increases to minutes and hours even for problem instances of 50x50. For bigger problem instances, the solver either runs out of memory again or does not yield a solution within several hours.

In real Social Cloud scenarios, the preference profiles can be quite diverse and include incompleteness and indifferences. Hence, the computation of an optimal solution through integer program solvers is not feasible for larger problem instances.

Calculating Approximate or Heuristic Solutions From a computational complexity perspective, the DA is the fastest algorithm with $O(n^2)$. Most of the approximation algorithms for the case of incomplete preferences are similarly fast, having runtimes of $O(mn^2)$, where m is an algorithm-specific factor.[17] The WO algorithm, provided that indifferences are broken first, has a runtime of $O(n^4)$.[18] Considering the studied heuristic algorithms, the TA also has a runtime of $O(mn^2)$. In this case, m is the number of changes to the solutions (number of thresholds multiplied with

[16] `http://www-01.ibm.com/software/commerce/optimization/cplex-optimizer/` – last accessed May 2014

[17] Shift is the only considered approximation algorithm with a different runtime. Given that the maximum length of ties is ψ, its runtime is $O(\psi^2 n^2)$.

[18] As mentioned before, this can be improved to an $O(n^{2.5} log\ n)$ bound by Feder (1992).

the repetitions per threshold). Similarly, the GA is $O(mpn^2)$, where m is the number of evolution rounds and p the size of the population. For both heuristics, the factor n^2 stems from calculating the stability of the current solution, for which no algorithm is known to have worst case time complexity better than $O(n^2)$. Overall, the actual runtime then seems to depend on the algorithm-specific factor m.

Table 5.4.: Comparison of Algorithm Runtime

Algorithm	Users					
	10x10	20x20	50x50	100x100	200x200	500x500
			Complete Preferences			
DA	<1 sec	<1 sec	<1 sec	<1 sec	<1 sec	<1 sec
WO	<1 sec	<1 sec	<1 sec	<1 sec	1 sec	34 sec
FE	<1 sec	<1 sec	<1 sec	<1 sec	1 sec	35 sec
GA	<1 sec	2 sec	7 sec	18 sec	58 sec	8 min
TA	<1 sec	2 sec	9 sec	25 sec	2 min	15 min
GATA	2 sec	4 sec	15 sec	43 sec	3 min	23 min
			Incomplete Preferences			
RSMA	<1 sec	<1 sec	<1 sec	<1 sec	<1 sec	5 sec
Király	<1 sec	<1 sec	<1 sec	<1 sec	<1 sec	1 sec
McDermid	<1 sec	<1 sec	<1 sec	<1 sec	<1 sec	2 sec
GSModified	<1 sec	<1 sec	<1 sec	<1 sec	<1 sec	3 sec
Shift	<1 sec	<1 sec	<1 sec	<1 sec	<1 sec	1 min
GA	<1 sec	1 sec	3 sec	6 sec	12 sec	1 min
TA	<1 sec	1 sec	5 sec	8 sec	15 sec	2 min
GATA	1 sec	3 sec	8 sec	15 sec	31 sec	5 min

Table 5.4 shows the average runtimes of the previously introduced approximation and heuristic algorithms for different (uncorrelated) preferences.[19] The table shows that for problem sizes up to 500 users on each side, the DA, WO, and approximation algorithms take less than or several seconds. GA, TA and GATA take longer, on average several seconds to compute. This is due to the large number of evolution steps which are an essential part of the heuristics. However, even for large problem sets finding a solution only takes a few seconds to a few minutes.

Overall, it can be seen that for most problem instances, runtimes of all the studied algorithms are in the range of seconds to minutes, which (especially for larger problem sizes) is more than acceptable considering the NP-hard optimization problem.

[19] In general, runtimes for correlated preferences seem to be slightly higher than for uncorrelated preferences.

5.4.3. Complete Preferences With Indifferences

If the preference profiles of users are complete yet contain indifferences, the same algorithms as in case of strict preferences can be applied by breaking the ties first. However, as shown in Table 5.1 applying the algorithms that are optimal in the case of strict preferences does not guarantee solution optimality anymore, and finding a welfare- or fairness-optimal stable solution is NP-hard. This scenario is the focus of this section, which is an extended version of (Haas et al., 2013). As the considered algorithms always yield a stable solution of maximum size in this case, it concentrates on finding a stable solution with good welfare or fairness characteristics.

Considering GA and GATA heuristics, the subscript "$-DA$" indicates that they are initialized only with DA solutions, whereas "$-MIXED$" means that a randomly created mixture of DA, WO and FE solutions are used. Note that both WO and FE were developed for symmetric problem sizes, and some of their routines in calculating the solution do not easily extend to non-symmetric settings. Hence, this case is not considered in this evaluation. At the same time, this shows the advantage of having flexible heuristics to calculate matching solutions: They can easily be applied to non-symmetric settings as well.

Unless stated otherwise, the statistical tests refer to non-parametric Wilcoxon signed-rank tests with Bonferoni p-value adjustment in order to account for multiple comparisons. The test is used due to the simulation design (algorithms have the same preference lists as input, leading to a paired design), as well as non-normally distributed data. The following figures refer to the average values over the 100 independent repetitions. As DA, WO and FE were run 50 times per repetition, additional bars indicate the average, best, and worst solution out of these 50 repetitions to study the dependency of algorithm performance on tie breaking.

Optimizing Stability and Welfare

The combination of stability and welfare maximization aims to find a stable solution with good welfare properties, i.e., where the average rank of the matched users is as close to the respective most preferred option as possible. As mentioned before, for SMT instances this is an NP-hard problem (and even hard to approximate), which means that finding a good solution is far from trivial. Hence, heuristics such as GA and TA might be able to yield better results than applying the algorithms developed for SM instances. The section only presents the most important results, detailed results and additional scenarios can be found in Tables C.1 and C.3 in Appendix C. For GA, TA, and GATA, the objective of welfare maximization with penalty on blocking pairs is used, which yields completely stable solutions for the given scenarios.

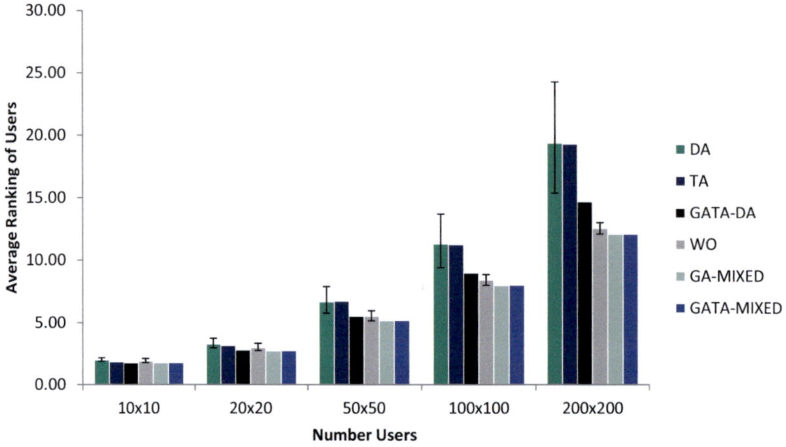

Figure 5.1.: Comparison of Welfare Performance for Complete Preferences

Uncorrelated Preferences Figure 5.1 shows the results for the different algorithms for problem sizes between 10x10 and 200x200 users, averaged over different tie-lengths. The results show that the average welfare becomes worse with an increasing number of participating users (indicated by an increasing score). This is not surprising, as an increase in users also increases the list of potential competitors for high-ranked users on the preference lists, thereby lowering the chance of being matched to a high ranked user.

Considering the performance of the algorithms, GA and GATA with mixed initial solutions perform best. Both are able to significantly increase the DA and average WO solutions, and the solutions are slightly better than the best WO solutions (at the level $p < 0.001$). This indicates that both GA and GATA are able to improve upon WO solutions and yield a superior solution quality. Additionally, the fairness scores of the GA and GATA solutions are on average slightly better than the WO (average and best) solutions.

Considering the GA performance with different initial solutions, the results show that the GA with only DA solutions is able to significantly improve upon the DA solutions, and also yields better solutions than WO for problem sizes up to 50x50. For larger number of users, the WO might yield better solutions, yet the increase in solution quality compared to the initial solutions is still significant ($p < 0.001$). If GA and GATA use mixed initial solutions, the heuristics are able to improve upon them as well. This shows two issues: First, the GA effectively improves the given starting solutions, showing its usefulness. Second, the quality of the starting solutions determine the quality of the heuristic solutions, which means that feeding the heuristics with promising initial solutions increases their performance.

Interestingly, the TA does not perform as well. In the given setting, the TA starts with a DA solution and then tries to find a better solution as specified in Section 5.3.3. Figure 5.1 shows that only for small problem instances the TA is able to significantly improve the solution quality of the starting DA solution. For larger problem instances, TA performs considerably worse compared to WO and GA. This indicates that starting with DA solutions is not promising for TAs, which might get stuck in local optima. In contrast, the GA with its ability to sample large search spaces is an adequate heuristic for SMT instances. Due to this, the performance of GA and GATA are basically the same as TA is not able to significantly improve the given solution.

Effect of Preference Correlation In this scenario, preferences are correlated with the factor $\xi = 25$, meaning that the set of user IDs is split into two sets of relative size 25% and 75%, and the 25% highest ranked users in all the preference profiles (of each side) are drawn from the same set.

Considering finding a welfare-optimal stable solution, Figure 5.2 compares the performance of DA, WO, GA, TA, and GATA. The results are qualitatively very similar to the case of uncorrelated preferences. In general, the results show that the average welfare decreases compared to the uncorrelated case, which is not surprising as the correlation means that some users are more likely to be matched with lower-ranking users as there is an increased competition for higher-ranked users. The relative ranking of the algorithm performance is practically the same. GA and GATA perform significantly better than the other algorithms on average ($p < 0.001$), and only the best WO solution yields comparable results (for all considered scenarios, the signed-rank test reveals a statistical difference between the best WO solution

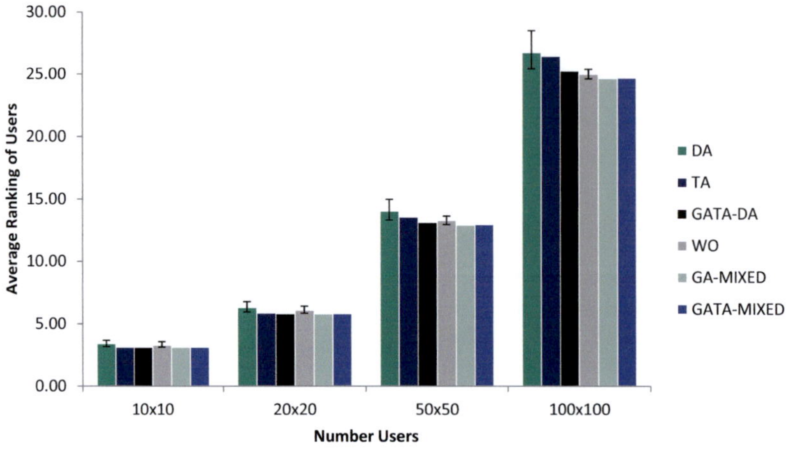

Figure 5.2.: Comparison of Welfare Performance for Complete and Correlated Preferences

and GA (GATA), although the absolute difference is negligible). Another interesting finding is that the spread in solution quality is smaller for correlated preferences, i.e., is less dependent on the way that ties are broken. This is indicated by the smaller range of best and worst solutions averaged over the 100 repetitions.

Sensitivity analyses were also performed on varying values for maximum tie lengths. The results indicate that the relative performance of GA and GATA is better than WO particularly for small tie lengths. However, the qualitative results are similar.

Optimizing Stability and Fairness

Besides welfare optimization, finding a stable and particularly fair solution is another common goal in two-sided matching. However, even for strict preferences this is an NP-hard problem, and the approximation algorithm FE can be applied in SM and SMT instances by appropriately breaking ties. This part of the evaluation aims to study the performance of the DA, FE, GA, TA, and GATA algorithms for finding stable and fair solutions. As before, it concentrates on the most important findings, and the detailed results can be found in Tables C.2 and C.4 in Appendix C. For GA, TA, and GATA, the objective of fairness maximization with penalty on blocking pairs is used, which yields completely stable solutions for the given scenarios.

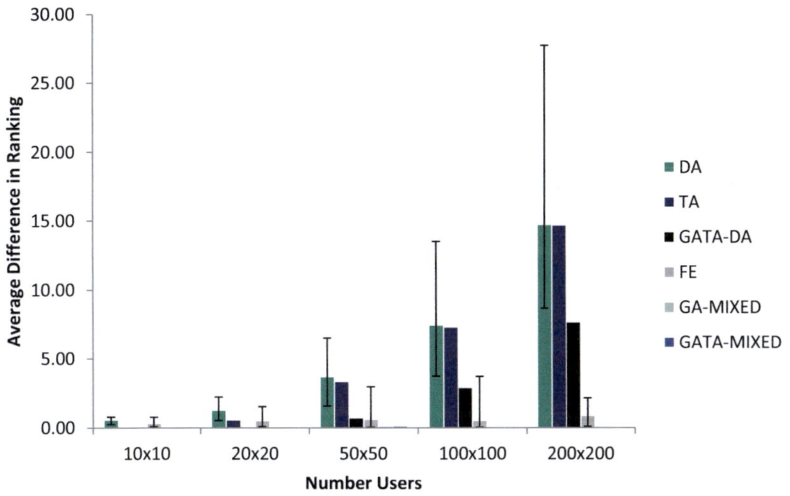

Figure 5.3.: Comparison of Fairness Performance for Complete Preferences

Uncorrelated Preferences Figure 5.3 presents the fairness performance of the considered algorithms. As expected from theory, the DA has the worst performance of the considered algorithms. Furthermore, as before TA finds improvements (in this case: fair solutions) only for small problem instances. For larger instances the TA performance considerably decreases. The figure also shows that the range of best and worst solutions can be considerably high, which indicates that especially for DA tie-breaking greatly affects the solution quality.

Comparing the performance of DA, FE and GA the results indicate that the GA and GATA yield significantly better results with respect to fairness if it is initialized with mixed solutions, and also outperforms the average FE solution. This is confirmed by Wilcoxon signed-rank tests at the level $p < 0.001$. Over all considered scenarios, the signed-rank test indicates a significant difference between the best FE solution and the GA solution with mixed initial solutions, although the practical effect size can be considered negligible. The performance of GATA-DA, initialized only with DA solutions, is significantly better than DA solutions ($p < 0.001$), yet, for all but very small problem sizes up to 20x20 users, it is worse than the average FE solution. Considering sensitivity with respect to input parameters, TA performs considerably better for larger tie lengths (see Tables C.2 and C.4 in Appendix C).

Another interesting result is the performance of the GA with equal weight on welfare and fairness. Tables C.1 - C.4 show that with this objective function, the fairness of the solutions can be substantially increased while resulting only in a small decrease in welfare performance. This points out one of the main advantages of using heuristics to solve two-sided matching problems: the ability to optimize several metrics simultaneously.

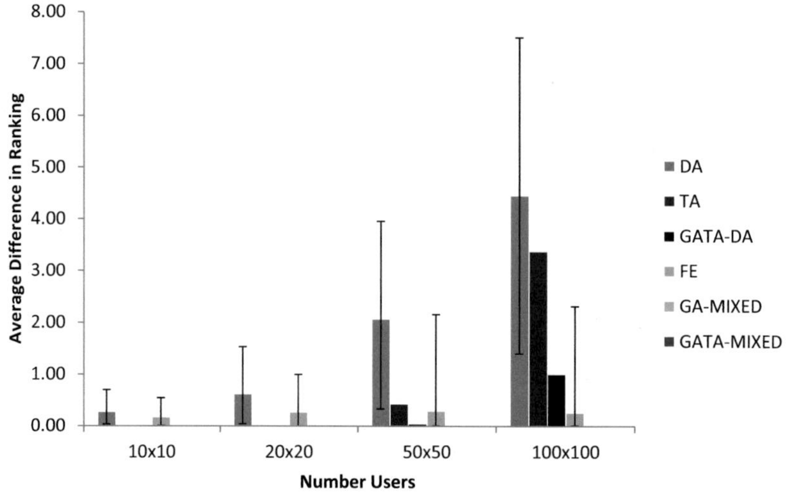

Figure 5.4.: Comparison of Fairness Performance for Complete and Correlated Preferences

Effect of Preference Correlation The results for correlated preferences are similar. Figure 5.4 shows that GA and GATA with fairness optimization and penalty for unstable pairs is able to yield almost perfectly fair solutions for the studied scenarios. The performance of GA and GATA with mixed initial solutions are significantly better with respect to fairness, as a Wilcoxon signed-rank test at the level $p = 0.01$ reveals. Furthermore, the TA performs slightly better for correlated preferences, and is able to provide comparably good results for problem sizes up to 50x50 users.

5.4.4. Incomplete Preferences With Indifferences

In the most general case, preference profiles can be both incomplete and contain indifferences, in which case the common goal of matching algorithms is to find a stable solution of maximum size. As shown in Table 5.1, there are several approximation algorithms and heuristics specifically developed for this case. The focus of this section is to study how GA, TA, and GATA heuristics perform against these specialized algorithms in different scenarios. For statistical evaluation, Wilcoxon signed-rank tests are used for the same reasons as in the previous section.

Comparing Solution Quality

To compare the overall efficiency of the algorithms, this section studies the ability of the mechanisms to compute a stable allocation of maximum size. The following figures represent the average values based on the 12*100 independent repetitions for each scenario, a more detailed analysis of the effects of preference structures on the results is presented subsequently. Similar to the previous section, for GATA the suffix $'' - MIXED''$ indicates that initial solutions are based on DA solutions plus an additional solution from applying Király, McDermid, and GSModified, respectively.[20] If no suffix is provided, GA and GATA are initialized only with DA solutions. Considering the optimization function, GA, TA, and GATA use a weighted function that emphasizes the number of matched pairs as main goal, and also tries to optimize welfare as secondary goal. More specifically, the goal is to minimize an objective function of the form $(Max\,(n_X, n_Y))^2 * (Min\,(n_X, n_Y) - NumPairs) + Welfare$. This ensures that the number of matched pairs is the dominant objective, yet still allows for the simultaneous optimization of welfare. For the evaluation and comparison with the approximation algorithm, such an optimization function represents a pessimistic comparison as the welfare scores tend to increase with a larger number of matched pairs, indicating that welfare and matched pairs are conflicting optimization goals.

Performance in this case can be measured in two ways. On one hand, the percentage of matched users can be considered as a proxy for algorithm performance. Depending on the preferences, however, it cannot be guaranteed that there is a stable solution where all users are matched. This suggests measuring the performance relative to the optimal solution as an indicator how close the algorithms are to the optimal outcome.

[20] As seen in Section 5.4.2, the runtime for the approximation algorithms is comparably short, hence using them in addition to the DA to get initial solutions does not increase the relative runtime of GA or GATA.

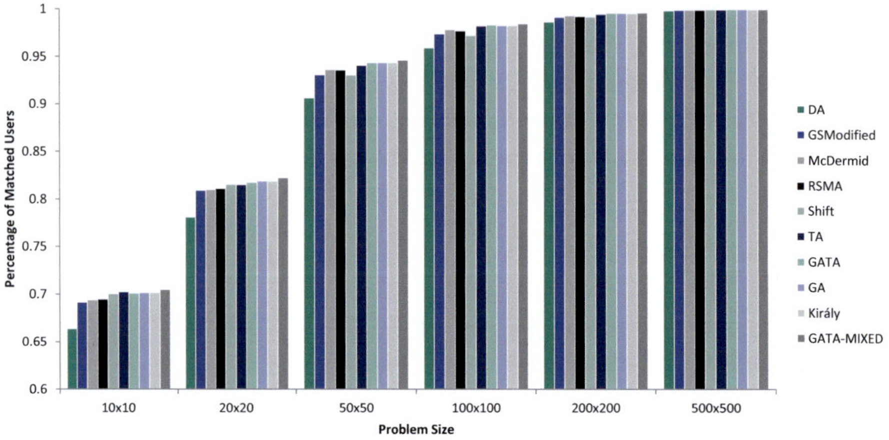

Figure 5.5.: Algorithm Performance in Number of Matched Pairs, Uncorrelated Preferences

Figure 5.5 displays the results for the first performance measure, the percentage of matched users. Averaged over the different parameter values for tie length and length of preference lists, the results show that with an increasing number of users, the percentage of matched users in the solutions increases as well. Especially for large problem sizes, the majority of users are matched (the next section shows that this seems to depend on the lengths of the preference lists). There are apparently considerable differences in the performance of the algorithms. DA performs worst, which is not surprising as it was not specifically developed for this scenario. Applying the RSMA improvement cycle on the DA solution is able to significantly increase the number of matched pairs. Considering the approximation algorithms described in Section 5.3.2, the Király algorithm performs best, while GSModified, McDermid and Shift are slightly worse. Considering the Shift algorithm, the extended results in Table C.5 in Appendix C show that it yields its best performance in case the maximum length of ties is 2, which is the core scenario for which it was developed. However, the Király algorithm usually provides better solutions, and for larger tie lengths the performance of Shift decreases considerably.

Both the GA and TA perform very well, being slightly outperformed only by Király. This indicates that in contrast to the previous scenario with complete preferences, TA is a useful heuristic in SMTI scenarios. Additionally, the results for GATA and GATA-MIXED show that instantiating the GATA with solutions from approximation algorithms can significantly increase the solution quality of GATA. In particular, GATA-MIXED on average outperforms even the best approximation algorithm, Király, in the considered scenarios. The statistical analysis with a Wilcoxon signed-rank test reveals that there is no significant difference between GA, GATA and Király, and that GA, GATA and Király are better than TA, Shift, McDermid, GSModified as well as RSMA ($p < 0.001$). Furthermore, GATA-MIXED yields better solutions than GA, GATA, and Király ($p < 0.001$).

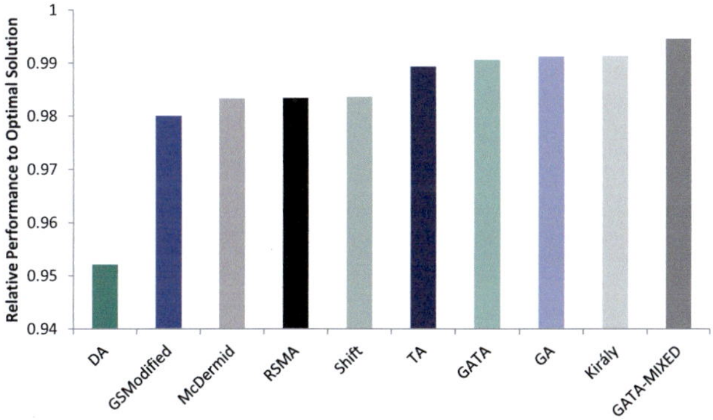

Figure 5.6.: Algorithm Performance Relative to Optimum, Uncorrelated Preferences, 10x10 to 100x100 users

Next, Figure 5.6 shows the relative performance of the considered algorithms with respect to the optimum solution calculated with the Integer Program formulation as shown in Section 5.3.1. Due to runtime and memory considerations, only the problem sizes with 10 to 100 users on each side are considered here. The graph shows that for all considered scenarios the algorithms are within 95% of the optimum solution, i.e., are able to find relatively large matches which are close to the optimal solution.

Table 5.5.: Algorithm Performance Relative to Optimal Solution, Incomplete Preferences, 10-100 Users per Side

Statistic	DA	GS-Mod.	Mc-Der.	RSMA	Shift	TA	GATA	GA	Király	GATA-MIXED
Mean	0.952	0.980	0.983	0.983	0.984	0.989	0.991	0.991	0.991	0.995
Median	0.965	1.000	1.000	1.000	1.000	1.000	1.000	1.000	1.000	1.000
S.D.	0.051	0.032	0.030	0.031	0.029	0.023	0.022	0.020	0.019	0.014
Min	0.500	0.778	0.667	0.667	0.750	0.750	0.667	0.750	0.857	0.857
Max	1.000	1.000	1.000	1.000	1.000	1.000	1.000	1.000	1.000	1.000
Opt. calc. (%)	0.228	0.619	0.660	0.669	0.684	0.731	0.763	0.759	0.754	0.813

Table 5.5 presents several statistics for the relative performance of the algorithms compared to the optimal solution. Interestingly, the heuristics not only perform well on average, they also calculate the optimal solution in more cases than the approximation algorithms. Furthermore, the standard deviation is lower as well. As approximation algorithms provide a guaranteed quality bound, i.e., worst case performance, Table 5.5 shows that the worst-case performance is best for Király and GATA-MIXED.[21]

Overall, similar to the previous findings about the percentage of matched users, the consideration of average and worst-case performance relative to the optimal solution shows that GATA-MIXED not only yields the best solutions, but also the solutions with the best worst-case performance. This is particularly interesting as it indicates that for the considered scenarios, the practical quality bounds of GA, GATA, and especially GATA-MIXED are comparable (or even better) to the quality bounds of the approximation algorithms. However, as heuristics are not able to provide definite quality bounds, there might be scenarios where the worst-case performance is lower than that of the approximation algorithms. Nevertheless, the performance of the studied heuristics is more than promising.

Table 5.6.: Algorithm Performance for Welfare and Fairness Relative to GATA-MIXED, Incomplete Preferences. Percentages indicate to what degree the GATA-MIXED solution improves upon the respective algorithm.

Size	DA	RSMA	GS-Mod.	Mc-Der.	Shift	Király	TA	GA	GATA
	Welfare Score Increase relative to GATA-MIXED								
10x10	10.2%	5.4%	5.7%	6.3%	1.1%	3.9%	0.0%	0.9%	0.4%
20x20	13.9%	13.6%	11.3%	14.5%	2.5%	7.1%	0.5%	1.1%	0.8%
50x50	13.7%	31.1%	14.9%	26.6%	3.4%	8.7%	4.9%	1.1%	0.8%
100x100	12.2%	52.1%	16.7%	38.5%	3.0%	8.7%	7.6%	1.0%	0.9%
200x200	13.4%	79.9%	20.0%	50.0%	12.5%	11.6%	11.8%	1.0%	1.1%
500x500	18.5%	125.2%	26.2%	60.9%	18.5%	18.3%	17.9%	1.2%	1.3%
	Fairness Score Increase relative to GATA-MIXED								
10x10	2.3%	4.7%	3.1%	5.1%	0.4%	2.5%	-0.2%	0.3%	0.1%
20x20	3.8%	21.4%	9.3%	19.8%	0.2%	4.7%	-0.7%	0.0%	0.0%
50x50	14.1%	89.5%	30.3%	68.8%	2.1%	14.8%	7.3%	0.7%	0.8%
100x100	35.5%	196.9%	63.6%	145.2%	4.7%	36.3%	30.5%	0.7%	1.8%
200x200	72.9%	338.0%	108.3%	224.7%	70.6%	72.4%	69.9%	4.5%	5.1%
500x500	75.5%	378.2%	102.6%	203.4%	75.9%	76.6%	73.3%	4.9%	5.0%

[21] The worst-case performance of 0.66 for McDermid is exactly the guaranteed 3/2 approximation factor of the considered approximation algorithm.

Besides the superior performance in the number of matched pairs, it is also interesting to consider the performance of the algorithms with respect to welfare and fairness characteristics, even though the approximation algorithms are not specifically developed for this combination of metrics. Table 5.6 presents the average welfare and fairness performance relative to GATA-MIXED. For example, a value of 50% indicates that the welfare score of an algorithm was 50% higher (i.e., worse) than the welfare of the GATA-MIXED solution. The results show that not only does GATA-MIXED yield better solutions with respect to the number of matched pairs, the solution quality with respect to welfare and fairness is considerably better than the approximation algorithms.[22] The relative improvements in welfare and fairness are particularly high for larger problem instances, which indicates that the respective solution quality can be considerably increased by the use of the proposed heuristics. For example, compared to the best approximation algorithm Király, welfare improvements of up to 18% and fairness improvements of up to 76% can be achieved, which means that users are on average matched to higher ranked partners, and that the solution treats both sides more equally. Table 5.6 also shows that RSMA, which focuses on finding improvements for users of one market side, yields comparably unfair solutions, and potential fairness and welfare improvements by using the heuristics can be substantial. These results show that the heuristics not only provide good solutions for the standard combinations of goals, but also for multiple objectives such as finding a maximum size stable match with good welfare or fairness properties. This can be especially important in social settings where such welfare and fairness aspects are of importance, making the proposed heuristics particularly beneficial in these settings.

Effect of Preference Structures and User Distributions

To study the sensitivity of the results on different design parameters, this section looks at the algorithm performance in case of different tie lengths, different preference lengths, and correlation in preferences.

Influence of Tie Lengths For the different maximum lengths of ties, Figure 5.7 shows that, as before, GA and TA perform quite well. In most cases their perfor-

[22] Interestingly, TA seems to find slightly better solutions for small problem instances. The relative improvement, however, is small, and taking into account the solution quality for larger problem instances, GATA-MIXED provides the overall best solution quality.

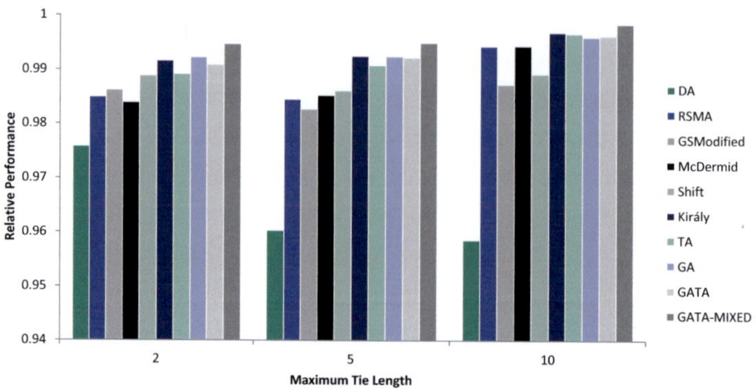

Figure 5.7.: Performance of Matching Algorithms, Random Preferences

mance is better than the approximation algorithms, and only Király yields better solutions. GATA-MIXED yields consistently the best performance in the considered scenarios. Overall, the relative performance differences become smaller with increasing tie lengths. These observations are confirmed by a statistical analysis applying Wilcoxon signed-rank tests. For small maximum tie lengths, $\psi = 2$ and $\psi = 5$, GA and Király are significantly better than TA, and GATA-MIXED is significantly better than GA and Király ($p < 0.001$). For $\psi = 10$, the performance of the algorithms is more similar overall. TA is in fact slightly better than GA ($p = 0.001$) and yields similar solutions than Király (no statistically significant difference), and GATA-MIXED is still better than Király at the level $p = 0.001$.

Influence of Preference Lengths Figure 5.8 shows the results for different average preference lengths, both for the percentage of matched users and relative to the optimal solution. For larger values of l, more users will be deleted from each others' preference profiles, thereby shortening the profiles and increasing the probability that some users might be unmatched in a solution. This is especially reflected in Figure 5.8a, which shows that the percentage of matched users considerably decreases if users have short preference lists. Per definition of parameter l, the preference length is measured proportionally to the number of users, which means that for larger problem sizes, the absolute preference lengths increase for the same l. This might explain the findings shown earlier in Figure 5.5, which showed that with increasing user size the percentage of matched users increases.

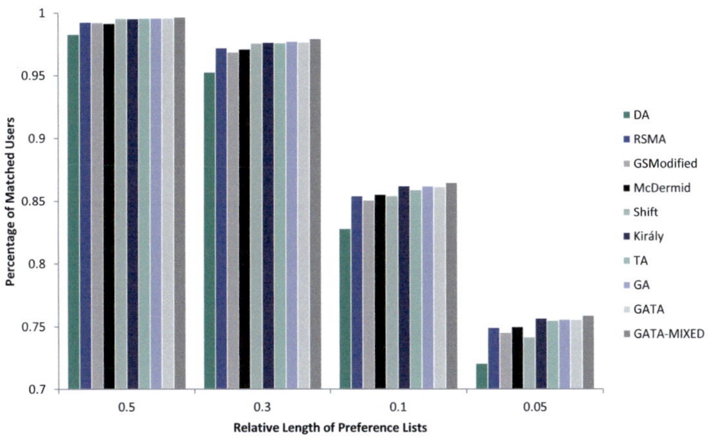

(a) Percentage Matched Users

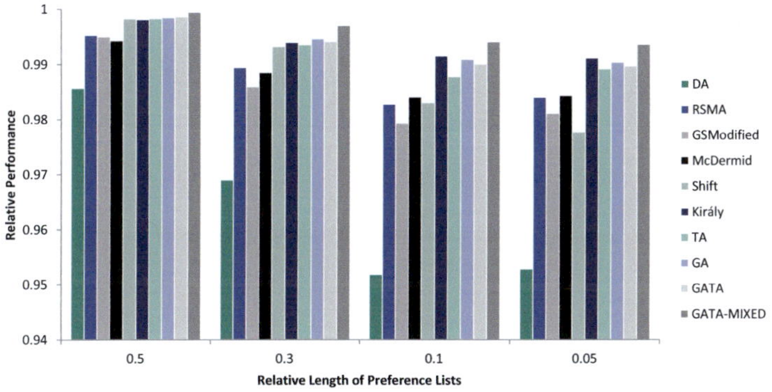

(b) Performance Relative to Optimum

Figure 5.8.: Comparison of Algorithms for Different Preference Lengths

In more detail, Table C.5 in Appendix C shows that the absolute number of matched pairs decreases with decreasing l, which was expected. Additionally, Figure 5.8b shows that with increasing l the relative performance of the algorithms, compared to the optimal solution decreases (slightly). Considering the relative performance of the algorithms, Figure 5.8 shows that Király is the best approximation algorithm. GA, TA, and GATA yield solutions similar to Király, yet often better than other approximation algorithms. As before, GATA-MIXED outperforms all other algorithms. This increase in solution quality is statistically significant for smaller values of l (at the level $p = 0.01$ for $l = 0.1$ and $l = 0.05$), yet relatively small. Especially for larger values of l, i.e., longer preference lists, it seems to be easier to find large stable matches which makes the differences between algorithms marginal. However, when users provide the preference ranks of other users manually in larger Social Clouds, smaller values for l are realistic as users might have time and cognitive limitations in providing the preference ranks.

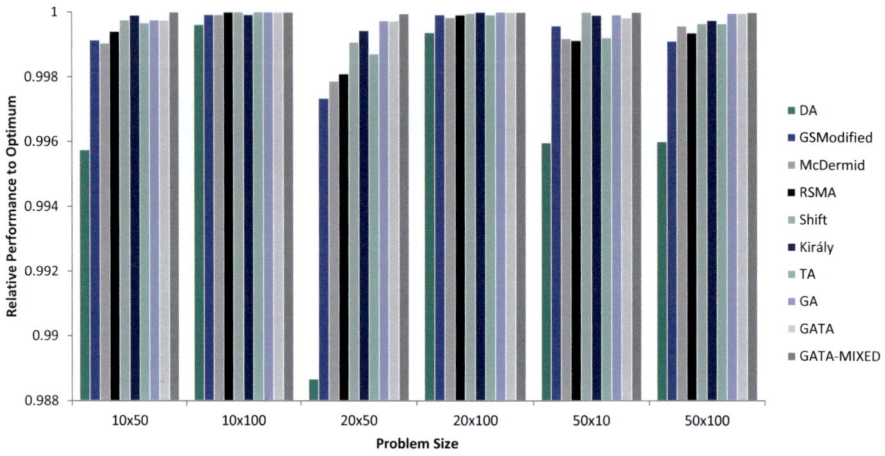

Figure 5.9.: Algorithm Performance, Asymmetric Problem Instances

Scenarios with Asymmetric Numbers of Users Figure 5.9 shows the performance of the algorithms relative to the optimal solution for problems where the numbers of requesting and providing users are unequal. The overall efficiency of the considered algorithms is better than in the case of symmetric problem instances. Furthermore, the higher the difference in size, the closer the relative performance of the algorithms. This can be expected, as the maximum number of agents matched is bounded by the number of users of the smaller side, and the probability to match all such users increases if (relatively) more users of the second side are present in the market. As a result, all algorithms calculate an optimal solution in 99% of the cases. Figure 5.9 also shows that, while the performance increase is comparably small, the performance of the GA, GATA, and GATA-MIXED heuristics is slightly better than the approximation algorithms, which confirms the previous findings. In particular, GATA-MIXED is able to find an optimum in all the studied problem instances.

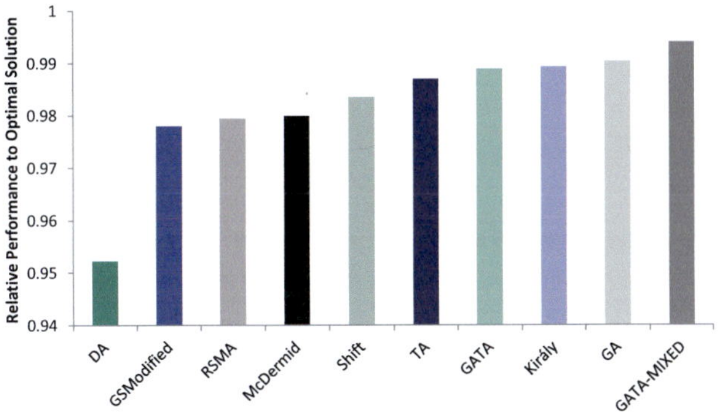

Figure 5.10.: Algorithm Performance, Correlated Preferences

Table 5.7.: Algorithm Performance Relative to Optimal Solution, Incomplete Correlated Preferences

Statistic	DA	GS-Mod.	Mc-Der.	RSMA	Shift	TA	GATA	GA	Király	GATA-MIXED
Mean	0.952	0.978	0.980	0.979	0.983	0.987	0.989	0.990	0.989	0.994
Median	0.962	1.000	1.000	1.000	1.000	1.000	1.000	1.000	1.000	1.000
S.D.	0.048	0.033	0.033	0.035	0.028	0.024	0.023	0.020	0.022	0.014
Min	0.500	0.750	0.667	0.500	0.750	0.818	0.818	0.857	0.800	0.857
Max	1.000	1.000	1.000	1.000	1.000	1.000	1.000	1.000	1.000	1.000
Opt. calc. (%)	0.205	0.588	0.618	0.618	0.683	0.690	0.730	0.745	0.721	0.799

Correlated Preferences For correlated preferences, Figure 5.10 shows the relative performance ranking of the algorithms over all combinations of problem size, lengths of preference lists, and maximum lengths of ties. Similar to the scenario with uncorrelated preferences, the heuristics perform exceptionally well. As before, GATA-MIXED yields on average the best solutions of the considered algorithms. Table 5.7 also shows that it has a low variance in solution quality, and that its worst case solution quality is better than Király and the other approximation algorithms. Whereas the general worst-case performance seems to be similar to the case of uncorrelated preferences, the number of times where the algorithms are able to find an optimal solution is lower. Compared to the findings in Table 5.5, the percentage of scenarios where an optimal solution was found decreases from up to 86% to 80% in the best case.

5.5. Summary

This chapter introduced the concept of preference-based resource matching and several algorithms that are used to calculate allocations with certain desired properties. Section 5.1 provided the necessary notation and fundamental theorems, and classified the matching problems according to preference structures and optimization metrics. Section 5.2 continued with an overview of related work, and Section 5.3 described the algorithms considered to calculate a solution for the matching problem. Section 5.4 evaluated the performance of the proposed heuristics and existing algorithms for various preference structures.

As the complexity to calculate such solutions is, for general preference types, NP-hard, either approximation algorithms or heuristics are needed as calculating the optimal solution might be infeasible. Heuristics provide the flexibility to consider various combinations of objective functions. To determine their performance relative to existing algorithms, Section 5.4 compared and evaluated the performance of the considered algorithms for several scenarios in order to address research question 2.1. For the scenario of complete preferences with indifferences, the evaluation showed that depending on the initial solutions, a genetic algorithm (potentially combined with a Threshold Accepting algorithm) improves upon the initial solutions, and on average yields similar or better solutions than existing algorithms. In case of incomplete preferences, the heuristics (especially GATA with mixed initial solutions) are able to yield better solutions on average than even the best approximation algorithms concerning the number of matched users, and this average improvement is also statistically significant. Furthermore, the solutions found by the heuristics outperform the solutions of approximation algorithms with respect to additional criteria such as welfare or fairness to a substantial degree. This is a particularly important result as platforms with social contexts, such as Social Clouds, might value welfare and fairness aspects in addition to the standard set of optimization goals for which approximation algorithms exist (stability and number of matched pairs). Users of a Social Cloud benefit from the application of the proposed heuristics as they are, on average, matched to a higher ranked partner, and the solution is fairer to both requesting and providing users.

Overall, this section showed that heuristic algorithms provide a useful, flexible and powerful tool to compute solutions for preference-based matching with a short runtime. Potentially, the solution quality of the heuristics can be even further improved by applying subsequent optimization steps such as RSMA (requester-optimal-stable-matching). Initial results indicate that this can be the case for some repetitions and scenarios. A conclusive study of the combination of the heuristics with existing algorithms (such as improvement cycles), thus, is an interesting area of further research. Another interesting aspect is the computational optimization of the algorithms. Especially GAs are considered suitable for parallelization, which might decrease their runtime and make them even more useful.

In the context of preference-based resource exchange in social contexts, the results are especially promising. The actual structure of user preferences can be diverse and likely includes incompleteness and indifferences, especially when users have larger social networks and cannot provide a definite rank for each single user (or do not want to share with certain users). For example, in the Social Cloud prototype (Section 2.1.4), the preference interface allows for the specification of "blocked" users with whom sharing is not wanted, and providing the same rank for several users indicates indifference. The absence of an explicitly provided rank can either be interpreted as being indifferent or also not wanting to be matched to these users. The latter decision will most likely affect the allocation, as not considering many users in the preference ranks leads to short preference lists. The heuristics are, however, well suited to handle such situations, and provide solutions that are on average closer to the optimal solution than the considered approximation algorithms (see Section 5.4.4).

Having identified that heuristics provide similar or superior performance to existing algorithms and are adaptable to various different scenarios, the next chapter considers two case studies on preference-based matching. The first case study considers the effects of strategic preference manipulation for the different algorithms, both from a system and a user perspective. Especially for participating users, this can be interesting as it possibly provides strategic guidelines of how to act in such a resource allocation market. The second case study considers the case of dynamic allocation of resources. In such a scenario, resource supply and demand is not matched in distinct, batch-like allocations, but continuously over time. As a frequent recalculation of the allocation, or migration of allocated resources might not be possible, the case study considers heuristics to cope with such dynamic supply and demand.

Chapter 6.

Incentive Compatibility and Dynamic Allocation

"It is difficult to advise participants in markets that use stable matching mechanisms when to behave straightforwardly (i.e. in a way that reveals their true preferences) and when there might be opportunities to behave strategically, and if so, how."

(Roth and Rothblum, 1999)

THE solution quality of two-sided matching problems, which was the focus of the last chapter, is an important consideration in preference-based resource allocation. Yet, there are other aspects that might be of interest when a two-sided matching approach is applied in practice. This chapter looks at two of these aspects, namely the manipulation of preferences and the dynamic allocation of resources.

The first aspect considered in this chapter is *preference manipulation*. The matching mechanisms studied in the last chapter all require the preference profiles of the participating users as input for their calculations, and the solution of the respective mechanisms depends on the profiles submitted by the users. An important observation in this case is that, in general, the submitted preference profiles might not be the true preference profiles of the users. Under the assumption that users want to be matched with a partner as highly ranked as possible, rational users might have an incentive to manipulate the submitted preference profiles in order to increase their chance of being matched with a higher-ranked partner.

This is the focus of Section 6.1, which considers the existence and the effects of preference manipulations for the mechanisms introduced in the previous chapter.

In particular, two aspects are considered: 1) the degree to which users can benefit (or be worse off) by manipulating their preferences; and 2) the effect of preference manipulation on the solution quality of different matching mechanisms.

As the calculation of a solution depends on the submitted preference profiles of all participating users, preference manipulation does not only affect the manipulating users, but other users as well. Furthermore, the matches calculated by the algorithms might be stable for the submitted preference profiles, but not for the true profiles of the users. The introduction of instability, considering the true profiles of the manipulating users, is therefore also considered as potential manipulation effect.

Besides studying the effects of preference manipulation on the market, for individual participants it might be interesting to know under which circumstances preference manipulation is useful, and what manipulation strategies are most promising. Due to the complexity of the matching problem and the multitude of potential manipulation types, straightforward strategy recommendations for participants in different markets do not exist, and existing results are limited to special circumstances (Roth and Rothblum, 1999). Another interesting issue is how robust the different mechanisms are against strategic manipulation. These two aspects are the focus of Section 6.1.3.

In the second part of this chapter, Section 6.2 considers the application of two-sided matching mechanisms in dynamic scenarios, using the prototype of a Social Compute Cloud (see Section 2.1.4). Matching mechanisms are usually applied in static settings, where users submit their preference profiles once or only at certain time intervals, and the mechanism calculates a solution for the given submitted profiles. In (social) resource exchange settings such as a Social Cloud, the allocation can be more dynamic in the sense that users might enter or leave the market in between the time intervals. This creates new, unallocated supply and/or demand (either by arriving users, or by freeing allocated resource offers/requests), which is denoted as *intermediate supply* and/or *demand* for the rest of this chapter. In such a case, the question arises how such intermediate supply and demand can be handled.

For technical and computational reasons, it might not be feasible to recompute the entire allocation every time a user enters or drops out. For example, users in existing matched pairs might have agreed that the allocation is valid for a certain time, and a reallocation might break up such a match. Hence, the second part of this chapter looks at the effects of dynamic supply and demand in preference-based resource allocation. In particular, Section 6.2 considers potential algorithms to match supply and demand, and investigates the effects of different algorithms for dynamic allocation on the market.

The chapter is structured as follows. Section 6.1 introduces the concept of preference manipulation and studies its effects on allocations in preference-based resource matching. Section 6.2 discusses and evaluates different algorithms to match intermediary supply and demand. Section 6.3 summarizes the findings and gives an outlook on potential next steps.

6.1. Strategic Manipulation in Resource Allocation

In centralized resource allocation mechanisms, the allocation is determined based on the information submitted by the participants. In general, this submitted information does not need to be truthful, i.e., it might not reflect the true valuation or preference of a participant. Depending on the mechanism, a participant might benefit from sending untruthful information, which in turn could lead to an allocation that does not reflect the true preferences in the market. Untruthful information about preferences can have serious implications in the real world, for example schools ranked low in the school choice problem have been closed due to the ranking (see Abdulkadiroğlu et al. (2009)). Such behavior can also lead to the emergence of blocking pairs with respect to the true preferences, i.e., if an allocation is calculated based on submitted preferences it does not necessarily have the same properties, such as stability, as under the true preferences. This section considers this issue in the context of preference based two-sided matching. Specifically, after introducing the necessary concepts and theoretical results, it studies the potential gains and losses of manipulating users, and compares the robustness of the considered matching mechanism against such strategic manipulation.

6.1.1. Theoretical Results and Manipulation Strategies

In the economic field of mechanism design, impossibility theorems provide guidance about which combinations of market goals can be achieved (see e.g. Parkes (2001) for an overview), and **incentive compatibility** is one of the most frequently considered properties of a mechanism. Participants have private information about their true preferences, and reveal parts of this information through interaction with the mechanism (e.g., through bids or submission of preference rankings). However, depending on the market mechanism it might not be best for them to reveal their true private information. The aspect of incentive compatibility in this case is defined as follows:

Definition 8 (**Incentive Compatibility in Two-Sided Matching**). *A two-sided matching mechanism is incentive compatible if submitting the true preference profile is the best strategy in equilibrium. If this applies for dominant strategies, then the mechanism is said to be strategy-proof.*

Note that incentive compatibility in general is defined for any equilibrium concept, such as Nash, Bayes, or dominant strategy equilibrium. In the context of two-sided matching, previous work has focused on dominant strategies, in which case strategy-proof would be the correct term. Adopting the standard of previous literature in this field, unless otherwise stated incentive compatibility will refer to dominant strategies in the subsequent considerations.

From the viewpoint of a market designer, achieving incentive compatibility (ideally in dominant strategies) is important for several reasons. On one hand, participants do not have to calculate complex strategies of how to act on a market, as it is in their best interest to act based on their true preferences. On the other hand, it guarantees that the solution quality calculated with submitted preferences is reflecting the true quality, e.g., stable solutions might not necessarily be stable if the private preferences differ from the submitted ones.

In the case of two-sided matching where participants have private information about their true preferences, incentive compatibility studies whether it is best for participants to reveal these true preferences while acting on the market or not. The fundamental result considering incentive compatibility in two-sided matching was developed by Roth (1982) and summarized in Roth and Sotomayor (1992):

Theorem 4 (**Roth, 1982**). *No stable matching mechanism exists for which stating the true preferences is a dominant strategy for every agent.*

This result has serious implications on the design of a two-sided matching mechanism. As stability is commonly (and empirically) considered the most important property of a two-sided matching mechanism (see e.g. Roth (2008)), incentive compatibility needs to be sacrificed if stability is to be guaranteed. Furthermore, Alcalde and Barberà (1994) show that strategy proofness is also incompatible with individual rationality and Pareto efficiency. Considering the DA, Roth and Sotomayor (1992) also show that the DA is strategy-proof for the proposing side, yet not the accepting side.

Although this seems to be a rather negative result, the implications of the impossibility of incentive compatibility for all participants are less clear. As Roth and Rothblum (1999) noted: "However the existing theoretical results do not generally allow us to address the considerable demand for practical advice about how to participate in such markets, once they are established. It is difficult to advise participants in markets that use stable matching mechanisms when to behave straightforwardly (i.e. in a way that reveals their true preferences) and when there might be opportunities to behave strategically, and if so, how. This also suggests that there are some gaps in our understanding of why stable matching mechanisms work so well in practice" (Roth and Rothblum, 1999, p.21). For example, as one of the few results in the literature, Roth and Rothblum (1999) find that only a small number of participants have incentives to reveal altered preference rankings. Additionally, Pini et al. (2011a) show that there can be non-strategy-proof matching mechanisms which are NP-hard to manipulate, i.e., finding a successful manipulation strategy can be a hard problem.

Related Work

Due to its practical relevance, e.g. in school choice and college-admission markets, preference manipulation has been subject of many studies. Most of these focus on preference manipulation either in the classic DA, or in the adapted mechanism for many-to-one matchings.

Considering its strategic properties, the DA is strategy-proof for the proposing side, yet not strategy proof for the accepting side (Roth and Sotomayor, 1992, p. 90). Moreover, not putting its most preferred alternative first is a dominated strategy for the users of the accepting side (Roth and Sotomayor, 1992, p. 105). Abdulkadiroğlu et al. (2009) show that (again in the case of strict preferences) for any tie breaking rule, there is no mechanism that is strategy-proof and dominates the DA. Ashlagi and Klijn (2012) consider manipulation in the DA and show that all weakly beneficial group manipulation strategies of accepting users are beneficial for all other accepting users and harmful for all proposing users. Furthermore, this is true if users from the accepting side apply a truncation of preferences. Studying the prevalence of manipulation in experimental settings, Echenique et al. (2009) show that truncation of preferences for the accepting side in a DA is applied only rarely.

In many-to-one settings, several studies looked at the effects of manipulation in the respective markets. Under certain conditions, the percentage of users that can successfully manipulate their preferences in a student-optimal stable matching converges to zero for large markets (Kojima and Pathak, 2009; Lee, 2011). Abdulkadiroğlu et al. (2009) discuss the effect of strategy-proofness on efficiency (measured in average rankings) in the school-choice problem using date from New York and Boston school districts. Furthermore, Kesten (2012) studies manipulation strategies in the school choice problems. In particular, he considers the option for schools to manipulate their submitted capacity (i.e., offering less capacity than available), and the possibility to pre-arrange matches in which case the involved student does not participate in the actual matching procedure. Whereas some of the studied mechanisms are immune to capacity manipulation, Kesten shows that all studied mechanisms are not immune to pre-arranged matches.

Fixed Strategies

In order to study the implications of a non-achievable incentive compatibility for different matching algorithms, the manipulation strategies need to be defined. Based on literature in this field, several strategy types are considered for the subsequent evaluation.

Re-ordering Matching algorithms cannot guarantee that each participant is matched to its most preferred alternative. Hence, one potential reasoning for this strategy is that if participants are not likely to be matched with their most preferred alternative, putting more preferred alternatives (in their true preferences) in lower ranks might result in a better match for them. For example, if a participant is on average matched to its third choice, putting their true first choice at rank 3 might yield a better result for them. However, as the matching depends on the preferences of the other participants, it is not straightforward to see whether such a strategy might be useful. Furthermore, for strict and complete preferences Roth and Sotomayor (1992) show that not putting the most preferred alternative first is a dominated strategy for the DA. The re-ordering or shuffle strategy applies this reasoning to create a new preference ranking: Given the degree of manipulation k, the strategy randomly shuffles the first k ranks. This strategy can be either applied alone or in combination with the truncation strategy.

Truncation Including lower ranked alternatives in one's preference ranking might increase the chance of being matched to them, as it increases the potential number of partners one can be matched with. By stating these lower ranked alternatives as unmatchable, a participant could end up being matched to a more preferred alternative, thus increasing its benefit. However, stating otherwise acceptable alternatives as unmatchable also increases the chance of the participant being unmatched in the final allocation, in case other participants have a higher ranking in the rankings of the remaining alternatives. This consideration describes the *truncation* strategy defined by Roth and Rothblum (1999). Given the true preference ranking of length n of user i, a truncation is defined as the preference ranking that contains the first k users, $k < n$, in the same order as the true preferences. Roth and Rothblum (1999) showed that truncation strategies dominate non-truncation strategies under certain assumptions for the preference rankings, making them an interesting candidate for the following evaluation.

Truncation strategies involve an inherent trade-off. Truncating to a high degree aims to avoid being matched to less preferred alternatives, yet simultaneously increases the probability of remaining unmatched. Roth and Rothblum (1999) showed that for a given preference set, the number of participants benefiting from truncation is small, yet its behavior under other algorithms or indifferences in preference rankings remain to be explored. Using analytical models, Ehlers (2008) extends the analysis of Roth and Rothblum (1999) for priority-based and linear programming mechanisms, and shows that under certain assumptions (symmetric information) the same result about truncation preferences holds.

Manipulation Learning

The previous two strategies are examples of fixed strategies. The downside of evaluating such strategies is that to be able to evaluate their performance, they would have to be compared to the theoretically best strategy with the highest gains for the manipulating users. Finding such an optimal strategy is a combinatorial problem, especially for preferences with indifferences or incompleteness. For example, for a preference list of length n, there are $n!$ different re-ordered lists. Hence, a proxy is needed as benchmark. One potential proxy is the use of learning algorithms which allow the manipulating participants to (try to) learn good strategies. With such an approach, manipulating participants are more flexible and not restricted to the provided or pre-specified strategies. It is also a more realistic representation of participants trying to actively game the matching mechanism by learning and adapting their strategies. Two learning algorithms are used in the following evaluation.

Evolutionary-based Learning The first is an evolutionary learning algorithm based on a genetic algorithm. As mentioned earlier, it has been previously shown that GA's work well in large search spaces, and the number of potential strategies for preference manipulation indeed is considerable. Furthermore, a similar learning algorithm has been successfully applied for other economic decision scenarios, see e.g. Haas et al. (2013). As a GA, the learning algorithm is initialized with a starting population of randomly created strategies, with an equal mix of truncation and re-ordering strategies. Each strategy is represented by the adjusted preference ranking. It uses standard mutation and crossover operators to evolve the initial population and selects the best performing strategy after the last evolution cycle. For crossover, a cycle-crossover operator is used to create new strategies. The mutation operator randomly applies either re-ordering or truncation, or adds users to the preference ranking (reverse truncation). The latter option is included in the mutation operator to allow users to potentially retract from too severe truncation.

Probe and Adjust The second learning algorithm is a simple learning algorithm similar to reinforcement learning, Probe and Adjust (PA). This type of algorithm has been previously used in several studies, for example learning in an oligopoly game (Kimbrough and Murphy, 2009) or learning in strategic contexts (Haas et al., 2013). It is an example of an adaptive local search learning algorithm. Starting from a given solution, the algorithm explores the neighborhood of the solution by slightly adjusting the current solution. After several rounds of exploration, during which the fitness of the new potential solutions are probed, the PA selects the best performing solution in the neighborhood (potentially the current solution) as the new solution. This is repeated for a certain number of adjustment rounds, after which the currently best solution is returned. Applied to learning manipulation strategies, PA starts with a neighborhood of randomly created truncated and re-ordered strategies, and selects the best performing one. Then, for each of the subsequent rounds, the neighborhood of the currently best strategy is created by truncating, re-ordering, or adding user rankings to the current preferences. The pseudocode of this learning algorithm is described in Algorithm 6 in Appendix D.

6.1.2. Effects of Preference Manipulation on Matching Outcome

Preference manipulation can have several effects on the outcome of preference-based matching:

- Potential gains and losses of manipulating users
- Effects on non-manipulating users
- Different solution quality under submitted and true preferences

Whereas the effects on the users, whether manipulating or not, are intuitive, the third point is very interesting as well. If manipulating users do not submit their true preferences, the resulting solution of the matching might, for example, not be stable under the true preferences. These effects are studied in the following evaluation.

Simulation Specifics
For the simulation-based evaluation, different scenarios are studied. For a given problem size, the main parameters that are varied are the percentage of manipulating users, and the type or degree of manipulation. For example, for a problem size of 20 users per side, the number of manipulating users is varied from 1 to 20. The evaluation only considers manipulation on one side, and manipulation from both requesting and providing users is not considered. The rationale behind this is that for the standard DA, manipulation is only (potentially) beneficial for one side, and

in order to be able to compare the results between algorithms, only one-sided manipulation is considered here. The manipulation type can be either a fixed strategy (in this section: truncation) or a strategy determined through a learning process. For truncation strategies, the degree of manipulation defines how much the preferences are truncated. For example, in a 20x20 scenario with initially complete preferences, truncation of degree 0.5 means that the truncated preferences have length 10. Similar to the simulations in the previous chapter, 100 independent repetitions are made for each scenario to ensure a certain robustness of the findings.

For the GA-learning parameters, the same parametrization as in the previous chapter is chosen. The population size is 50, the mutation rate 0.2, and the crossover probability 0.6. In total, the learning was evolved for 20 rounds[1], and in every round each solution of the population was evaluated twice to get an estimate of its fitness. For PA-learning, two settings are studied to examine the effect of the available learning time on the outcome. In the first setting, each potential solution in the neighborhood is evaluated twice, and 20 rounds of adjustments are simulated. In the second setting, the solutions are evaluated four times, and 50 adjustment rounds are studied.

The following results involve complete preferences with indifferences (maximum group size of 2) for non-manipulating users. Obviously, in case of truncation strategies the problem transforms into a setting with incomplete preferences (with the manipulating users submitting incomplete preference lists). Complete preferences were chosen because users can only remain unmatched if other users manipulate, which makes the comparison with the baseline case easier where all users are matched. In addition, small indifference groups potentially improve the benefits from manipulation, as it is easier to switch between the indifference groups. Hence, this represents an optimistic setting in which benefits from manipulation can potentially be higher. Starting with incomplete preferences is, of course, also possible in general.

Manipulation Effects with Truncation Strategies Figure 6.1 shows the average gain or loss of manipulating and non-manipulating users (measured in absolute rank differences) for two different problem sizes if they apply truncation strategies

[1]The number of learning rounds is, for a GA, rather small. However, up to 1000 different manipulation strategies are considered in this setting, and the GA seem to converge to a certain manipulation strategy after this number of rounds.

and the solution is calculated with GATA. Green colors indicate an average gain, and yellow and red colors an average loss. Figure 6.1a shows that depending on the number of manipulating users and the degree of truncation there are scenarios where applying these strategies are, on average, beneficial for manipulating users. However, the figure also shows two aspects to applying truncation strategies: on one hand, the average gain is quite low, which makes the average benefit of manipulation doubtful. On the other hand, especially when the profiles are truncated to a high degree, the expected outcome from truncation is an actual loss (measured in the absolute difference of preference ranks) compared to submitting the true preferences. This is not surprising, as higher truncation leads to an increased likelihood of being unmatched in the solution.

Similar results can be seen in Figure 6.1b, which considers the same setting for a 50x50 scenario. Interestingly, in this case truncating the preferences only to a small degree is less beneficial than in the 20x20 case. As the absolute gain or loss is small, however, this should not be overemphasized. The benefit of truncation for a medium range of truncation seems to be consistent over the two studied problem sizes.

Considering the effects on non-manipulating users, Figure 6.2 shows that in most cases, manipulation of other users has detrimental effects on users that submit their preferences truthfully. Especially when a large number of users are manipulating, the chances for them to remain unmatched increases, which also increases the chance of a non-manipulating user to be unmatched. There are some cases in which manipulation leads to an average gain, but the very small absolute amount indicates that these gains occur as other solutions are calculated, which potentially result in a better welfare for all users. This can happen as GATA is a heuristic and potentially leads to different solutions once it is recalculated.

Additionally, the average gain in ranking for manipulating users has been compared for several matching algorithms. Tables 6.1 and 6.2 show the results for different degrees of truncation and number of manipulating users, respectively. Over all scenarios, i.e., all combinations of number of manipulating users and degree of manipulation, the absolute gains are smallest for GATA. This result is also statistically significant using Wilcoxon signed-rank test at the level $p = 0.001$ for the non-normally distributed data. Detailed results for the interplay of truncation degree and number of manipulating users can be found in Tables D.1 and D.2 in Appendix D.

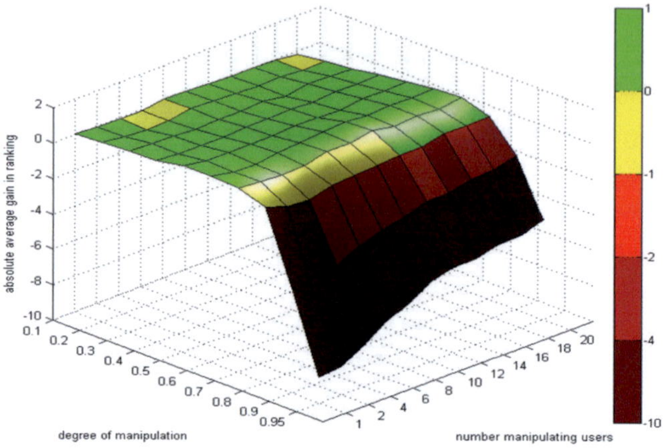

(a) 20x20 scenario

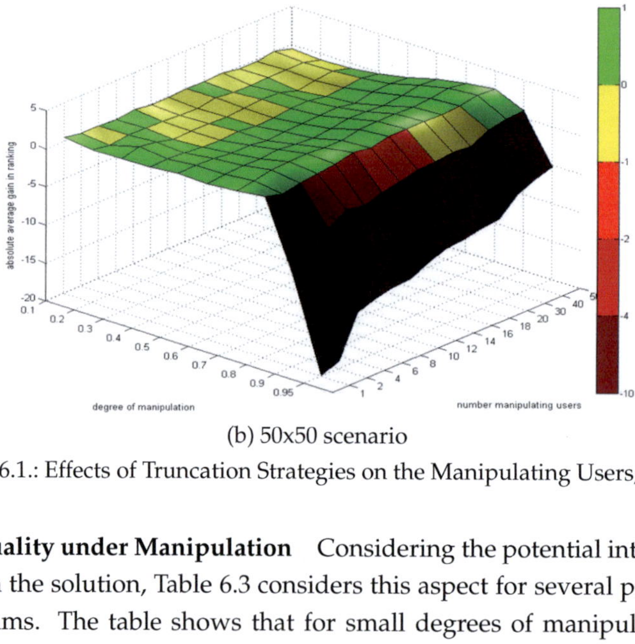

(b) 50x50 scenario

Figure 6.1.: Effects of Truncation Strategies on the Manipulating Users, GATA

Solution Quality under Manipulation Considering the potential introduction of instability in the solution, Table 6.3 considers this aspect for several problem sizes and algorithms. The table shows that for small degrees of manipulation, i.e., if manipulating users only truncate the last users in their preference ranking, the resulting solution is still stable. However, as the degree of truncation increases, the number of blocking pairs that are introduced when the true preferences are considered increases considerably. This effect can be observed over all matching algorithms, which indicates that it is an inherent property of user manipulation.

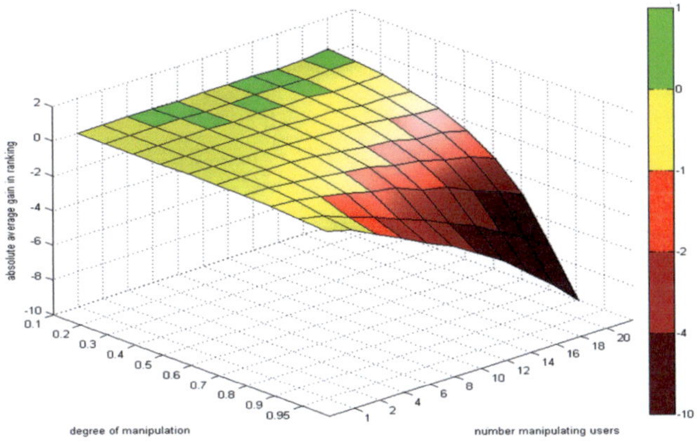

(a) 20x20 scenario

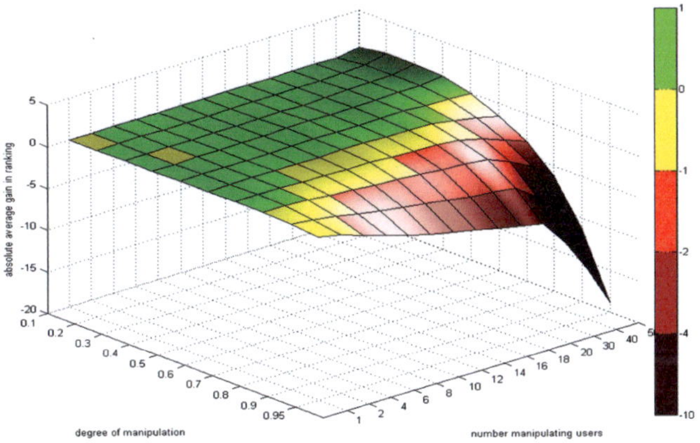

(b) 50x50 scenario

Figure 6.2.: Effects of Truncation Strategies on the Nonmanipulating Users, GATA

This result is interesting for practical reasons. Firstly, while the matching algorithms still calculate solutions which are stable under the submitted preferences, they are potentially unstable under the true preferences if some users manipulate. Hence, there might be opportunities for users to act on these unstable pairs, which would break up the matching solution. Secondly, as Knuth (1997) discusses, even a small number of unstable pairs can have substantial consequences on the market, and allocations that contain blocking pairs can lead to a failure of the entire market. For example, it can lead to behavior where users prearrange matches before the actual allocation takes place (see Sönmez (1999); Kagel and Roth (2000)).

An interesting extension of this observation is to examine which users are involved in these unstable pairs. Theoretically, if unmatched users realize that they can find

Table 6.1.: Absolute Preference Gain for Truncation Strategies for Different Truncation Degrees, 20x20 Users

Truncation Degree	DA	RSMA	Király	Shift	GATA
0.95	-5.12	-3.89	-4.49	-4.91	-6.13
0.9	-1.79	-0.58	-0.94	-1.40	-2.70
0.8	0.98	2.10	1.58	1.22	-0.06
0.7	1.84	2.84	2.18	1.76	0.56
0.6	1.87	2.77	2.11	1.63	0.57
0.5	1.74	2.50	1.85	1.42	0.44
0.4	1.39	2.01	1.44	1.10	0.26
0.3	1.10	1.66	1.10	0.81	0.14
0.2	0.72	1.12	0.73	0.55	0.03
0.1	0.30	0.53	0.30	0.21	0.00

Table 6.2.: Absolute Preference Gain for Truncation Strategies for Different Numbers of Manipulating Users, 20x20 Users

Truncation Degree	DA	RSMA	Király	Shift	GATA
1	-1.04	.18	-.61	-.23	-1.06
2	-0.53	.08	-.15	-.36	-1.26
4	-0.23	.40	.01	-.12	-1.11
6	-0.03	.87	.32	-.07	-0.91
8	0.21	1.05	.54	.07	-0.70
10	0.67	1.34	.81	.33	-0.57
12	0.78	1.50	.98	.42	-0.44
14	0.67	1.54	.96	.50	-0.53
16	0.85	1.68	1.13	.60	-0.35
18	0.86	1.67	1.19	.72	-0.38
20	1.11	1.85	1.29	.78	-0.28

other users which would prefer to be matched with them, there could be an iterative process of users breaking up and forming new pairs. It is unclear, however, if such an iterative process would lead to a stable match or not. Hence, it is hard to predict what actual effects such unstable pairs which were introduced by manipulated preferences have on the market (Knuth, 1997).

6.1.3. Robustness of Matching Algorithms against Manipulation

Simulation Specifics

As before, the effects of manipulation are studied with varying parameters for the number of manipulating users, and the type of manipulation. In this section, the two different learning procedures (GA-Learning and Probe-and-Adjust-Learning)

Table 6.3.: Effects of Manipulation on Stability, Measured in Number of Blocking Pairs

Problem Size	Degree Truncation	DA	RSMA	Király	Shift	GATA
20x20	0.95	45.65	44.92	43.60	42.90	43.28
	0.9	23.14	22.31	19.98	19.74	20.52
	0.8	8.23	7.58	6.61	5.95	6.48
	0.7	2.88	2.65	2.23	1.74	2.11
	0.6	1.29	1.10	0.86	0.67	0.79
	0.5	0.53	0.46	0.37	0.23	0.28
	0.4	0.26	0.23	0.20	0.10	0.14
	0.3	0.08	0.07	0.05	0.04	0.04
	0.2	0.03	0.02	0.02	0.00	0.01
	0.1	0.01	0.01	0.00	0.00	0.00
50x50	0.95	104.50	102.35	93.19	93.29	93.75
	0.9	30.65	29.37	25.96	23.94	24.71
	0.8	7.19	6.70	5.71	3.79	4.13
	0.7	2.10	1.86	1.46	0.71	0.86
	0.6	0.61	0.48	0.42	0.09	0.14
	0.5	0.13	0.05	0.05	0.02	0.01
	0.4	0.05	0.01	0.00	0.00	0.00
	0.3	0.01	0.00	0.00	0.00	0.00
	0.2	0.00	0.00	0.00	0.00	0.00
	0.1	0.00	0.00	0.00	0.00	0.00

are used. For complexity reasons, only one or two manipulating users are considered. As before, for each scenario 100 independent repetitions are made to study the robustness of the results. In addition to the previously considered algorithms, GATA-MIXED (GATA with starting solutions from DA and approximation algorithms, see Section 5.4.4) is included in the following evaluation to study the dependency of the results on the GATA starting solutions.

Effectiveness of Manipulation

Previous results for DA suggest that the number of users who can actually benefit from manipulation is small. Hence, this aspect is considered first. Table 6.4 shows for a given market setting, how many times manipulating users can actually benefit from manipulation. The table can be separated into three scenarios. The first scenario studies truncation strategies for different problem sizes and algorithms. The second and third scenarios are a small number of manipulating users applying GA- or PA-Learning, respectively.

The table shows that, averaged over the independent repetitions the probability of successful manipulation, i.e. an actual gain in welfare for the manipulating users, varies with the manipulation strategy. For both GA- and PA-learning, the actual

Table 6.4.: Manipulation Effectiveness

Scenario	Man. Users	Strategy	DA	RSMA	Király	Shift	GATA	GATA-MIXED
Probability of Successful Manipulation								
20x20	1	GA	0.540	0.540	0.560	0.440	0.436	.570
	2	GA	0.560	0.578	0.584	0.460	0.448	.485
	1	PA	0.540	0.620	0.550	0.480	0.401	.480
	2	PA	0.555	0.610	0.605	0.470	0.448	.555
	1-20	Truncation	0.269	0.334	0.287	0.257	0.176	0.271
	1	Truncation	0.120	0.205	0.143	0.159	0.117	0.127
	2	Truncation	0.182	0.235	0.205	0.191	0.114	0.184
50x50	1-50	Truncation	0.335	0.387	0.342	0.314	0.210	0.337
	1	Truncation	0.142	0.194	0.146	0.149	0.130	0.146
	2	Truncation	0.172	0.216	0.185	0.175	0.138	0.164
Average Gain in Case of Successful Manipulation								
20x20	1	GA	5.23	6.22	5.28	5.84	2.82	5.07
	2	GA	3.94	4.51	3.92	3.61	2.12	3.49
	1	PA	4.62	6.08	5.09	4.56	2.75	5.04
	2	PA	3.09	4.17	3.68	3.10	1.71	2.94
	1-20	Truncation	3.01	3.56	3.10	2.80	1.99	3.08
	1	Truncation	6.80	8.23	6.91	7.82	5.73	7.73
	2	Truncation	4.86	4.66	5.02	4.26	3.21	4.68
50x50	1-50	Truncation	6.92	7.84	6.93	5.78	3.82	6.71
	1	Truncation	17.74	18.72	16.89	14.07	8.74	16.86
	2	Truncation	12.07	12.05	12.32	9.82	6.76	9.77

manipulation is successful in 40%-62% of the cases, depending on the applied matching algorithm. For truncation strategies, the success probabilities are considerably smaller (between 11% and 39%). In other words, this means that even for users with the ability to learn and adjust their manipulation strategy, the chances of actually benefiting from such manipulation are comparably small. Interestingly, the success probability is smallest for GATA. A potential explanation for this result is that GATA can find multiple solutions of the same or similar quality and randomly selects one of them. This additional random element could make it harder for users to learn a successful manipulation strategy.

Another related question is the degree to which they can improve their position in the cases where manipulation is indeed successful. The second part of Table 6.4 provides the results for the given scenarios. Interestingly, the potential improvements in case of truncation strategies are higher than for the learning strategies.

A likely explanation for this behavior is that, in the truncation cases, users might gain considerably if they submit a highly truncated preference list. However, as the table only shows actual improvements, not average gains, such heavily truncated strategies might also lead to being unmatched in other cases (thus potentially leading to lower average gains). In contrast, when users have to learn a manipulation strategy, they might not learn these extreme truncation strategies as they potentially involve a higher risk of being unmatched.

Considering the influence of the the small size of indifference groups that are used in this scenario, it can be expected that the previous results are optimistic in the sense that larger indifference groups could make it less likely to benefit from manipulation (as the chances for being matched within the same indifference groups are higher). In total, it can be seen that users can gain several preference ranks if their manipulation is successful, yet the probability of a successful manipulation is comparably small. This indicates that even if there are cases in which (as predicted by theory) manipulation is possible, the likelihood and incentives of users to actually manipulate are rather small. In particular, they might not outweigh the risk of being worse off from manipulation.

Robustness Against Learning

Figure 6.3 shows the effects when the manipulating users apply a GA-Learning algorithm to learn successful manipulation strategies. There are several interesting facts than can be observed. First, the actual number of benefiting users, as shown in Figure 6.3b, is roughly similar for the studied allocation mechanisms, yet both GATA and Shift seem to have a lower probability of successful manipulation. Averaged per user, the likelihood that a manipulating user is actually benefiting is between 44-58%. Second, Figure 6.3a reveals considerable differences in the profitability of manipulation. Manipulation is less beneficial if GATA is used as an allocation mechanism, compared to the other algorithms (statistically significant at the level $p = 0.001$, using Wilcoxon signed-rank tests and accounting for multiple comparisons). One potential explanation is that due to the high number of random elements, thus unpredictability, of the GATA mechanisms, it is harder to achieve substantial gains for manipulating users in these settings. Interestingly, GATA-MIXED performs similarly to the other algorithms and is more beneficial for manipulating users. A potential explanation for this finding is that the solutions found by GATA-MIXED are structurally similar to the solutions of the approximation algorithms such as Király, whereas the GATA solutions are less similar.[2]

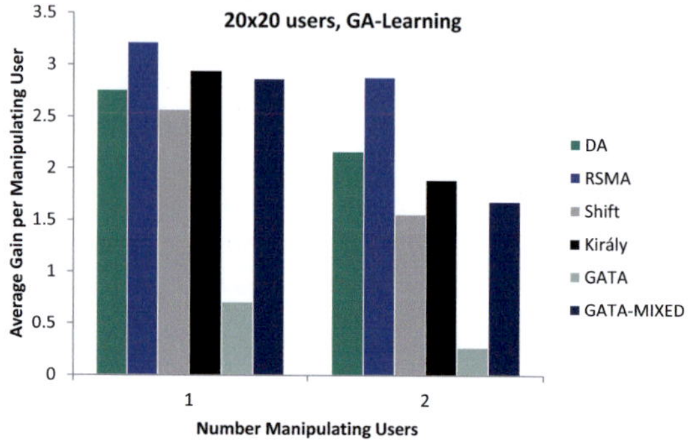

(a) Gain in Ranking, GA-Learning

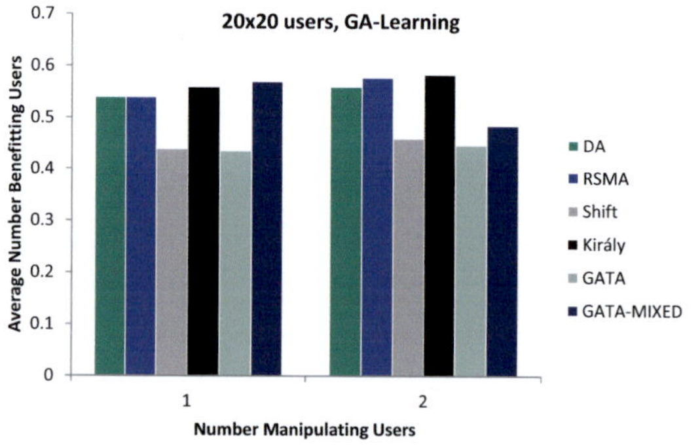

(b) Number of Benefiting Users, GA-Learning

Figure 6.3.: Average Gain and Number Benefiting Users for GA-Learning, 20x20 users

In particular, manipulation gains are lower for GATA than for Király, which indicates that the former is more robust against manipulation as the potential gains are lower. This affects the corresponding trade-off between potential gain and potential loss that a manipulating user faces, making it less appealing to try preference manipulation.

[2]In other words, the final GATA-MIXED solutions can be similar to the solutions found by the approximation algorithms as they are, on average, better than DA solutions for scenarios with incomplete preferences, thus being more likely to be propagated through the evolution rounds of GATA. As the standard GATA uses only DA starting solutions, the variety of different propagated solutions might be higher, thus decreasing predictability and the probability of successful manipulation.

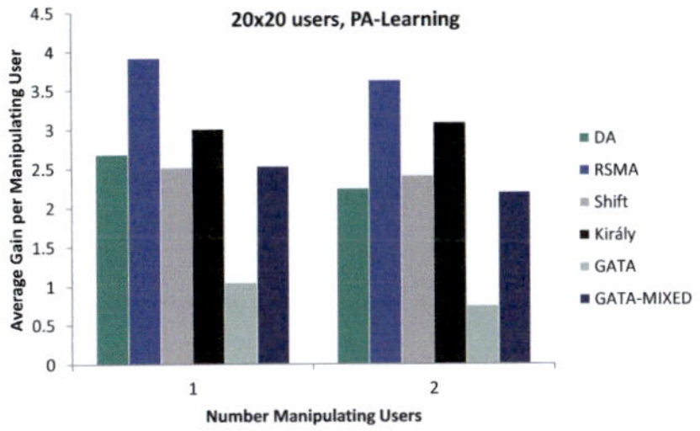

(a) Gain in Ranking, PA-Learning, 20 Adjustment Rounds

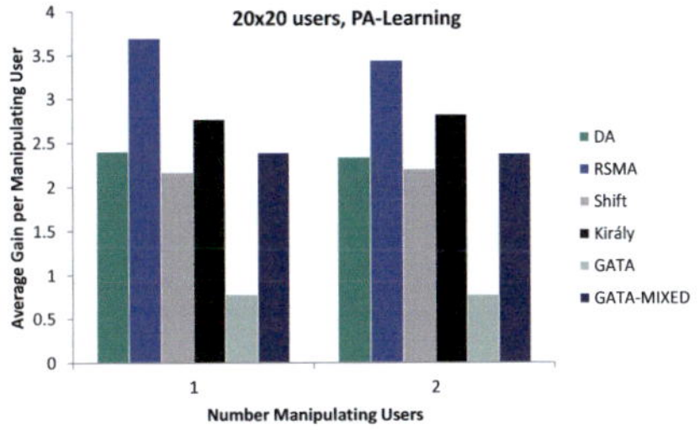

(b) Gain in Ranking, PA-Learning, 50 Adjustment Rounds

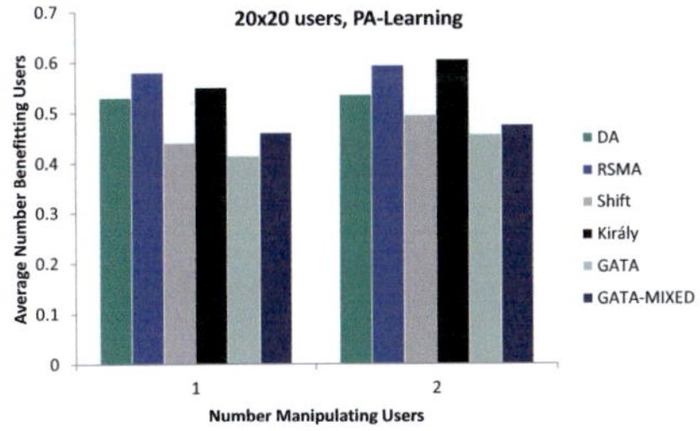

(c) Number of Benefiting Users, PA-Learning, 20 Adjustment Rounds

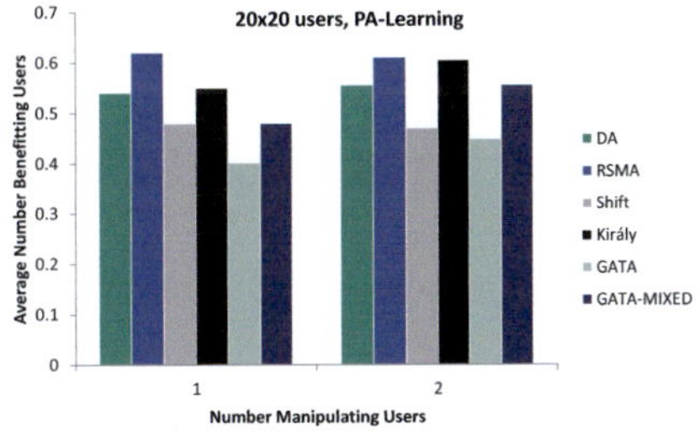

(d) Number of Benefiting Users, PA-Learning, 50 Adjustment Rounds

Figure 6.4.: Average Gain and Number Benefiting Users for PA-Learning, 20x20 users

To compare the robustness of the previous findings, another learning procedure, Probe and Adjust, is used as well. Figure 6.4 shows the results of this scenario. Compared to the GA-learning case, PA-learning yields similar results. The number of adjustment rounds does not have a significant impact on the number of benefiting users. Figures 6.4a and 6.4b show that the average gain from manipulation is very similar. Furthermore, the results show that the average gain from manipulation is smallest for GATA. In fact, the average gain in the GATA case is statistically significantly smaller than the gains for Király and the other algorithms (Wilcoxon signed-rank test, $p = 0.001$). GATA-MIXED performs similarly to the other algorithms and worse than GATA, which again indicates that the solutions found by GATA-MIXED seem to be more similar to the other approximation algorithms rather than GATA. The findings are particularly interesting as Király performed best among the approximation algorithms, and GATA-MIXED yielded the best overall results (see Section 5.4.4). The findings indicate that there is no difference in the strategic properties of Király and GATA-MIXED, yet GATA is more robust against manipulation (lower gains for manipulating users). This implies an interesting trade-off between algorithm performance and strategic considerations.

6.1.4. Discussion

This section considered the effects of preference manipulation for the algorithms presented in Chapter 5. There are several interesting insights that can be derived from the results.

First, the results in Section 6.1.2 indicate that manipulation through preference truncation can be beneficial for users, yet the average gains of successful manipulation are rather small (see Table 6.1). In many cases, manipulation has negative effects on non-manipulating users. Furthermore, instability can be introduced through manipulation, indicated by the number of blocking pairs in Table 6.3. Due to the unpredictable consequences of these blocking pairs, this can be a potentially serious challenge for the applicability and sustainability of the allocation mechanism in a Social Cloud.

Second, the evaluation in Section 6.1.3 shows that the number of cases in which manipulation actually is successful is rather small (in most cases between 11 and 62%), and that learning-based algorithms are more successful than pure truncation strategies. This indicates that, while manipulation is possible in such markets, finding a successful manipulation strategy is a non-trivial problem. Comparing different learning algorithms, for the studied scenarios the average gain from manipulation is smaller for GATA than for the other algorithms, in particular the best performing approximation algorithm (Király). This means that users can gain less from manipulating, thereby potentially lowering their incentive to pursue such manipulation. Considering the combined results with respect to performance (see Section 5.4.4) and strategic properties, GATA provides similar performance as the best performing approximation algorithm, and simultaneously is more robust against manipulation. If performance aspects are of higher importance, GATA-MIXED can be used as it yields a superior solution quality while retaining similar strategic properties as, e.g., Király.

6.2. Dynamic Resource Allocation in a Social Compute Cloud

Commonly, preference-based resource allocation mechanisms assume that all participating users in a market submit their preference profiles to the mechanism, and a solution is calculated through a specific algorithm in a batch-like procedure. This only applies if the allocation happens once, or at certain time intervals in which all users are free and can be re-matched. Realistic scenarios, however, might be more dynamic. For example, during two time intervals where the matching is calculated, some users might enter or leave the market, thereby creating intermediate supply and demand. Another example is if certain matched users agree to be matched longer than a time period, in which case they might not be available in the next matching calculation (i.e., they form an "unbreakable" pair).

In such scenarios, the question is how such intermediate demand is handled. For the purpose of this case study, *intermediate supply or demand* is defined as newly arriving or freed resource offers or requests that occur when either new users arrive or existing matched users leave, thereby creating additional resource offers or requests in the system. As mentioned before, breaking current pairs and re-matching all users on the market might not be feasible for technical (e.g., if a calculation on a machine cannot be interrupted) or complexity reasons (i.e., recalculating the optimal allocation takes too long). The option to not consider intermediate demand leads to a potentially considerable amount of idle resources, depending on the length of the time intervals. On the other hand, matching only the available intermediate supply and demand might lead to the creation of blocking pairs, especially with respect to the currently matched pairs.

This dynamic allocation of resources in a two-sided matching setting is the focus of this section, which is an extended version of (Caton et al., 2014). Building on the description of the Social Compute Cloud prototype presented in Chapter 2.1.4, this case study uses the prototype for the dynamic allocation scenario. The additional heuristics that are used to match intermediate supply and demand are described in Section 6.2.1. Section 6.2.2 evaluates these mechanisms that can be used to capture intermediate supply and demand. A discussion of the findings in Section 6.2.3 concludes this case study.

6.2.1. Approaches to Capture Intermediate Supply and Demand

The matching algorithms discussed in related literature are usually assumed to be batch jobs. In this case, allocations are computed after certain time intervals. For example, economic studies of allocation mechanisms in Cloud Computing often assume that allocations are computed hourly, often referring to Amazon EC2 where users buy resources based on hourly usage. In the case of a Social Compute Cloud, one can say that the allocation is calculated every x hours, where x is the predetermined lease period of a compute vessel.

While this type of allocation computation yields good results for the supply and demand given at the time of the computation, it is unclear what happens in the case of new or changing supply and demand. For example, users can offer/request new resources or retract offers/requests in between two calculation intervals. It is clear that if allocations are only (re)computed at predetermined time intervals, resources will be idle and requests will be left (or become) unsatisfied. Existing preference-based matching literature does not consider such settings. Therefore the following solutions for dynamic supply and demand are proposed.

Disregard The "worst" solution would be to **disregard** any new incoming supply or demand until the next time the allocation is computed. In this case, new supply/demand would be idle until the next batch allocation, even if there were corresponding demand/supply.

Optimal The "optimal" solution would be the **immediate rematching** of the entire supply and demand. In this case, no (new) supply would be idle if an allocation was available, and the resulting allocation would always be stable (given the right algorithms are used). However, this places additional requirements on the system. Firstly, computing resources (e.g. VM's) would have to be migratable at any given point in time, and, secondly, the runtime of the allocation mechanism has to be short. For the implementation of the Social Compute Cloud prototype, this is currently unachievable, as the underlying framework does not yet support migration. Hence, this approach should be considered the best benchmark from a system perspective, i.e. with respect to performance criteria such as stability, welfare, and fairness.

Random Given the intermediate offers and requests at a given time, **random allocation** randomly matches offers and requests with the constraint that the matched users have to be mutually acceptable. As only one constraint is used in the calculation, this algorithm has a fast runtime, yet cannot guarantee specific properties of the resulting match (such as stability).

Greedy In **greedy allocation**, an incoming or freed provider or requester is matched, if applicable, to a currently unmatched, acceptable requester or provider of the highest possible rank. It is greedy in the sense that it tries to find the best intermediate match for the incoming or freed user. Similar as the random allocation, properties such as stability cannot be guaranteed.

As the Random and Greedy heuristics are applied each time a new offer or request arrives, or a matched user leaves, they particularly have to have a fast runtime in order to cope with potentially frequent changes in the system. Note that both Random and Greedy are likely to yield unstable solutions, i.e., the consumer-provider pairs in the market at the end of the lease period would not be the pairs that a stable allocation algorithm would yield. However, if it is assumed that matched pairs cannot be migrated in between two batch allocations, this does not, per se, affect the practical stability in between batch computations.

A final approach is to check if there is a match that would yield a stable solution, yet does not require other users to be reallocated. It can be argued that this approach would be subsumed by the above approaches, as the probability of achieving a stable solution is low, and in the absence of a stable match, another approach would be applied.

6.2.2. Evaluating the Effects of Dynamic Allocation

To study the applicability of the previously mentioned approaches to match intermediate supply and demand in a Social Cloud, the following evaluation shows the effects of the approaches on standard preference-based matching solution characteristics: the number of matched pairs, stability, welfare, and fairness.

Simulation Specifics

For the evaluation, a Social Cloud with 200 users (100 on each side) with incomplete preferences and indifferences is simulated (with an average preference list length of 50). To model dynamic supply and demand, real user resource availability distributions derived from donations and resource availability in SETI@home (Javadi et al., 2009, 2011) are used in the evaluation. The data from SETI@home represents statistical clusters of users, that can be used in the simulator to define both when a resource will become available and for how long, as well as when users will request resources.

Considerations for Stochastic Participation

To study stochastic supply and demand, the four approaches mentioned above are simulated to study how they support the system with new supply/demand in between two batch-allocation computations. Intuitively, immediate rematching should yield the best solutions, whereas leaving resources idle should be worst. Random and greedy should be somewhere in between.

In the simulation, each user is drawn an (un)availability distribution from the SETI@home distribution, which determines when and how long they will be (un)available. Only available users are taken into account for resource matching. At time points 155, 265 and 410, the batch allocation algorithm is run for the current supply/demand.

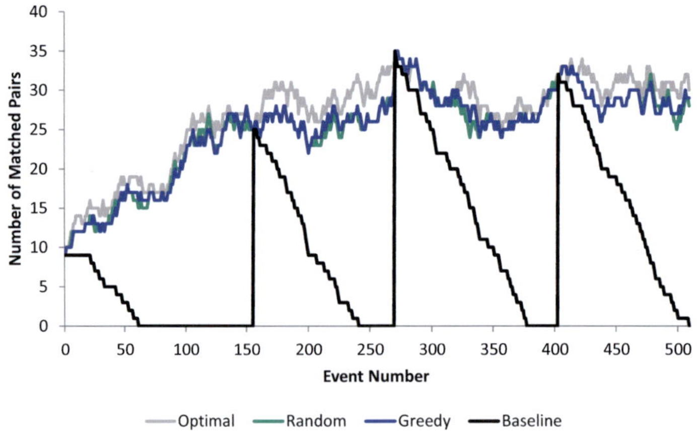

Figure 6.5.: Number of Matched Pairs for Intermediate Supply and Demand

Figure 6.5 shows that the number of matched users fluctuates over time, and users arrive and leave from the allocation depending on their (un)availability pattern. It can be seen that, most of the time, the "optimal" matching yields the highest number of matched pairs, and both random and greedy yield fewer matched pairs. This can be explained by the lack of choice that incoming users have: in random and greedy, only the currently unmatched users are suitable for matching, whereas the "optimal" rematching can consider all available users at that time. Figure 6.5 also shows the baseline scenario in which allocation only happens at pre-determined time intervals. In this case, new requests and offers are only considered at predetermined time intervals, and if matched users become unavailable, the corresponding request/offer is freed without being automatically reallocated. Hence, the baseline scenario depicts the worst case, quasi-static scenario where intermediate demand is not considered. It can be easily seen in Figure 6.5 that not considering intermediate supply/demand can lead to a significant amount of unused, unallocated resources.

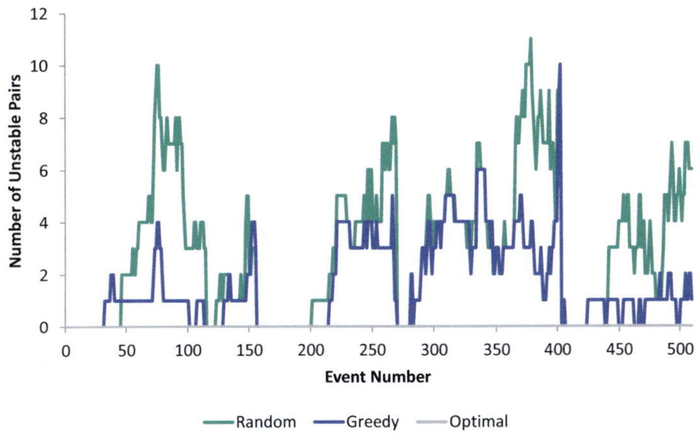

Figure 6.6.: Instability Effects for Intermediate Supply and Demand

Figures 6.6, 6.7a, and 6.7b show the results for stability, welfare, and fairness respectively. These figures show that the immediate rematching performs well with respect to welfare (allocating users close to their highest preference) and fairness (balancing the two market sides), and always yields stable outcomes. Furthermore, the greedy strategy often provides better welfare than the random strategy (Figure 6.6), and is computationally as efficient. Whereas the runtime for GATA per allocation is around 10 seconds, both random and greedy run almost instantly, i.e., take milliseconds to compute. Similar results are obtained for the number of unstable pairs, which are most often lower for the greedy strategy. Figure 6.7b shows that both greedy and random strategy are more beneficial for consumers, indicated by the lower scores, especially compared to the optimal matching. This finding,

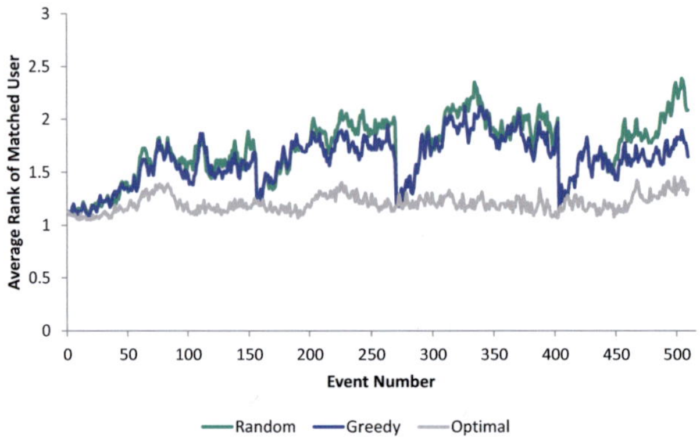

(a) Welfare: Average Rank of Matched Users

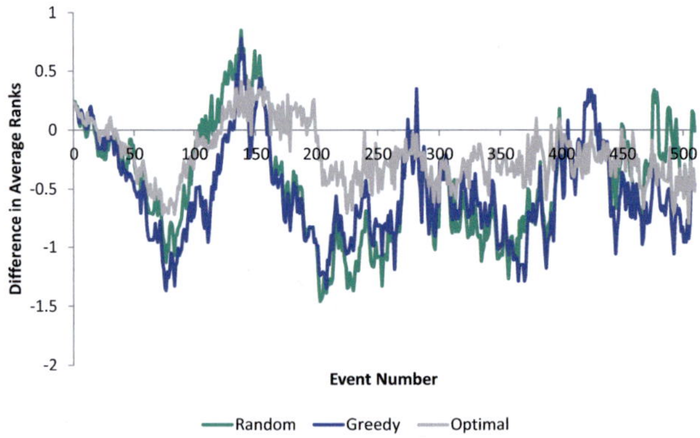

(b) Fairness: Welfare Distribution. Negative scores represent solutions more beneficial to consumers.

Figure 6.7.: Comparison of Matching Heuristics for Intermediate Supply and Demand

along with the fact that greedy can sometimes yield worse results for welfare as well, is not surprising as it primarily aims to give new, incoming users their highest priority, without considering the preferences of other users.

Overall, the results suggest that approaches for the intermediate rematching of supply/demand are necessary, and that on average the greedy heuristic performs well with respect to welfare, despite one side being favored in the matching. This is especially interesting if immediate rematching is not technically feasible.

6.2.3. Discussion

Section 6.2.2 shows convincing evidence that dynamic supply and demand between batch allocation times, caused by leaving and arriving users, has to be considered. While these results show that the solution quality tends to be very good and even close to optimal it is clear that continuously running the algorithms might not be feasible due to their computational overhead. Hence, fast heuristics are needed that are able to deal with changing supply and demand, although these heuristics usually lack the solution quality of the other algorithms. For small problem sizes, it might still be feasible to run algorithms such as the GATA in a continuous setting.

One potential strategy to improve both allocation quality and runtime would be to compute an initial solution with a fast algorithm, e.g. DA, and then leverage users' provided computational power to improve solution quality. This would give users an incentive to provide resources for a co-operative infrastructure (Haas et al., 2013).

Another issue with the matching algorithms considered here is that they currently support only one-to-one matchings, i.e., they do not yet support multi-unit allocations. In some settings, users might contribute or request multiple units of resources (e.g., several VMs to run a compute-intensive job). This is particularly interesting if intermediate demand can be captured by (potentially already matched) users with remaining capacity. This extension is an area of future work.

6.3. Summary

Besides the pure performance characteristics of the algorithms, there are several other interesting aspects that can be studied in the context of preference-based resource allocation mechanisms. This chapter presented two case studies, each of which investigating and highlighting such an aspect. Section 6.1 presented the first case study which considers the manipulation of preferences and the effects on the allocation and the users. After introducing existing results and commonly studied manipulation strategies, the evaluation shows that users might benefit from manipulation, but the probability of successful manipulation is rather small. In addition, both manipulating and non-manipulating users face the risk of being worse off from manipulation. This highlights the essential trade-off that users have to consider in this context: Weighing the chances of improving one's outcome versus potentially increasing the chances of not being allocated.

Considering the difference between matching algorithms, GATA is more robust against manipulation as the average gains from manipulation are smaller compared to other algorithms, for example Király. This is interesting, as lower (average) gains also provide lesser incentives for preference manipulation in the first place, especially considering the potential drawback of being unmatched if manipulation is not successful.

Section 6.2 considered aspects of dynamic allocation in case users arrive or leave in between the calculation of allocations. This might be relevant if either the recalculation of the allocation is infeasible from a time-perspective, or if existing matched pairs cannot be broken up due to technical reasons. The evaluation shows that even very simple heuristic algorithms to match such intermediate supply or demand only introduce a small number of unstable pairs.

The findings have several implications for resource sharing in Social Clouds. First, the study on incentive compatibility shows that not only do heuristics prove to be robust against manipulation, the potential benefits that users can achieve with such preference manipulation is small and often outweighed by potential losses (not being matched, or being matched to a less preferred partner). This is a promising result as it is in line with the social philosophy of a Social Cloud: sharing should be voluntary and strategic considerations should be of lesser importance. Second, the dynamic allocation scenario shows that preference-based matching is also suitable for Social Clouds with fluctuating user participation (and thus, resource offers and requests). The type of heuristic used for resource allocation should depend on the available time and technical considerations (e.g., the feasibility of VM migration). As the effects of leaving new resources idle (i.e., not allocating them until the next allocation interval) can be severe, the studied heuristics provide the means to use provided resources in a Social Cloud in an efficient manner. For the participating users, the matching of intermediate demand and supply implies that resources can be allocated and used once available, thereby avoiding cases of not utilized, offered resources.

These two case studies present a good starting point to investigate further topics of interest. For example, in the context of preference manipulation, the question of robust strategies is important. Given different scenarios and matching algorithms, a manipulation strategy can be considered robust if it consistently provides good results (improvements to non-manipulation) in many scenarios. The existence of such robust strategies is a topic for further research.

In summary, Chapters 5 and 6 showed how heuristics can be used to implement preference-based resource allocation in Social Clouds. Their flexibility allows for the adjustment to different scenarios and optimization goals, and users benefit from a similar or improved performance in comparison to existing matching algorithms. They provide little incentives to manipulate preference rankings as the respective probability to actually benefit from manipulation is small. Furthermore, they are able to handle dynamic allocation scenarios when user participation (and thus, resource offers and requests) is stochastic.

As this thesis focused on one-to-one allocations, the presented work can be extended in order to adapt the heuristics for many-to-one or many-to-many scenarios, when multiple resources can be matched to one offer/request. This is particularly interesting if a resource offer can satisfy several requests, or a request requires a large amount of resources such that it cannot be covered with one offer (e.g., complex calculations requiring several VMs). Similar to this work, the comparison of the adapted heuristics with existing mechanisms for many-to-one allocations, as well as the consideration of incentive compatibility in such settings, are topics that require further research.

Part IV.

Finale

Chapter 7.

Conclusion

THE types of resources that are shared and exchanged on online platforms is as varied as the platforms themselves. The engineering of such platforms is a complex task, and several challenges have to be addressed. This includes the technical implementation, the design of a resource allocation mechanism, the need to provide incentives for user participation, and the consideration of potential user behavior and its effects on the platform. This thesis considered resource sharing through the concept of Social Clouds, where the exchange of resources involves non-monetary mechanisms on the basis of underlying social relationships. In such a system, existing direct and indirect connections correspond to a certain level of trust, which can have various effects on the sharing behavior of users (e.g., the relevance of specific incentives, and the applicability of certain allocation mechanisms), and thus also affects the design of such a platform with its corresponding challenges.

This thesis focused on two coordination challenges in the design of a Social Cloud: user incentives for participation, and non-monetary allocation mechanisms based on two-sided matching. As achieving a critical mass of actively participating users is crucial for a sharing platform, the first part of the thesis focused on the understanding of relevant user incentives and the design of incentive schemes that take into account the social setting of the platform. In the second part, the thesis analyzed two-sided matching heuristics for the non-monetary allocation of resources. In particular, it focused on aspects of solution quality, strategic considerations, and dynamic allocation.

Section 7.1 summarizes the contributions of the thesis. Section 7.2 critically discusses the assumptions and limitations of this work, and closes with an overview of future work.

7.1. Contribution

The design of coordination mechanisms for Social Clouds, specifically the identification and study of participation incentives as well as the design of mechanisms for resource allocation, was the focus of this thesis. Its contributions to the design of a social sharing platform are threefold: 1) the technical implementation of a simulation tool as complementary methodology to study such systems; 2) the understanding of relevant incentives for participation as well as the engineering of incentive schemes; 3) the design of preference-based matching heuristics as a means to allocate resources on a non-monetary basis. The three contribution aspects are discussed in more detail in the subsequent sections.

7.1.1. Simulation-based Approach to Study Social Clouds

Social Clouds and other resource sharing concepts are complex systems. Different types of users (with respect to resource endowment, sharing motivations, preferences, etc.) participate on such platforms and influence the overall system outcome through their individual interactions with each other. Due to this complexity, the study of Social Clouds presents methodological challenges. While analytical modeling and prediction of (dynamic) system effects might be possible only for small systems, the (prototypical) implementation of the platform provides the opportunity to receive feedback from real users, their characteristics and behaviors. Similarly, certain effects such as influence of self-representation on the sharing behavior can be studied through laboratory experiments. However, not all problems can be addressed with the mentioned methodologies. For example, it can be necessary to predict effects of rule changes on the system before they are implemented, or stress-tests need to be run to study scalability behavior.

For these reasons, this thesis advocated the use of a simulation-based approach as complementary methodology for Social Clouds and similar systems. The simulation tool described in Chapter 2.2 provides added value to the methodological toolkit for the study of social sharing systems. It provides functionality to model the relevant aspects of Social Clouds, ranging from users, underlying relationships and networks, and a variety of allocation mechanisms, and is easily extendable to capture new scenarios. The usefulness of the simulation tool and its applicability for Social Cloud scenarios was shown throughout the thesis. Chapter 4 applied the simulation tool to study effects of different incentive schemes on (heterogeneous) user types and overall system performance. Chapters 5 and 6 used the tool to analyze the performance of different two-sided matching mechanisms for resource allocation.

Due to its architecture and extensibility, the simulation tool is not only usable for Social Cloud settings, but is also able to capture a variety of other resource sharing scenarios in the future. However, as mentioned before, such a simulation-based approach can be seen as complementary methodology and does not replace prototypes, experiments or theoretical analysis. As simulation results crucially depend on the correct modeling of assumptions of input parameters, several steps such as verification and validation of the simulation model as well as sensitivity analyses of the results need to be pursued to ensure the correctness of simulation studies.

7.1.2. Understanding Incentives for Participation

To achieve a critical mass of participating users, a resource sharing platform such as a Social Cloud needs to provide appropriate incentives to potential users. This was the focus of research question 1:

RESEARCH QUESTION 1 ≺PARTICIPATION AND CONTRIBUTION INCENTIVES≻ *What are relevant user participation incentives for Social Clouds and how can they be leveraged in the design of tailored participation and contribution schemes?*

The first step to address this research question is to analyze how users interact with a Social Cloud in order to determine different participation stages. As the relevance of certain incentives might change over the time of user participation on the platform, research question 1.1 aimed at distinguishing these participation stages and identifying relevant incentives for the different stages.

RESEARCH QUESTION 1.1 ≺INCENTIVE ENGINEERING≻ *What are the stages of participation and the corresponding relevant incentives that users exhibit in Social Clouds?*

Three different stages of participation can be identified that are relevant for Social Clouds: the registration on the platform, the active participation on the platform, and the adherence to social norms and behavior (see Section 3.2). Through a web survey, relevant incentives for the first two stages were identified (Section 3.3). For user registration and participation, a direct invitation from friends, general altruistic traits, and the perceived benefits from joining were considered most important, whereas the prospect of monetary compensation was considered least important. In addition, the setting of the sharing scenario, i.e., whether sharing occurs in private settings between friends or in professional settings between colleagues, also influenced the relative importance of certain incentives such as monetary compensation or fun from participation.

Having identified different stages of user participation and the need to potentially emphasize different incentives in these stages, as a next step this knowledge can be applied to design incentive schemes for active user participation on the platform. This thesis advocated the use of the previously mentioned simulation tool as complementary methodology for the engineering of such incentive schemes. To exemplify the usefulness of the simulation-based approach, Chapter 4 presented two case studies. The aim of the first case study was to study the effects of an incentive scheme on different user types, as stated in research question 1.2.

RESEARCH QUESTION 1.2 ≺INCENTIVE SCHEME DESIGN≻ *How can a simulation-based approach be leveraged in the design of incentive schemes for participation?*

The simulation tool was used to study a complex Social Cloud scenario where resources were shared between heterogeneous user groups. The aim of the case study was to analyze the effects a trading constraint on the users and the system. As an analytical approach was not feasible due to the number of considered users and their heterogeneity, the (dynamic) effects of the trading constraint on different user types were studied in Section 4.2. The simulation revealed interesting effects on the different user types, which were affected differently to a substantial degree. In particular, it showed that selfish users suffer most from the introduction of a participation constraint, while altruistic and other user types generally are also affected to some degree. The case study also showed that the results are sensitive with respect to the distribution of user types, which is an important input factor that has to be considered in the design process of Social Clouds. Overall, the case study showed that a simulation-based approach can be used to study and predict dynamic effects in Social Clouds, and to find robust parameters for an incentive scheme by analyzing different user type distributions.

The second case study in Section 4.3 proposed an economic model how infrastructure resources that are needed to host a Social Cloud can be co-operatively provided by the users of the platform themselves. In such a scenario, the incentives to provide resources to the infrastructure determine the amount of platform resources and thus the applicability of such an approach. Therefore, research question 1.3 studied different contribution schemes how users can provide resources to the infrastructure, and examined how the feasibility of the approach is determined by the characteristics of the user base.

RESEARCH QUESTION 1.3 ≺CO-OPERATIVE INFRASTRUCTURES≻ *What are the effects of different contribution schemes on co-operatively provided infrastructure resources for Social Clouds?*

The contribution schemes distinguished between required contribution (in which case each user has to provide a certain amount of resources) and voluntary contribution (users choose their level of contribution according to their specific characteristics). The results for the different contribution schemes showed that schemes with required contribution mostly lead to a sufficient number of contributed resources and guarantee a high level of platform availability and performance. In contrast, the applicability of voluntary contribution schemes largely depends on the characteristics of the underlying user base. For example, in systems with a high number of selfish users, required contribution schemes are more promising. The results also showed, however, that the utility for users is higher in case of voluntary contributions, as they themselves determine their optimal level of resource contribution.

Addressing research question 1, the findings showed that three distinct stages for user participation in a Social Cloud can be distinguished, and that non-monetary incentives such as altruism, fun, and expected reciprocity are the most relevant incentives in such a setting. Additionally, a simulation-based approach can be used to design incentive schemes and study dynamic effects on the Social Cloud. The presented results are, however, only a first step for the engineering of incentives for actual Social Clouds. As shown in the case studies, the effectiveness of a particular incentive scheme depends on the distribution of user types, hence it is necessary to identify the actual distribution for a given setting. In addition, it remains a largely open question how incentives can be tailored to individual users or user groups in Social Clouds.

7.1.3. Heuristics for Preference-based Resource Allocation

The design of resource allocation mechanisms for Social Clouds was the second coordination challenge addressed by this thesis. Due to the underlying social connections between users, a preference-based, two-sided matching approach was considered as a means to allocate resources through a non-monetary mechanism.

In preference-based matching, users are split into two sides: users requesting resources, and users providing resources. Each user specifies a preference ranking with whom of the other (market) side they want to be matched. Based on these preference rankings, a two-sided matching algorithm then calculates a solution that determines which users are matched. The thesis focused on one-to-one matches, i.e., one provider is matched with one requester. The complexity of calculating a solution depends on both the structure of the submitted preferences and the desired goals that the solution should satisfy. Preferences can be categorized in complete and incomplete preferences, depending if all users of the other side are matched or not, and having indifferences between certain users or not. The standard goal in preference-based matching is to calculate a stable solution, which means that no two users can both benefit by bilaterally breaking from the solution and forming a new pair. Other commonly considered goals are welfare, measuring the rank that the average user is matched with, and fairness, which considers if welfare is distributed equally between the two sides.

In the general case where preferences can include either incomplete lists or indifferences, finding a solution that satisfies the standard goals (e.g., finding a stable solution with best welfare) is NP-hard for all but a small number of scenarios. Furthermore, for certain combinations of preference structures and goals, approximation algorithms have been developed. However, the downside of current approximation algorithms is that they are specialized on a certain set of preference structures and goals, and are not designed to handle other cases. Furthermore, there are scenarios for which no approximation algorithms exist. Hence, the focus of this part of the thesis was following research question:

RESEARCH QUESTION 2 ≺RESOURCE ALLOCATION≻ *Which types of algorithms provide a good combination of performance, flexibility, and strategic properties for non-monetary, preference-based resource allocation?*

As this is a multifaceted question and the performance of the considered algorithms can be studied from different points of view, several other research questions have to be answered first. These questions each consider a specific aspect of algorithm performance or properties.

Especially in light of social resource sharing platforms, the goals of the platform can be diverse and change over time. For this reason, and due to the computational complexity of the underlying problem, heuristic algorithms to calculate a solution to the preference-based matching were proposed in Chapter 5. Two heuristics were considered to calculate solutions for preference-based matching: a Genetic Algorithm (GA) and a Threshold Accepting (TA) algorithm, as well as the combination of the two. For the applicability of these heuristics, particularly with respect to the quality of their solutions, research question 2.1 considered the performance of heuristics and existing algorithms in different settings.

RESEARCH QUESTION 2.1 ≺PERFORMANCE OF PREFERENCE-BASED MATCHING≻ *What is the performance of heuristics for preference-based matching compared to existing matching mechanisms?*

For different preference structures (complete and incomplete preferences with indifferences), the heuristics were compared with existing algorithms for the specific setting, focusing on standard metrics such as stability, welfare, fairness, and the number of matched pairs. For complete preferences, depending on the type of solutions with which it is initialized, the GA is able to improve the solution quality of the initial solutions, and in particular provides better solutions in comparison to the standard algorithms in this case. Similar results were obtained for the combination of GA and TA. TA alone, however, is not a fitting heuristic for this scenario as its solution quality is worse than GA (Section 5.4.3). For incomplete preferences, the relative performance of the heuristics is even better. Both GA and TA are useful heuristics in this scenario, and their respective solution quality is similar to the average quality of the best approximation algorithm. Furthermore, the combined GA and TA algorithm with mixed initial solutions consistently yields significantly better results than all other algorithms (Section 5.4.4). In addition to increasing the number of matched pairs, the heuristics also yield solutions with considerably better welfare and fairness properties.

Overall, the results showed that heuristics do not only provide flexibility to cope with various preference and goal combinations, but also perform similarly or better than existing algorithms. Combined with a relatively short runtime, heuristics provide an ideal combination of flexibility, runtime, and solution quality for the calculation of preference-based matching allocations. For resource sharing in social contexts, both the platform and the users benefit from the application of the proposed heuristics (through an increased number of shared resources, and being matched to a more preferred partner, respectively).

Besides solution quality, strategic behavior of users is another important aspect in preference-based resource matching. Matching mechanisms determine the allocation on the basis of the submitted preferences. However, if the mechanism is not incentive compatible, users might not submit their true preferences. One of the fundamental results in preference-based matching states that there can be no algorithm that always yields a stable solution and for which no user has incentives to manipulate the submitted preferences to the algorithm (Roth, 1982). In other words, for the algorithms considered in this thesis, at least some users theoretically can benefit from preference manipulation. The existence of manipulation has been studied for only a few of the considered algorithms, and the effect of manipulation considering the heuristics and different scenarios was an open question. This was the focus of research question 2.2.

RESEARCH QUESTION 2.2 ≺INCENTIVE COMPATIBILITY≻ *What are the effects of preference manipulation on the manipulating users, non-manipulating users, and the solution quality?*

Submitting manipulated preferences has complex effects on the matching solution. It can be beneficial for the manipulating user by being matched to a more preferred partner, yet it is also possible that the manipulating user is matched to a less preferred partner or even remains unmatched. The results of the corresponding evaluation in Section 6.1.2 showed that preference manipulation can indeed lead to being matched with better partners for the manipulating users, as predicted by theory. However, the likelihood of a successful manipulation is relatively small (between 40-44% for the combination of GA and TA), and severe manipulation can lead to the user remaining unmatched. Furthermore, the results showed that preference manipulation can introduce instability in the solution. For example, a solution which is stable under the submitted (manipulated) preferences can be unstable under the true preferences.

The robustness of the heuristics and best performing approximation algorithms was considered as well. For two scenarios with different numbers of users, the results indicate that potential (average) gains from manipulation are smallest for the combination of GA and TA. This indicates that it is harder for manipulating users to find a beneficial manipulation strategy if heuristic algorithms are used (Section 6.1.3).

The third aspect of algorithm performance in preference-based matching was the study of their applicability in dynamic allocation scenarios. In contrast to standard preference-based matching which assumes batch-like calculations of the solution at certain time intervals, in between these time intervals new users might enter or leave the platform, thereby creating new (intermediate) supply and demand. Research question 2.3 studied the effects of such dynamic supply and demand on preference-based matching.

RESEARCH QUESTION 2.3 ≺DYNAMIC ALLOCATIONS≻ *What are options to allocate dynamic supply and demand, taking into account potential existing matches?*

Section 6.2 showed that not acknowledging this intermediate supply and demand might leave a considerable amount of resources idle. Depending on the problem size, the runtime of the algorithms, or technical restrictions considering the migration of data or entire Virtual Machines, it might not be feasible to immediately recalculate the entire solution with all users that are currently matched. Hence, two additional heuristics were suggested to cope with such intermediate supply and demand. The evaluation in Section 6.2.2 showed that these heuristics are able to match the otherwise unutilized resources, yet introduce some level of instability in the (overall) solution and have varying effects on welfare and fairness. If the allocation does not have to be calculated instantaneously, the recalculation with GA and TA leads to the best results. Overall, however, the suggested heuristics for intermediate allocation are a valid option to match resources in dynamic scenarios.

Summarizing the results, the studied heuristics are superior to existing algorithms considering their ability to adapt to different preference structures and goal combinations. For example, the heuristics can be easily adjusted to optimize combinations of goal metrics that existing algorithms do not or cannot consider. Their performance for commonly considered metrics is equal or superior to existing algorithms, they offer good characteristics with respect to strategic behavior of users, and their runtime allows the application in dynamic scenarios. Due to this, the heuristics provide benefits for the resource allocation in Social Clouds. Depending on the setting, the optimization goals of the allocation can be flexibly adjusted while the resulting solution quality of the allocation remains consistently high. In particular, the improvements to existing (approximation) algorithms imply benefits for the system and the users (e.g., through better welfare and fairness properties of a solution).

However, despite these positive results, there are some limitations to the presented approach. Heuristics, in contrast to exact or approximation algorithms, do not guarantee certain bounds for solution quality. Although the results in Chapter 5 indicate otherwise, there might be cases where the worst-case performance of the heuristics is worse than the lower quality bounds of approximation algorithms. In addition, this thesis considered one-to-one matching scenarios. The heuristics can be easily adapted for many-to-one scenarios, yet their performance evaluation in such settings requires further evaluation. Two-sided matching with complex preference structures such as multiple attributes also remains an open topic. These issues are addressed in the next section on open research questions and future work.

7.2. Future Work

This section critically discusses the assumptions and limitations of this work and presents an outlook on future work.

7.2.1. User Participation Incentives

Participation Incentives: Feedback from Prototypes and Real Platforms
The identification of different participation stages in Section 3.2 is based on a conceptual model derived from literature research and a comparison with similar systems and models. The web-based survey on the relevance of certain incentive types

for different users, as presented in Section 3.3, does not claim to be representative of the actual user population, which limits the generalizability of the results. Both steps are necessary in the design of participation incentives for Social Clouds, and the results provided in Chapters 3 and 4 can be considered a first step towards a more comprehensive coverage of this topic. In particular, the relevance of the incentives studied in the web survey in Chapter 3 have to be extended to capture users of an actually implemented (prototype) platform, in order to derive insights for the specific platform.

The results can be extended by using prototype implementations or actual platforms to gain feedback about user behavior, their participation incentives and other user characteristics. This can help to both refine the model of participation stages as well as to obtain useful insights about the importance of the studied incentive types for certain user groups. The technical prototype implementation of a Social Compute Cloud as presented in Section 2.1.4 provides an ideal starting point for such research. As a next step, this prototype can be made accessible to users with the goal to obtain feedback about the usage and the relevance of certain participation incentives.

Agreement Design for Social Clouds

The relevant motivations and incentives to exchange and share resource in social settings, in particular on a non-monetary basis, are different from the primarily monetary-based resource exchange systems such as the procurement of services from service providers. In the latter case, the details of the exchange are often specified in Service Level Agreements (SLA) which determine the functional and non-functional properties of the given exchange. That is, SLAs specify the attributes of the service that is exchanged and the relevant payments. Also, penalties in case of unsuccessful service provisioning are defined.

In a more social context, the use of standard SLAs and monetary-based penalties might be detrimental or have serious consequences on the existing relationships between the providing and consuming users. Hence, a new form of socially-aware SLAs has to be developed to cope with such situations, and still be able to specify certain properties of the exchanged resources and services. First steps in this direction have been pursued by Michalk and Haas (2011), who discuss why social aspects should be considered in the definition of SLAs in social contexts. Additionally, potential options and details how such agreements can be represented in a Social Cloud are discussed by Thal (2013).

Sustainable Infrastructures for Social Clouds

The model for co-operative infrastructure provisioning as discussed in Section 4.3 only considers the trade-off between providing resources to the platform and keeping resources for other usage. In addition, the sensitivity analyses of the model with respect to different user characteristics assumed the existence of certain types of utility functions, which might not necessarily reflect the real user behavior.

An immediate extension, in particular in the context of Social Clouds, is the augmentation of the model to capture not only the contribution to the platform, but potential resource sharing between users as well. In this case, users have the option to either reserve resources for own usage, donate them to the infrastructure, or share them with other users on the platform. Users might also have different preferences and incentives with respect to these options. To create a necessarily realistic model and evaluation of such a combined approach, a Social Cloud prototype with said capabilities seems to be the best approach to evaluate actual user behavior and its effects on the co-operative infrastructure model. A second extension is a feasibility study of having a sustainable user-contributed infrastructure for volunteer computing. Usually, the infrastructure for BOINC-like projects is centralized, and only the computing jobs are sent and retrieved from clients. However, it might also be an viable option to host the project infrastructure itself on the client resources.

System Development and User Interface Design

This thesis concentrated on identifying participation incentives for Social Clouds, as well as algorithms to match offers and requests. In the design of a Social Cloud, there are further tasks that require attention. The concepts of perceived usefulness and perceived ease of use, which are the two central constructs of the Technology Acceptance Model (Venkatesh et al., 2003), are essential in the adoption of new technology, and also new platforms. Hence, one of the necessary areas of design is the development of good user interfaces. For example, Seuken et al. (2010) discuss user interface design in the context of P2P storage sharing. In the context of Social Clouds, the influence of user interfaces on user behavior (e.g., with respect to specifying sharing preferences) is of particular interest.

7.2.2. Preference-based Resource Allocation

Multi-Attributive Two-Sided Matching

Preference-based matching is a suitable approach to allocate resources on a non-monetary basis. The considered algorithms in this thesis focus on one-to-one matching, where one requesting user is matched with one providing user. This model assumes that resources are either homogeneous, or that a match is only allowed if the provided resource is able to fulfill the request (e.g., the provided VM satisfies all requirements with respect to computational power, memory, etc.). This simple representation might not be suitable to capture more complex scenarios. For example, users providing a certain part of their computer as VM might be able to split this VM into smaller instances and satisfy multiple smaller requests simultaneously. A direct extension of the one-to-one model, thus, would be to capture such many-to-one matching algorithms.

In the case of heterogeneous resources, multiple attributes are often used to characterize the resources' properties. For example, a VM can be described by the number of cores, the provided memory and storage, its availability, etc. In such a scenario, users might have different preferences for the attributes, i.e., weight the relative importance of the attributes. If alternatives are ranked differently with respect to the attributes, i.e., the ranking of alternatives is not the same for all attributes, the question arises how a resource allocation can be found. One approach, in this case, is to aggregate the preference rankings for the attributes into one ranking based on the relative weight for the attributes. Another approach is to define necessary requirements for the considered attributes that the alternatives have to fulfill, and rank the alternatives according to the fulfillment of these requirements.

The allocation of seminar slots to students is another example where such a multi-attributive approach can be useful. In such a scenario, students have a preference for certain seminars they want to attend, and seminar leaders also have preferences which students they want to have in the seminar. Diebold et al. (2014) study the application of stable matching algorithms on course allocation problems. Decentralized allocation, in this case, can be quite complex and lead to considerable inefficiencies. For example, to increase their chances of getting a seminar slot students might apply for many seminars in parallel, and only accept the slots that they like most, leading to potentially open slots in seminars where allocated students are not interested in the slot anymore. A centralized allocation mechanism can help to alleviate this situation. For example, seminar leaders can state their preferences for students (e.g., grade average, number of relevant lectures attended, etc.), and students can rank the seminars according to their liking. The centralized mechanism can then find an allocation that matches students to seminar slots such that the overall allocation efficiency (e.g., with respect to stability or welfare) is increased compared to decentralized allocation. Such an approach can utilize additional constraints, such as the guarantee that each student is allocated a minimum number of seminar slots. The analysis of stability and other performance metrics is an interesting case study in such a scenario.

Weighted Preferences

The two-sided matching algorithms considered in this thesis focus on unweighted preferences, i.e., preference rankings represent qualitative priority structures that can be represented as rank order lists. For example, preference rank 1 denotes the most preferred alternative, rank 2 the second most preferred alternative, etc. While this is a common assumption in two-sided matching literature, a more quantitative preference representation can be useful in certain scenarios. For example, Irving et al. (1987) propose weighted preference lists where, instead of preference ranks, users are ranked according to a numerical score. Through such a representation, users are able to express preferences in more details. For example, a users might consider the difference between the two most preferred alternatives as considerably higher than the difference between the two least preferred alternatives. By providing scores instead of priorities, such a more complex representation is achievable.

When weighted preferences are considered, several aspects need to be addressed. Pini et al. (2011b) argue that the performance metrics should be adjusted to capture the new preference representation. Considering algorithms for finding solutions to the matching problem, the performance of the studied algorithms needs to be evaluated for such a setting. Although the heuristics can be easily adapted to capture weighted preferences, their performance with respect to the optimal solution, or in comparison with other algorithms, are an interesting topic for future research.

Robust Strategies for Two-Sided Matching

The aim of studying strategic preference manipulation in this thesis was to gain insight in the potential effects of manipulation as well as the robustness of the considered mechanisms against manipulation. With this foundation, the following interesting question lends itself: What is a good strategy for manipulation in two-sided preference-based matching markets? As seen in Chapter 6.1, theoretical results suggest that in certain scenarios truncation of preferences is superior to both random reordering as well as submitting the true preferences. Yet, this does not answer the question how much the preferences should be truncated, and how such a strategy depends on the strategies of other, potentially also manipulating participants. Considering the practical importance of such manipulation, it is also of interest if there are robust strategies that work well in (many) different settings, thus providing useful guidelines for participants and market designers alike.

The evaluation in Section 6.1 can be considered a first step in studying such robust strategies. A potential research direction is to apply evolutionary computing to determine successful manipulation strategies. Alternatively, a tournament in the spirit of Axelrod's strategy tournament for the Prisoner's Dilemma game can be held, where strategies are played against each other to determine the most robust strategy (Axelrod and Hamilton, 1981; Axelrod, 1997).

Dynamic Preference Rankings and Feedback Integration

The preference-based matching algorithms presented in Chapters 5 and 6 take as input the preference profiles of participating users. These profiles do not need to be static, and thus can potentially change over time. For example, in a network with providing and requesting users, the relative ranking of other users might be influenced by the previous interaction and sharing experiences as well as the feedback about such past interactions from other users.

A potential way to rank users in the preferences is to use a trust network with local or global trust values for the users. These trust networks incorporate the feedback of other users in addition to own experiences about transactions with other users (see e.g. Petri et al. (2012) for the use of trust networks in P2P clouds). If users did not interact with certain other users before, it might be difficult to obtain a preference ranking due to the lack of knowledge about these other users. By using trust networks and the corresponding trust values, users might be able to improve the accuracy of their preference rankings over time. Two aspects are of particular interest in this case. On the one hand, the relative positions of users in preference rankings can by dynamic and change based on their previous transactions as well as user feedback. Hence, it is necessary to study the factors that influence this dynamic ranking. On the other hand, the feedback itself might not always be reliable itself, or even be manipulated by maliciously behaving users. The effects of different feedback types on the resulting solution, thus, is an important topic that requires attention.

Preference Creation and Elicitation

Preference rankings submitted by users are the main input of the two-sided matching algorithms in this thesis. From the perspective of the users and the platform designer, the creation and elicitation of these preference rankings is an interesting aspect. In a Social Cloud, the data about the underlying social network and connections between users can be used in the creation of preference rankings. However, as the representation of connections is often binary, the interpretation of a user's social ties for the purposes of allocation is not immediately clear. There is no single unified methodology for the interpretation of social ties, and which to use is often context dependent. To create a preference ranking from the social ties, several methods could be applied either separately or in combination with one another: 1) ask users to rank their friends; 2) leverage methods from social network analysis to identify features of social ties that can be used to (artificially) construct preferences; and 3) use social network and interaction theories to construct a social sharing and interaction model, and tune this model over time based upon observed interactions within the social network platform and the Social Cloud. Each of these approaches have their advantages and disadvantages, and there might be other methods which are not listed above as well.

The use of user generated lists has the advantages that it is easy to implement, requires no special permissions (other than access to the list of friends), and should be closest to capturing the true preferences of the user. However, given the recent trends in social network usage, the average Facebook user currently has 190 friends (Backstrom et al., 2012), this approach would not scale as more friends joined the Social Cloud, as it cannot be expected that users rank large numbers of friends. In contrast, the use of computational methods has the main advantage that these approaches can be scaled as the Social Cloud grows. The challenge, however, is in the identification of appropriate methods and indicators. These approaches also require more data from the social network platform, and are thus more invasive into the user's private sphere, which cannot be understated. A simple example that can be used in a preference-like manner are constructs like circles in Google+ or relationship lists in Facebook, as these are often created or at least curated by the user, and represent either specific (sub)groups in the social network and/or relationship types that are "similar" in some way. It is also possible to compose more complicated methods of assessing social ties with the use of indicators to assess the properties of a social tie. Overall, however, identifying the best implementation(s) for the creation and elicitation of preferences remains an interesting and open challenge.

Part V.

Appendix

Appendix A.

Additional Material for Incentive Survey

Survey Questions

1) Have you ever shared (provided and/or received) resources online? (Examples for resources: files, programs, photos, lectures notes, (working) documents, sample solutions, storage, ...)

- o Yes
- o No

2) Over which platforms and/or communication channels have you shared (providedand/or received) resources? (multiple answers allowed)

- o Social network (private, e.g. Facebook)
- o Social network (professional, e.g. Xing)
- o DropBox
- o Own server (FTP)
- o Google Drive
- o Microsoft SkyDrive
- o P2P-Tools (BitTorrent, eMule, Limewire, ...)
- o E-Mail
- o Other:

3) Which of the following resources have you already shared (provided and/or received)online? (multiple answers allowed)

- o Files
- o Programs
- o Music
- o Photos
- o Movies
- o Lecture Notes
- o Sample Solutions
- o (Working) Documents
- o Storage
- o Other:

4) With whom have you shared (provided and/or received) resources so far? (multiple answers allowed)

- o Family
- o Friends (real life)
- o Friends (online)
- o Friends of Friends
- o Classmates
- o Colleagues
- o Other:

5) How often do you share (provide and/or receive) resources on average? (multiple answers allowed)

- o More often than once per day
- o Once per day
- o A few times a week
- o Once per week
- o A few times a month
- o Once per month
- o frequently than once per month
- o Dependent on certain events
- o Please specify, if it is dependent on certain events:

6) What are (would be) your reasons for sharing (providing and/or receiving) resources? (1 = disagree strongly, . . ., 7 = agree strongly)

- o Direct request
- o Helpfulness
- o Own benefit
- o Monetary compensation
- o Other compensation (e.g. favor)
- o Prestige / Reputation
- o Other (please specify):

7) In addition to the resources, which you have already shared, are there any other resources you would like to share if the appropriate technology was available? (Except for any illegal share activities)

- o No
- o Don't know
- o Yes, the following:

8) Are you interested in sharing (providing and/or receiving) resources in general? (Examples for resources could be files, programs, photos, lectures notes, (working) documents, sample solutions, storage, ...)

- o No
- o Don't know
- o Yes, the following:

9) Which incentives would be important/crucial for you to register with that network? (In this case, registration does not imply active usage, only the general access to the network to, for example, see the offered resources. 1 = disagree strongly, . . ., 7 = agree strongly)

- o Request of closer friends
- o Monetary Compensation
- o Prestige / Reputation
- o Curiosity / Fun
- o Helpfulness / favor
- o Own benefit
- o Other (please specify)

10) Please now imagine that you are registered in such a sharing network with friends. Which incentives would be important/crucial to be an active user, i.e. to actively participate and share resources? (1 = disagree strongly, ..., 7 = agree strongly)

o Request of closer friends
o Prestige / Reputation
o Helpfulness / favor
o Other (please specify)
o Monetary Compensation
o Curiosity / Fun
o Own benefit

11) Please imagine that classmates, colleagues or acquaintances from a professional platform, e.g. Xing, participate in a closed sharing network. Which incentives would now be important/crucial for you to register to that network? (In this case, registration does not imply active usage, only the general access to the network to, for example, see the offered resources. 1 = disagree strongly, ..., 7 = agree strongly)

o Request of closer friends
o Prestige / Reputation
o Helpfulness / favor
o Other (please specify)
o Monetary Compensation
o Curiosity / Fun
o Own benefit

12) Please now imagine that you are already member of such a sharing network with acquaintances, classmates or colleagues. Which incentives would be important/crucial to be an active user, i.e. to actively participate and share resources? (1 = disagree strongly, ..., 7 = agree strongly)

o Request of closer friends
o Prestige / Reputation
o Helpfulness / favor
o Other (please specify)
o Monetary Compensation
o Curiosity / Fun
o Own benefit

13) Imagine a scenario where it is possible to provide storage on your hard disk to other people for storing their data (e.g. backups, documents, photos, etc.) and access it online. You can be sure that there is sufficiently high security so that only the owner of the data can create, read, update and delete their data and that you are protected from viruses/malware and legal liability for the data stored on your hard disk. To which groups would you provide your storage (independent of compensation)? (multiple answers allowed)

o Nobody
o Closer Friends
o Classmates / Colleagues
o Other (please specify)
o Relatives
o Friends of Friends
o Everybody

14) Now you would like to store your own (personal) data (backups, documents, photos, ...) on another's hard disk. The data is encrypted, so that only you can can create, read, update and delete your data. Which type of relationship must exist between you and the provider of the storage? (multiple answers allowed)

- o Relatives
- o Closer Friends (in real life)
- o Closer Friends (online)
- o Friends of Friends
- o Classmates / Colleagues
- o Other (please specify)

15) In the previous scenario, "storage" was the resource shared between users. Imagine now that you share (provide and/or receive) another resource (e.g. photos, lecture notes, (working) documents,...). Would the group of people with whom you share resources change?

- o No
- o Yes:

16) Here are a number of personality traits that may or may not apply to you. Please mark as appropriate to indicate the extent to which you agree or disagree with that statement. You should rate the extent to which the pair of traits applies to you, even if one characteristic applies more strongly than the other.
I see myself as... (1 = disagree strongly, ..., 7 = agree strongly)

- o Extroverted, enthusiastic
- o Critical, quarrelsome
- o Dependable, self-disciplined
- o Anxious, easily upset
- o Open to new experiences, complex
- o Reserved, quiet
- o Sympathetic, warm
- o Disorganized, careless
- o Calm, emotionally stable
- o Conventional, uncreative

17) Please choose your age.

- o < 20
- o 20 - 25
- o 26 - 30
- o 31 - 40
- o 41 - 50
- o > 50
- o Prefer not to say

18) Please choose your gender.

- o Female
- o Male

19) What is the highest degree or level of school you have completed? If currently enrolled, mark the previous grade or highest degree received.

- o Nursery-high school, no diploma
- o High school diploma
- o Some college, no degree
- o Bachelor's degree (for example: BA, AB, BS)
- o Master's degree (for example: MA, MS, MEng, MEd, MSW, MBA)
- o Professional degree (for example: MD, DDS, DVM, LLB, JD)
- o Doctorate degree (for example: PhD, EdD)
- o Post-doctoral education
- o Other (please specify):

20) Please choose your profession.

- o Trainee
- o Student
- o Employee
- o Self-employed
- o Prefer not to say
- o Other (please specify):

SurveyDesign

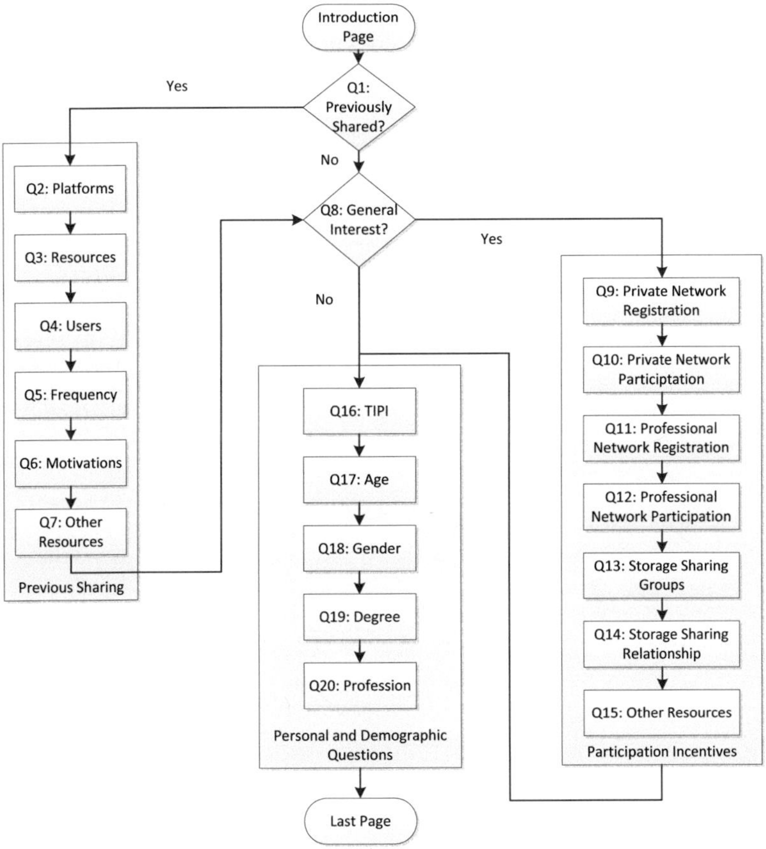

Figure A.1.: Incentive Survey Logic

Additional Survey Data

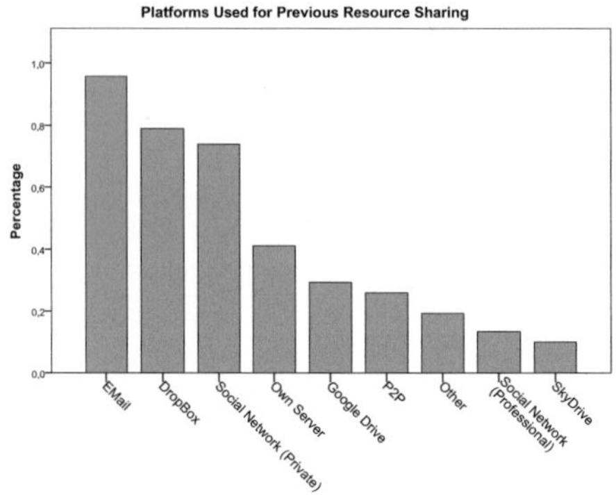

Figure A.2.: Platforms Used for Previous Online Resource Sharing

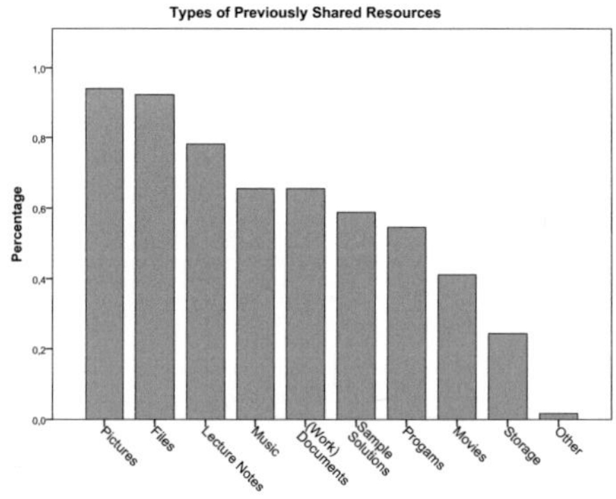

Figure A.3.: Resource Types Previously Shared Online

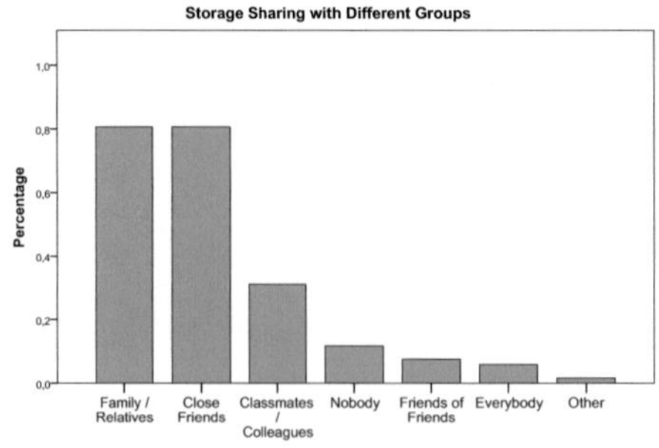

Figure A.4.: User Groups with which Storage would be Shared

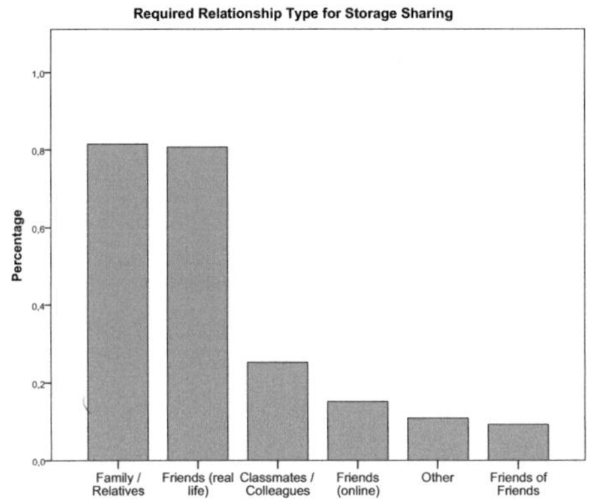

Figure A.5.: Required Relationships for Sharing Storage

Correlation Tables for Incentive Survey

	Ext.	Agr.	Consc.	Emoti.	Open.
Ext.	1.000	-0.080	,190*	,216*	,373**
Agr.	-0.080	1.000	0.023	0.031	0.152
Consc.	,190*	0.023	1.000	,229*	0.104
Emoti.	,216*	0.031	,229*	1.000	0.114
Open.	,373**	0.152	0.104	0.114	1.000
Req.	-0.016	-0.077	,228*	0.159	0.065
Help.	0.115	0.071	,188*	0.055	,199*
Benefit	0.170	0.000	0.045	0.043	0.115
Monet.	0.109	-0.180	0.000	0.044	0.127
Other	,223*	-0.092	-0.097	0.165	0.095
Rep.	0.157	0.066	-0.023	-0.018	0.134

Table A.1.: Spearman-Rho Correlation Table for Incentives for Previous Sharing, Part 1

	Req.	Help.	Benefit	Monet.	Other	Rep.
Ext.	-0.016	0.115	0.170	0.109	,223*	0.157
Agr.	-0.077	0.071	0.000	-0.180	-0.092	0.066
Consc.	,228*	,188*	0.045	0.000	-0.097	-0.023
Emoti.	0.159	0.055	0.043	0.044	0.165	-0.018
Open.	0.065	,199*	0.115	0.127	0.095	0.134
Req.	1.000	,301**	,224*	-0.044	0.086	-0.026
Help.	,301**	1.000	0.176	-0.027	0.100	,349**
Benefit	,224*	0.176	1.000	0.163	,214*	0.072
Monet.	-0.044	-0.027	0.163	1.000	,317**	,281**
Other	0.086	0.100	,214*	,317**	1.000	,508**
Rep.	-0.026	,349**	0.072	,281**	,508**	1.000

Table A.2.: Spearman-Rho Correlation Table for Incentives for Previous Sharing, Part 2

	TIPI					Correlations Private Network Participation						Active Sharing					
	Ext.	Agr.	Consc.	Emoti.	Open.	Req.	Mon.	Rep.	Cur.	Help.	Benefit	Req.	Mon.	Rep.	Cur.	Help.	Benefit
Ext.	1.000	-0.080	.190*	.216*	.373**	0.069	.215*	.205*	.204*	0.126	.206*	.280**	.189*	.249**	.219*	-0.002	.199*
Agr.	-0.080	1.000	0.023	0.031	0.152	0.126	-0.091	0.089	0.123	.214*	0.020	0.077	0.027	.220*	0.168	.312**	0.096
Consc.	.190*	0.023	1.000	.229*	0.104	0.096	0.097	0.112	0.074	0.009	0.015	0.138	0.069	0.095	0.006	0.143	0.018
Emoti.	.216*	0.031	.229*	1.000	0.114	-0.040	-0.058	-0.043	-0.002	0.004	0.067	0.080	0.022	-0.005	0.013	0.146	.193*
Open.	.373**	0.152	0.104	0.114	1.000	0.108	-0.064	0.063	0.102	0.133	0.137	0.157	0.036	0.110	0.156	.257**	.191*
Req.	0.069	0.126	0.096	-0.040	0.108	1.000	0.101	.322**	.230*	.286**	0.122	.583**	0.075	.308**	.314**	0.088	.231*
Mon.	.215*	-0.091	0.097	-0.058	-0.064	0.101	1.000	.371**	-0.019	.202*	0.162	0.105	.772**	.367**	0.066	0.010	.222*
Rep.	.205*	0.089	0.112	-0.043	0.063	.322**	.371**	1.000	.388**	.350**	0.108	.204*	.290**	.731**	.409**	0.119	0.128
Cur.	.204*	0.123	0.074	-0.002	0.102	.230*	-0.019	.388**	1.000	.387**	0.166	.261**	-0.047	.380**	.660**	.263**	0.106
Help.	0.126	.214*	0.009	0.004	0.133	.286**	.202*	.350**	.387**	1.000	0.053	.204*	0.124	.386**	.348**	.520**	0.003
Ben.	.206*	0.020	0.015	0.067	0.137	0.122	0.162	0.108	0.166	0.053	1.000	.231*	.205*	0.150	-0.054	0.052	.760**
Req.	.280**	0.077	0.138	0.080	0.157	.583**	0.105	.204*	.261**	.204*	.231*	1.000	0.084	.279**	.272**	.243**	.375**
Mon.	.189*	0.027	0.069	0.022	0.036	0.075	.772**	.290**	-0.047	0.124	.205*	0.084	1.000	.378**	0.071	0.133	.253**
Rep.	.249**	.220*	0.095	-0.005	0.110	.308**	.367**	.731**	.380**	.386**	0.150	.279**	.378**	1.000	.418**	.188*	0.167
Cur.	.219*	0.168	0.006	0.013	0.156	.314**	0.066	.409**	.660**	.348**	-0.054	.272**	0.071	.418**	1.000	.242**	0.103
Help.	-0.002	.312**	0.143	0.146	.257**	0.088	0.010	0.119	.263**	.520**	0.052	.243**	0.133	.188*	.242**	1.000	0.137
Ben.	.199*	0.096	0.018	.193*	.191*	.231*	.222*	0.128	0.106	0.003	.760**	.375**	.253**	0.167	0.103	0.137	1.000

Table A.3.: Spearman-Rho Correlation Table for Participation in Private Networks

	TIPI					Correlations Professional Network Participation						Active Sharing					
	Extr.	Agr.	Consc.	Em. Stab.	Open.	Req.	Monet.	Rep.	Cur.	Help.	Ben.	Req.	Monet.	Rep.	Cur.	Help.	Ben.
Ext.	1.000	-0.080	,190*	,216*	,373**	,207*	0.006	0.171	,328**	0.168	,259**	,320**	0.085	,200*	,351**	0.151	,287**
Agr.	-0.080	1.000	0.023	0.031	0.152	-0.075	-0.178	0.123	0.126	0.142	-0.106	0.048	-0.124	0.137	0.118	,300**	0.007
Consc.	,190*	0.023	1.000	,229*	0.104	0.134	0.142	0.076	0.149	0.051	0.025	0.141	0.103	0.055	0.161	0.039	0.038
Emoti.	,216*	0.031	,229*	1.000	0.114	0.023	-0.135	-0.085	0.138	-0.059	0.084	0.000	-0.061	-0.098	0.053	-0.030	0.099
Open.	,373**	0.152	0.104	0.114	1.000	0.038	-0.151	0.069	,215*	0.180	0.145	0.161	-0.023	0.099	,182*	,235*	,232*
Req.	,207*	-0.075	0.134	0.023	0.038	1.000	,268**	,378**	,367**	,348**	,424**	,684**	,330**	,338**	,359**	,308**	,445**
Mon.	0.006	-0.178	0.142	-0.135	-0.151	,268**	1.000	,451**	-0.058	,195*	,298**	0.163	,807**	,333**	0.029	0.102	,305**
Rep.	0.171	0.123	0.076	-0.085	0.069	,378**	,451**	1.000	0.173	,287**	,342**	,309**	,521**	,833**	,220*	,248**	,428**
Cur.	,328**	0.126	0.149	0.138	,215*	,367**	-0.058	0.173	1.000	,369**	,196*	,440**	0.005	0.139	,779**	,350**	,234*
Help.	0.168	0.142	0.051	-0.059	0.180	,348**	,195*	,287**	,369**	1.000	,228*	,339**	0.171	,226*	,339**	,726**	,276**
Ben.	,259**	-0.106	0.025	0.084	0.145	,424**	,298**	,342**	,196*	,228*	1.000	,453**	,363**	,291**	,193*	,268**	,842**
Req.	,320**	0.048	0.141	0.000	0.161	,684**	0.163	,309**	,440**	,339**	,453**	1.000	,284**	,290**	,351**	,356**	,487**
Mon.	0.085	-0.124	0.103	-0.061	-0.023	,330**	,807**	,521**	0.005	0.171	,363**	,284**	1.000	,429**	0.023	0.089	,438**
Rep.	,200*	0.137	0.055	-0.098	0.099	,338**	,333**	,833**	0.139	,226*	,291**	,290**	,429**	1.000	,280**	,278**	,355**
Cur.	,351**	0.118	0.161	0.053	,182*	,359**	0.029	,220*	,779**	,339**	,193*	,351**	0.023	,280**	1.000	,444**	,197*
Help.	0.151	,300**	0.039	-0.030	,235*	,308**	0.102	,248**	,350**	,726**	,268**	,356**	0.089	,278**	,444**	1.000	,336**
Ben.	,287**	0.007	0.038	0.099	,232*	,445**	,305**	,428**	,234*	,276**	,842**	,487**	,438**	,355**	,197*	,336**	1.000

Table A.4.: Spearman-Rho Correlation Table for Participation in Professional Networks

Appendix B.

Extended Result Tables for Co-operative Infrastructures

Table B.1.: Simulation Results for Enforced Fixed Contribution

Number Users	$x \times \rho^*$	Avg. Sys. Availability Worst Case	Avg. Sys. Availability Average Case	Avg. Contribution Worst Case	Avg. Contribution Average Case	Ratio Prov. / Req. Worst Case	Ratio Prov. / Req. Average Case
10	1	0.799	0.813	0.242	0.231	1.962	1.849
	1.1	0.839	0.851	0.266	0.253	2.164	2.022
	1.2	0.893	0.908	0.317	0.301	2.561	2.418
	1.5	0.960	0.968	0.468	0.444	3.780	3.542
20	1	0.971	0.953	0.145	0.170	2.317	2.218
	1.1	0.982	0.969	0.160	0.187	2.554	2.441
	1.2	0.992	0.986	0.192	0.224	3.059	2.935
	1.5	0.999	0.998	0.288	0.333	4.585	4.352
50	1	1.000	0.999	0.096	0.138	2.846	2.392
	1.1	1.000	1.000	0.106	0.151	3.123	2.635
	1.2	1.000	1.000	0.127	0.182	3.757	3.165
	1.5	1.000	1.000	0.190	0.272	5.636	4.747
100	1	1.000	1.000	0.084	0.147	2.979	2.259
	1.1	1.000	1.000	0.092	0.161	3.279	2.481
	1.2	1.000	1.000	0.110	0.194	3.939	2.978
	1.5	1.000	1.000	0.166	0.290	5.903	4.465
200	1	1.000	0.990	0.094	0.178	2.885	1.974
	1.1	1.000	0.993	0.103	0.196	3.174	2.170
	1.2	1.000	1.000	0.124	0.236	3.807	2.604
	1.5	1.000	1.000	0.185	0.353	5.708	3.909
400	1	1.000	0.990	0.116	0.230	2.568	1.667
	1.1	1.000	0.991	0.127	0.253	2.824	1.833
	1.2	1.000	1.000	0.153	0.304	3.388	2.199
	1.5	1.000	1.000	0.229	0.451	5.086	3.262

Table B.2.: Simulation Results for Variable Fixed Contribution

Number Users	ρ	Avg. Sys. Availability Worst Case	Avg. Sys. Availability Average Case	Avg. Contribution Worst Case	Avg. Contribution Average Case	Ratio Prov. / Req. Worst Case	Ratio Prov. / Req. Average Case
10	0.1	0.013	0.017	0.206	0.192	0.385	0.371
	0.2	0.255	0.283	0.188	0.186	0.686	0.715
	0.3	0.198	0.269	0.105	0.121	0.565	0.683
	0.4	0.144	0.135	0.046	0.042	0.349	0.324
	0.5	0.195	0.166	0.045	0.030	0.414	0.309
20	0.1	0.119	0.230	0.211	0.198	0.637	0.738
	0.2	0.505	0.602	0.173	0.175	1.032	1.266
	0.3	0.430	0.591	0.102	0.114	0.941	1.273
	0.4	0.185	0.261	0.048	0.045	0.561	0.660
	0.5	0.219	0.355	0.039	0.041	0.576	0.750
50	0.1	0.231	0.851	0.202	0.209	0.826	1.437
	0.2	0.836	0.971	0.179	0.175	1.474	2.437
	0.3	0.672	0.896	0.105	0.103	1.286	2.093
	0.4	0.262	0.560	0.043	0.046	0.708	1.261
	0.5	0.341	0.579	0.041	0.037	0.816	1.253
100	0.1	0.036	0.980	0.204	0.208	0.727	1.713
	0.2	0.831	1.000	0.180	0.183	1.295	2.972
	0.3	0.631	0.986	0.106	0.104	1.127	2.535
	0.4	0.139	0.732	0.047	0.045	0.659	1.472
	0.5	0.183	0.735	0.038	0.037	0.675	1.543
200	0.1	0.000	0.987	0.203	0.203	0.522	1.443
	0.2	0.296	1.000	0.180	0.181	0.922	2.588
	0.3	0.159	0.998	0.107	0.105	0.820	2.243
	0.4	0.002	0.801	0.046	0.047	0.471	1.360
	0.5	0.003	0.738	0.039	0.038	0.496	1.351
400	0.1	0.000	0.633	0.205	0.204	0.345	1.042
	0.2	0.000	1.000	0.180	0.177	0.603	1.810
	0.3	0.000	0.988	0.105	0.106	0.532	1.617
	0.4	0.000	0.403	0.047	0.047	0.319	0.960
	0.5	0.000	0.412	0.038	0.038	0.318	0.955

Table B.3.: Simulation Results for Voluntary Variable Contribution, Baseline User Distribution

		Avg. Sys. Availability		Avg. Contribution		Ratio Prov. / Req.	
Number Users	Relative Price	Worst Case	Average Case	Worst Case	Average Case	Worst Case	Average Case
	1.00	0.213	0.181	0.072	0.071	0.602	0.545
	1.25	0.049	0.038	0.044	0.044	0.370	0.373
10	1.50	0.003	0.000	0.029	0.027	0.251	0.212
	2.00	0.000	0.000	0.012	0.012	0.096	0.103
	3.00	0.000	0.000	0.004	0.004	0.036	0.032
	1.00	0.531	0.479	0.075	0.073	1.118	1.028
	1.25	0.225	0.147	0.043	0.047	0.700	0.616
20	1.50	0.036	0.012	0.027	0.027	0.410	0.357
	2.00	0.000	0.000	0.013	0.013	0.203	0.177
	3.00	0.000	0.000	0.004	0.004	0.065	0.054
	1.00	0.914	0.664	0.071	0.070	2.190	1.247
	1.25	0.644	0.203	0.042	0.045	1.219	0.763
50	1.50	0.263	0.010	0.027	0.028	0.804	0.491
	2.00	0.000	0.000	0.013	0.012	0.378	0.215
	3.00	0.000	0.000	0.004	0.004	0.123	0.071
	1.00	0.993	0.643	0.074	0.074	2.626	1.132
	1.25	0.907	0.062	0.044	0.045	1.593	0.697
100	1.50	0.422	0.000	0.027	0.029	0.959	0.434
	2.00	0.000	0.000	0.013	0.013	0.441	0.200
	3.00	0.000	0.000	0.004	0.004	0.144	0.064
	1.00	0.999	0.138	0.073	0.073	2.244	0.817
	1.25	0.911	0.000	0.044	0.043	1.350	0.486
200	1.50	0.175	0.000	0.028	0.028	0.849	0.308
	2.00	0.000	0.000	0.013	0.013	0.398	0.145
	3.00	0.000	0.000	0.004	0.004	0.125	0.046
	1.00	0.999	0.000	0.074	0.073	1.656	0.538
	1.25	0.447	0.000	0.044	0.044	0.984	0.319
400	1.50	0.000	0.000	0.027	0.028	0.609	0.202
	2.00	0.000	0.000	0.013	0.013	0.285	0.092
	3.00	0.000	0.000	0.004	0.004	0.090	0.030

Table B.4.: Simulation Results for Voluntary Variable Contribution, Selfish User Distribution

		Avg. Sys. Availability		Avg. Contribution		Ratio Prov. / Req.	
Number Users	Relative Price	Worst Case	Average Case	Worst Case	Average Case	Worst Case	Average Case
	1.00	0.650	0.593	0.176	0.168	1.512	1.313
	1.25	0.403	0.376	0.118	0.114	0.933	0.867
10	1.50	0.306	0.238	0.092	0.089	0.778	0.681
	2.00	0.134	0.106	0.061	0.056	0.521	0.462
	3.00	0.025	0.015	0.040	0.040	0.334	0.313
	1.00	0.934	0.902	0.173	0.174	2.769	2.269
	1.25	0.818	0.725	0.117	0.113	1.835	1.486
20	1.50	0.639	0.558	0.087	0.089	1.337	1.164
	2.00	0.454	0.349	0.064	0.064	0.999	0.859
	3.00	0.139	0.069	0.038	0.039	0.594	0.502
	1.00	1.000	0.997	0.175	0.176	5.169	3.002
	1.25	0.997	0.953	0.111	0.111	3.368	1.962
50	1.50	0.988	0.896	0.092	0.090	2.721	1.638
	2.00	0.927	0.576	0.064	0.064	1.938	1.108
	3.00	0.639	0.117	0.040	0.039	1.172	0.690
	1.00	1.000	1.000	0.176	0.177	6.154	2.747
	1.25	1.000	0.974	0.114	0.113	3.993	1.736
100	1.50	1.000	0.880	0.090	0.089	3.212	1.390
	2.00	0.994	0.435	0.063	0.063	2.229	0.971
	3.00	0.864	0.017	0.039	0.040	1.385	0.619
	1.00	1.000	1.000	0.176	0.172	5.490	1.915
	1.25	1.000	0.890	0.115	0.112	3.549	1.243
200	1.50	1.000	0.482	0.091	0.090	2.821	0.999
	2.00	0.998	0.007	0.063	0.063	1.928	0.703
	3.00	0.798	0.000	0.040	0.038	1.207	0.426
	1.00	1.000	0.983	0.175	0.176	3.853	1.277
	1.25	1.000	0.040	0.113	0.114	2.495	0.840
400	1.50	1.000	0.000	0.089	0.090	1.996	0.660
	2.00	0.992	0.000	0.063	0.063	1.398	0.460
	3.00	0.162	0.000	0.040	0.039	0.886	0.288

Appendix C.

Extended Results for Preference-based Matching

Example for Preference Encoding and Genetic Operators of the Genetic Algorithm

Example: Encoding, Crossover Operator, and Mutation Operator
Chromosome 1: $(\langle i_2, j_1\rangle, \langle i_1, j_3\rangle, \langle i_4, j_2\rangle, \langle i_5, j_5\rangle, \langle i_3, \emptyset\rangle, \langle \emptyset, j_4\rangle)$
Chromosome 2: $(\langle i_2, j_3\rangle, \langle i_1, j_1\rangle, \langle i_4, j_5\rangle, \langle i_5, j_2\rangle, \langle i_3, \emptyset\rangle, \langle \emptyset, j_4\rangle)$

After cycle crossover starting with the first gene:
New Chromosome 1: $(\langle i_2, j_1\rangle, \langle i_1, j_3\rangle, \langle i_4, j_5\rangle, \langle i_5, j_2\rangle, \langle i_3, \emptyset\rangle, \langle \emptyset, j_4\rangle)$
New Chromosome 2: $(\langle i_2, j_3\rangle, \langle i_1, j_1\rangle, \langle i_4, j_2\rangle, \langle i_5, j_5\rangle, \langle i_3, \emptyset\rangle, \langle \emptyset, j_4\rangle)$

Mutation operator, example for selecting two matched pairs and switching two users:
$\langle i_2, j_1\rangle, \langle i_1, j_3\rangle \rightarrow \langle i_2, j_3\rangle, \langle i_1, j_1\rangle$

Mutation operator, example for selecting a mutation cycle:
$\langle \emptyset, j_4\rangle, \langle i_1, j_3\rangle, \langle i_3, \emptyset\rangle \rightarrow \langle i_1, j_4\rangle, \langle i_3, j_3\rangle$

Extended Result Tables for Preference-based Matching

Size	MGS	PM	DA (Best-Worst)	WO (Best-Worst)	GA-MIXED (EW)	TA	GATA-DA	GATA-MIXED
10x10	2	S	0.00 (0.00,0.00)	0.00 (0.00,0.00)	0.00 (0.00)	0.00	0.00	0.00
		W	2.83 (2.74,2.91)	2.65 (2.58,2.74)	2.53 (2.61)	0.00	2.55	2.54
		F	0.73 (0.67,0.80)	0.44 (0.41,0.53)	0.43 (0.16)	0.00	0.44	0.41
	5	S	0.00 (0.00,0.00)	0.00 (0.00,0.00)	0.00 (0.00)	0.00	0.00	0.00
		W	2.27 (1.97,2.61)	2.10 (1.79,2.52)	1.74 (1.82)	0.00	1.75	1.75
		F	0.63 (0.42,0.92)	0.40 (0.29,0.52)	0.28 (0.07)	0.00	0.30	0.30
	10	S	0.00 (0.00,0.00)	0.00 (0.00,0.00)	0.00 (0.00)	0.00	0.00	0.00
		W	1.67 (1.22,2.27)	1.50 (1.17,2.06)	1.14 (1.16)	0.00	1.14	1.14
		F	0.40 (0.12,0.88)	0.26 (0.10,0.45)	0.08 (0.04)	0.00	0.08	0.08
20x20	2	S	0.00 (0.00,0.00)	0.00 (0.00,0.00)	0.00 (0.00)	0.00	0.00	0.00
		W	4.27 (4.15,4.40)	3.92 (3.82,4.01)	3.79 (3.88)	0.00	3.85	3.79
		F	1.42 (1.24,1.61)	0.61 (0.60,0.60)	0.58 (0.21)	0.00	0.74	0.57
	5	S	0.00 (0.00,0.00)	0.00 (0.00,0.00)	0.00 (0.00)	0.00	0.00	0.00
		W	3.59 (3.11,4.23)	3.18 (2.77,3.69)	2.73 (2.84)	0.00	2.81	2.80
		F	1.36 (0.78,2.28)	0.57 (0.38,0.74)	0.37 (0.07)	0.00	0.48	0.47
	10	S	0.00 (0.00,0.00)	0.00 (0.00,0.00)	0.00 (0.00)	0.00	0.00	0.00
		W	2.84 (2.08,3.82)	2.39 (1.89,3.00)	1.76 (1.86)	0.00	1.84	1.84
		F	1.11 (0.36,2.33)	0.46 (0.33,0.69)	0.25 (0.04)	0.00	0.26	0.26
50x50	2	S	0.00 (0.00,0.00)	0.00 (0.00,0.00)	0.00 (0.00)	0.00	0.00	0.00
		W	7.79 (7.35,8.19)	6.54 (6.40,6.69)	6.39 (6.48)	0.00	6.76	6.48
		F	3.94 (3.11,4.69)	0.85 (0.77,0.94)	0.77 (0.37)	0.00	1.95	0.78
	5	S	0.00 (0.00,0.00)	0.00 (0.00,0.00)	0.00 (0.00)	0.00	0.00	0.00
		W	6.91 (5.76,8.52)	5.67 (5.23,6.18)	5.21 (5.34)	0.00	5.56	5.46
		F	3.71 (1.59,6.32)	0.82 (0.59,1.12)	0.57 (0.06)	0.00	1.33	0.98
	10	S	0.00 (0.00,0.00)	0.00 (0.00,0.00)	0.00 (0.00)	0.00	0.00	0.00
		W	5.91 (4.50,8.06)	4.58 (4.01,5.22)	3.92 (4.07)	0.00	4.29	4.27
		F	3.44 (1.23,6.47)	0.73 (0.53,1.12)	0.45 (0.05)	0.00	0.85	0.81
100x100	2	S	0.00 (0.00,0.00)	0.00 (0.00,0.00)	0.00 (0.00)	0.00	0.00	0.00
		W	12.31 (11.26,13.44)	9.37 (9.18,9.57)	9.18 (9.29)	0.00	10.35	9.36
		F	7.66 (5.95,9.39)	1.01 (0.88,1.05)	0.85 (0.27)	0.00	4.25	1.07
	5	S	0.00 (0.00,0.00)	0.00 (0.00,0.00)	0.00 (0.00)	0.00	0.00	0.00
		W	11.59 (9.35,14.56)	8.60 (8.13,9.10)	8.11 (8.27)	0.00	8.99	8.53
		F	7.66 (3.76,11.89)	0.99 (0.73,1.32)	0.74 (0.08)	0.00	2.79	1.20
	10	S	0.00 (0.00,0.00)	0.00 (0.00,0.00)	0.00 (0.00)	0.00	0.00	0.00
		W	10.30 (7.69,13.99)	7.33 (6.75,7.95)	6.69 (6.86)	0.00	7.63	7.25
		F	7.11 (2.55,12.04)	0.95 (0.59,1.30)	0.57 (0.07)	0.00	2.61	1.05
200x200	2	S	0.00 (0.00,0.00)	0.00 (0.00,0.00)	0.00 (0.00)	0.00	0.00	0.00
		W	20.51 (17.70,23.70)	13.61 (13.34,13.87)	13.34 (13.48)	0.00	16.36	16.31
		F	15.09 (11.01,19.33)	1.15 (0.96,1.15)	0.96 (0.18)	0.00	8.92	8.76
	5	S	0.00 (0.00,0.00)	0.00 (0.00,0.00)	0.00 (0.00)	0.00	0.00	0.00
		W	19.53 (15.17,24.99)	12.66 (12.16,13.17)	12.16 (12.33)	0.00	14.64	14.64
		F	14.93 (8.24,21.88)	1.12 (0.89,1.50)	0.88 (0.11)	0.00	7.29	7.43
	10	S	0.00 (0.00,0.00)	0.00 (0.00,0.00)	0.00 (0.00)	0.00	0.00	0.00
		W	18.10 (13.27,24.10)	11.36 (10.78,11.97)	10.76 (10.95)	0.00	13.15	13.10
		F	14.29 (6.90,21.72)	1.12 (1.01,1.45)	1.00 (0.11)	0.00	6.90	6.69

Table C.1.: Complete Preferences, Welfare Optimization

Size	MGS	PM	DA (Best-Worst)	FE (Best-Worst)	GA-MIXED (EW)	TA	GATA-DA	GATA-MIXED
10x10	2	S	0.00 (0.00,0.00)	0.00 (0.00,0.00)	0.00 (0.00)	0.00	0.00	0.00
		W	2.82 (2.78,2.83)	2.73 (2.75,2.70)	2.76 (2.61)	2.75	2.77	2.77
		F	0.74 (0.59,0.92)	0.42 (0.27,0.57)	0.10 (0.16)	0.25	0.11	0.11
	5	S	0.00 (0.00,0.00)	0.00 (0.00,0.00)	0.00 (0.00)	0.00	0.00	0.00
		W	2.27 (2.17,2.30)	2.19 (2.23,2.42)	2.47 (1.82)	2.41	2.39	2.38
		F	0.64 (0.19,1.14)	0.36 (0.02,1.02)	0.00 (0.07)	0.02	0.00	0.00
	10	S	0.00 (0.00,0.00)	0.00 (0.00,0.00)	0.00 (0.00)	0.00	0.00	0.00
		W	1.68 (1.53,1.33)	1.57 (1.54,1.94)	1.94 (1.16)	1.82	1.95	1.88
		F	0.40 (0.03,0.33)	0.23 (0.00,0.76)	0.00 (0.04)	0.00	0.00	0.00
20x20	2	S	0.00 (0.00,0.00)	0.00 (0.00,0.00)	0.00 (0.00)	0.00	0.00	0.00
		W	4.29 (4.19,4.40)	4.08 (4.06,4.12)	3.98 (3.88)	4.24	4.04	4.02
		F	1.43 (1.13,1.91)	0.58 (0.29,0.92)	0.14 (0.21)	1.15	0.28	0.18
	5	S	0.00 (0.00,0.00)	0.00 (0.00,0.00)	0.00 (0.00)	0.00	0.00	0.00
		W	3.59 (3.29,4.16)	3.35 (3.29,3.85)	3.25 (2.84)	3.54	3.37	3.40
		F	1.33 (0.41,2.79)	0.55 (0.01,2.01)	0.01 (0.07)	0.54	0.03	0.03
	10	S	0.00 (0.00,0.00)	0.00 (0.00,0.00)	0.00 (0.00)	0.00	0.00	0.00
		W	2.82 (2.49,3.01)	2.59 (2.50,3.11)	2.71 (1.86)	3.10	2.72	2.66
		F	1.09 (0.09,1.98)	0.46 (0.00,1.69)	0.00 (0.04)	0.03	0.00	0.00
50x50	2	S	0.00 (0.00,0.00)	0.00 (0.00,0.00)	0.00 (0.00)	0.00	0.00	0.00
		W	7.78 (7.38,7.93)	6.77 (6.71,6.91)	6.55 (6.48)	7.74	6.87	6.65
		F	3.92 (3.03,4.33)	0.62 (0.12,1.40)	0.35 (0.37)	3.73	1.54	0.25
	5	S	0.00 (0.00,0.00)	0.00 (0.00,0.00)	0.00 (0.00)	0.00	0.00	0.00
		W	6.92 (5.97,8.93)	5.93 (5.81,6.91)	5.62 (5.34)	6.91	5.94	5.87
		F	3.71 (1.13,6.95)	0.64 (0.01,3.84)	0.02 (0.06)	3.57	0.52	0.15
	10	S	0.00 (0.00,0.00)	0.00 (0.00,0.00)	0.00 (0.00)	0.00	0.00	0.00
		W	5.94 (4.77,9.31)	4.87 (4.77,5.96)	4.59 (4.07)	5.82	4.92	4.88
		F	3.47 (0.60,8.26)	0.60 (0.01,3.69)	0.01 (0.05)	2.77	0.14	0.04
100x100	2	S	0.00 (0.00,0.00)	0.00 (0.00,0.00)	0.00 (0.00)	0.00	0.00	0.00
		W	12.26 (11.26,12.68)	9.58 (9.54,9.88)	9.36 (9.29)	12.38	10.48	9.53
		F	7.58 (5.78,8.34)	0.50 (0.08,1.81)	0.23 (0.27)	7.80	4.14	0.33
	5	S	0.00 (0.00,0.00)	0.00 (0.00,0.00)	0.00 (0.00)	0.00	0.00	0.00
		W	11.60 (9.36,15.59)	8.84 (8.71,9.97)	8.56 (8.27)	11.33	9.22	8.79
		F	7.66 (3.30,12.96)	0.54 (0.01,4.60)	0.03 (0.08)	7.27	2.61	0.35
	10	S	0.00 (0.00,0.00)	0.00 (0.00,0.00)	0.00 (0.00)	0.00	0.00	0.00
		W	10.30 (7.77,20.30)	7.56 (7.49,8.86)	7.30 (6.86)	10.15	7.90	7.49
		F	7.11 (2.11,19.20)	0.52 (0.01,4.72)	0.02 (0.07)	6.89	1.98	0.25
200x200	2	S	0.00 (0.00,0.00)	0.00 (0.00,0.00)	0.00 (0.00)	0.00	0.00	0.00
		W	20.46 (17.77,20.12)	13.81 (13.77,13.93)	13.60 (13.48)	20.48	16.41	16.33
		F	15.01 (11.00,14.56)	0.88 (0.18,1.67)	0.13 (0.18)	15.01	8.74	8.70
	5	S	0.00 (0.00,0.00)	0.00 (0.00,0.00)	0.00 (0.00)	0.00	0.00	0.00
		W	19.50 (15.14,29.27)	12.87 (12.83,13.10)	12.64 (12.33)	19.53	14.80	14.78
		F	14.90 (8.10,26.51)	0.88 (0.06,2.11)	0.04 (0.11)	14.98	7.42	7.42
	10	S	0.00 (0.00,0.00)	0.00 (0.00,0.00)	0.00 (0.00)	0.00	0.00	0.00
		W	18.02 (13.35,43.24)	11.58 (11.51,11.90)	11.38 (10.95)	17.90	13.27	13.24
		F	14.20 (6.91,42.15)	0.87 (0.06,2.70)	0.03 (0.11)	14.06	6.85	6.68

Table C.2.: Complete Preferences, Fairness Optimization

Size	MGS	PM	DA (Best-Worst)	WO (Best-Worst)	GA-MIXED (EW)	TA	GATA-DA	GATA-MIXED
10x10	2	S	0.00 (0.00,0.00)	0.00 (0.00,0.00)	0.00 (0.00)	0.00	0.00	0.00
		W	3.85 (3.74,3.95)	3.74 (3.67,3.81)	3.64 (3.70)	0.00	3.64	3.64
		F	0.50 (0.44,0.60)	0.38 (0.36,0.38)	0.34 (0.12)	0.00	0.34	0.34
	5	S	0.00 (0.00,0.00)	0.00 (0.00,0.00)	0.00 (0.00)	0.00	0.00	0.00
		W	3.32 (3.05,3.68)	3.22 (3.00,3.60)	2.99 (3.05)	0.00	2.99	2.99
		F	0.36 (0.22,0.62)	0.26 (0.18,0.36)	0.18 (0.06)	0.00	0.18	0.18
	10	S	0.00 (0.00,0.00)	0.00 (0.00,0.00)	0.00 (0.00)	0.00	0.00	0.00
		W	2.98 (2.71,3.42)	2.89 (2.68,3.29)	2.68 (2.69)	0.00	2.68	2.68
		F	0.24 (0.06,0.50)	0.16 (0.06,0.27)	0.05 (0.02)	0.00	0.05	0.05
20x20	2	S	0.00 (0.00,0.00)	0.00 (0.00,0.00)	0.00 (0.00)	0.00	0.00	0.00
		W	6.93 (6.79,7.08)	6.70 (6.62,6.80)	6.58 (6.67)	0.00	6.63	6.58
		F	0.92 (0.73,1.09)	0.41 (0.36,0.46)	0.37 (0.08)	0.00	0.43	0.37
	5	S	0.00 (0.00,0.00)	0.00 (0.00,0.00)	0.00 (0.00)	0.00	0.00	0.00
		W	6.31 (5.89,6.84)	6.08 (5.79,6.49)	5.75 (5.85)	0.00	5.78	5.75
		F	0.73 (0.37,1.30)	0.38 (0.28,0.48)	0.29 (0.03)	0.00	0.29	0.29
	10	S	0.00 (0.00,0.00)	0.00 (0.00,0.00)	0.00 (0.00)	0.00	0.00	0.00
		W	5.73 (5.22,6.43)	5.49 (5.13,5.96)	5.05 (5.12)	0.00	5.08	5.05
		F	0.57 (0.20,1.33)	0.28 (0.16,0.42)	0.12 (0.03)	0.00	0.14	0.12
50x50	2	S	0.00 (0.00,0.00)	0.00 (0.00,0.00)	0.00 (0.00)	0.00	0.00	0.00
		W	14.82 (14.43,15.25)	14.08 (13.92,14.25)	13.91 (14.02)	0.00	14.18	13.91
		F	2.46 (1.79,3.20)	0.62 (0.57,0.64)	0.59 (0.05)	0.00	1.28	0.59
	5	S	0.00 (0.00,0.00)	0.00 (0.00,0.00)	0.00 (0.00)	0.00	0.00	0.00
		W	14.05 (13.26,15.18)	13.33 (12.97,13.75)	12.95 (13.08)	0.00	13.17	12.95
		F	2.23 (0.95,4.04)	0.57 (0.44,0.76)	0.43 (0.03)	0.00	0.86	0.43
	10	S	0.00 (0.00,0.00)	0.00 (0.00,0.00)	0.00 (0.00)	0.00	0.00	0.00
		W	13.16 (12.23,14.53)	12.40 (11.97,12.89)	11.86 (12.00)	0.00	12.06	11.86
		F	1.96 (0.69,3.89)	0.51 (0.36,0.70)	0.29 (0.02)	0.00	0.55	0.29
100x100	2	S	0.00 (0.00,0.00)	0.00 (0.00,0.00)	0.00 (0.00)	0.00	0.00	0.00
		W	27.68 (26.72,28.83)	25.93 (25.71,26.18)	25.73 (25.85)	0.00	26.39	25.73
		F	4.88 (3.17,6.70)	0.68 (0.56,0.77)	0.52 (0.06)	0.00	2.48	0.52
	5	S	0.00 (0.00,0.00)	0.00 (0.00,0.00)	0.00 (0.00)	0.00	0.00	0.00
		W	26.92 (25.49,28.88)	25.14 (24.76,25.56)	24.81 (24.96)	0.00	25.37	24.81
		F	4.85 (2.25,7.75)	0.70 (0.56,0.79)	0.53 (0.04)	0.00	1.94	0.53
	10	S	0.00 (0.00,0.00)	0.00 (0.00,0.00)	0.00 (0.00)	0.00	0.00	0.00
		W	25.68 (24.12,27.81)	23.93 (23.44,24.46)	23.45 (23.64)	0.00	24.04	23.45
		F	4.31 (1.52,7.23)	0.64 (0.51,0.85)	0.44 (0.02)	0.00	1.57	0.44

Table C.3.: Complete and Correlated Preferences, Welfare Optimization

Size	MGS	PM	DA (Best-Worst)	FE (Best-Worst)	GA-MIXED (EW)	TA	GATA-DA	GATA-MIXED
10x10	2	S	0.00 (0.00,0.00)	0.00 (0.00,0.00)	0.00 (0.00)	0.00	0.00	0.00
		W	3.83 (3.76,3.90)	3.81 (3.80,3.77)	3.84 (3.70)	3.83	3.82	3.84
		F	0.50 (0.35,0.66)	0.28 (0.14,0.41)	0.07 (0.12)	0.08	0.08	0.07
	5	S	0.00 (0.00,0.00)	0.00 (0.00,0.00)	0.00 (0.00)	0.00	0.00	0.00
		W	3.34 (3.27,3.58)	3.28 (3.30,3.45)	3.48 (3.05)	3.48	3.45	3.48
		F	0.37 (0.07,0.81)	0.23 (0.01,0.65)	0.00 (0.06)	0.01	0.00	0.00
	10	S	0.00 (0.00,0.00)	0.00 (0.00,0.00)	0.00 (0.00)	0.00	0.00	0.00
		W	2.97 (2.87,3.31)	2.93 (2.92,3.18)	3.12 (2.69)	3.06	3.10	3.12
		F	0.23 (0.01,0.65)	0.15 (0.00,0.50)	0.00 (0.02)	0.00	0.00	0.00
20x20	2	S	0.00 (0.00,0.00)	0.00 (0.00,0.00)	0.00 (0.00)	0.00	0.00	0.00
		W	6.93 (6.84,7.02)	6.82 (6.81,6.80)	6.82 (6.67)	6.86	6.82	6.82
		F	0.90 (0.61,1.22)	0.33 (0.14,0.60)	0.04 (0.08)	0.17	0.11	0.04
	5	S	0.00 (0.00,0.00)	0.00 (0.00,0.00)	0.00 (0.00)	0.00	0.00	0.00
		W	6.31 (6.19,6.73)	6.20 (6.22,6.39)	6.24 (5.85)	6.37	6.22	6.24
		F	0.73 (0.08,1.60)	0.31 (0.00,1.10)	0.00 (0.03)	0.01	0.00	0.00
	10	S	0.00 (0.00,0.00)	0.00 (0.00,0.00)	0.00 (0.00)	0.00	0.00	0.00
		W	5.73 (5.55,6.39)	5.60 (5.61,5.92)	5.84 (5.12)	5.96	5.71	5.84
		F	0.58 (0.02,1.50)	0.25 (0.00,0.95)	0.00 (0.03)	0.00	0.00	0.00
50x50	2	S	0.00 (0.00,0.00)	0.00 (0.00,0.00)	0.00 (0.00)	0.00	0.00	0.00
		W	14.80 (14.47,15.21)	14.27 (14.24,14.44)	14.21 (14.02)	14.70	14.28	14.21
		F	2.43 (1.55,3.28)	0.29 (0.02,1.31)	0.02 (0.05)	1.94	0.83	0.02
	5	S	0.00 (0.00,0.00)	0.00 (0.00,0.00)	0.00 (0.00)	0.00	0.00	0.00
		W	14.05 (13.52,15.08)	13.53 (13.51,14.01)	13.48 (13.08)	14.07	13.54	13.48
		F	2.23 (0.49,4.07)	0.30 (0.00,2.19)	0.00 (0.03)	1.04	0.13	0.00
	10	S	0.00 (0.00,0.00)	0.00 (0.00,0.00)	0.00 (0.00)	0.00	0.00	0.00
		W	13.17 (12.52,14.46)	12.61 (12.55,13.18)	12.62 (12.00)	13.30	12.76	12.62
		F	1.99 (0.25,3.90)	0.29 (0.00,2.15)	0.00 (0.02)	0.13	0.00	0.00
100x100	2	S	0.00 (0.00,0.00)	0.00 (0.00,0.00)	0.00 (0.00)	0.00	0.00	0.00
		W	27.67 (26.74,28.78)	26.19 (26.15,26.53)	26.08 (25.85)	27.49	26.51	26.08
		F	4.87 (2.92,6.70)	0.29 (0.01,1.88)	0.02 (0.06)	4.51	2.24	0.02
	5	S	0.00 (0.00,0.00)	0.00 (0.00,0.00)	0.00 (0.00)	0.00	0.00	0.00
		W	26.91 (25.59,28.87)	25.42 (25.36,25.88)	25.34 (24.96)	26.81	25.54	25.34
		F	4.85 (1.88,7.85)	0.28 (0.01,2.52)	0.01 (0.04)	4.38	1.49	0.01
	10	S	0.00 (0.00,0.00)	0.00 (0.00,0.00)	0.00 (0.00)	0.00	0.00	0.00
		W	25.65 (24.27,27.83)	24.22 (24.23,24.68)	24.12 (23.64)	25.55	24.42	24.12
		F	4.26 (1.16,7.35)	0.26 (0.01,2.21)	0.00 (0.02)	2.88	0.78	0.00

Table C.4.: Complete and Correlated Preferences, Fairness Optimization

Size	MGS	PD	Opt	DA	RSMA	GS-Modified	Király	Mc-Dermid	Shift	GA	TA	GATA	GATA-MIXED
10x10	2	0.5	9.71	9.32	9.37	9.48	9.58	9.39	9.57	9.58	9.61	9.58	9.66
		0.7	8.80	8.32	8.56	8.51	8.64	8.52	8.69	8.68	8.69	8.67	8.74
		0.9	5.48	5.27	5.44	5.42	5.48	5.46	5.46	5.48	5.48	5.46	5.48
		0.95	3.70	3.64	3.68	3.70	3.70	3.66	3.69	3.69	3.70	3.70	3.70
	5	0.5	9.93	9.24	9.74	9.67	9.84	9.65	9.83	9.86	9.87	9.89	9.90
		0.7	9.33	8.34	9.00	8.88	9.17	8.97	9.09	9.10	9.17	9.11	9.25
		0.9	5.62	5.34	5.54	5.54	5.59	5.56	5.58	5.59	5.56	5.58	5.61
		0.95	3.75	3.68	3.74	3.74	3.75	3.75	3.74	3.75	3.74	3.73	3.75
	10	0.5	10.00	9.37	9.98	9.91	9.98	9.97	9.99	10.00	10.00	10.00	10.00
		0.7	9.35	8.36	9.18	8.98	9.28	9.20	9.21	9.27	9.27	9.23	9.30
		0.9	5.77	5.44	5.75	5.73	5.76	5.74	5.76	5.76	5.76	5.76	5.77
		0.95	3.43	3.34	3.40	3.43	3.43	3.42	3.43	3.43	3.43	3.42	3.43
20x20	2	0.5	19.85	19.57	19.66	19.61	19.74	19.57	19.78	19.75	19.67	19.75	19.82
		0.7	19.36	18.39	18.61	18.70	18.83	18.50	18.83	18.88	18.76	18.84	19.05
		0.9	14.88	14.01	14.38	14.46	14.73	14.44	14.49	14.71	14.56	14.60	14.80
		0.95	10.42	10.04	10.28	10.34	10.38	10.19	10.34	10.41	10.33	10.34	10.40
	5	0.5	20.00	19.56	19.80	19.86	19.98	19.78	19.98	20.00	19.97	20.00	20.00
		0.7	19.97	18.41	19.34	19.21	19.58	19.34	19.49	19.67	19.65	19.66	19.76
		0.9	15.81	14.22	15.28	15.26	15.64	15.33	15.42	15.59	15.38	15.52	15.72
		0.95	11.04	10.44	10.91	10.95	11.01	10.93	11.00	10.99	10.94	10.99	11.04
	10	0.5	20.00	19.55	19.97	19.95	20.00	19.93	20.00	19.99	19.99	19.99	20.00
		0.7	19.94	18.55	19.87	19.62	19.92	19.86	19.88	19.93	19.87	19.93	19.94
		0.9	15.82	14.21	15.52	15.24	15.69	15.48	15.53	15.59	15.55	15.58	15.77
		0.95	11.09	10.44	11.06	10.99	11.04	11.04	11.03	11.06	11.03	11.04	11.09
50x50	2	0.5	50.00	49.94	49.95	49.90	49.94	49.94	50.00	50.00	49.95	50.00	50.00
		0.7	49.94	49.28	49.44	49.37	49.52	49.28	49.68	49.76	49.44	49.75	49.80
		0.9	46.87	44.27	44.91	44.99	45.63	44.96	45.21	45.64	45.14	45.56	45.91
		0.95	40.61	37.96	39.16	39.31	39.85	39.13	39.02	39.83	39.34	39.54	40.11
	5	0.5	50.00	49.91	49.96	49.97	50.00	49.95	50.00	50.00	49.98	50.00	50.00
		0.7	50.00	49.21	49.50	49.56	49.93	49.61	49.96	50.00	49.67	50.00	49.99
		0.9	49.35	44.22	46.83	46.42	47.90	46.96	46.59	47.99	47.69	48.03	48.10
		0.95	42.84	37.70	41.00	40.52	41.69	41.05	40.13	41.70	41.53	41.67	41.97
	10	0.5	50.00	49.91	50.00	50.00	50.00	49.98	50.00	50.00	50.00	50.00	50.00
		0.7	50.00	49.26	49.98	49.88	50.00	49.92	50.00	50.00	49.99	50.00	50.00
		0.9	49.60	44.38	48.80	47.59	49.00	48.81	47.21	48.84	49.10	49.04	49.24
		0.95	43.20	37.78	41.98	40.86	42.49	42.14	40.44	42.24	42.48	42.38	42.78
100x100	2	0.5	100.00	100.00	99.99	99.99	100.00	99.99	100.00	100.00	99.99	100.00	100.00
		0.7	100.00	99.74	99.78	99.86	99.91	99.81	99.96	99.96	99.76	99.96	99.99
		0.9	99.04	95.59	96.16	96.11	96.89	96.18	96.67	97.10	96.36	97.07	97.31
		0.95	94.04	88.36	89.84	90.06	91.17	89.70	89.67	91.09	90.44	90.80	91.47
	5	0.5	100.00	99.99	100.00	100.00	100.00	100.00	100.00	100.00	100.00	100.00	100.00
		0.7	100.00	99.80	99.92	99.87	99.99	99.92	100.00	100.00	99.94	100.00	100.00
		0.9	99.98	95.77	97.10	97.52	98.68	97.74	98.07	98.83	98.72	98.96	99.02
		0.95	98.44	88.08	93.14	92.74	95.36	93.81	91.32	95.24	95.51	95.54	95.74
	10	0.5	100.00	100.00	100.00	100.00	100.00	100.00	100.00	100.00	100.00	100.00	100.00
		0.7	100.00	99.79	100.00	99.94	100.00	99.99	100.00	100.00	100.00	100.00	100.00
		0.9	99.98	95.84	99.52	98.54	99.78	99.63	98.53	99.74	99.79	99.86	99.87
		0.95	98.89	88.11	97.20	94.15	97.56	97.26	92.39	97.07	98.07	97.74	98.10

Table C.5.: Incomplete Preferences, 10x10 - 100x100 Users

Size	MGS	PD	Opt	DA	RSMA	GS-Modified	Király	Mc-Dermid	Shift	GA	TA	GATA	GATA-MIXED
200x200	2	0.5	-	200.00	200.00	200.00	200.00	200.00	200.00	200.00	200.00	200.00	200.00
		0.7	-	199.98	199.98	199.98	199.99	199.99	200.00	200.00	199.98	200.00	200.00
		0.9	-	197.88	198.06	198.07	198.50	198.23	198.59	199.07	197.99	199.07	199.17
		0.95	-	191.40	192.60	192.43	193.87	192.50	192.78	194.09	192.92	193.93	194.27
	5	0.5	-	200.00	200.00	200.00	200.00	200.00	200.00	200.00	200.00	200.00	200.00
		0.7	-	199.99	199.99	199.99	199.99	199.98	200.00	200.00	199.99	200.00	200.00
		0.9	-	197.99	198.73	198.55	199.52	198.76	199.46	199.67	199.26	199.71	199.86
		0.95	-	191.42	194.13	194.89	197.85	195.40	194.67	197.44	197.56	197.65	197.94
	10	0.5	-	200.00	200.00	200.00	200.00	200.00	200.00	200.00	200.00	200.00	200.00
		0.7	-	199.98	200.00	199.99	200.00	199.99	200.00	200.00	199.99	200.00	200.00
		0.9	-	197.88	199.72	199.16	199.87	199.80	199.87	199.90	199.95	199.93	199.95
		0.95	-	191.33	199.00	196.60	199.50	199.00	195.35	199.25	199.63	199.54	199.65
500x500	2	0.5	-	500.00	500.00	500.00	500.00	500.00	500.00	500.00	500.00	500.00	500.00
		0.7	-	500.00	500.00	500.00	500.00	500.00	500.00	500.00	500.00	500.00	500.00
		0.9	-	499.68	499.78	499.66	499.75	499.75	499.94	499.99	499.69	499.99	499.99
		0.95	-	496.81	497.28	496.90	497.84	497.13	497.72	498.67	497.06	498.67	498.73
	5	0.5	-	500.00	500.00	500.00	500.00	500.00	500.00	500.00	500.00	500.00	500.00
		0.7	-	500.00	500.00	500.00	500.00	500.00	500.00	500.00	500.00	500.00	500.00
		0.9	-	499.69	499.88	499.73	499.97	499.89	500.00	500.00	499.80	500.00	500.00
		0.95	-	496.73	498.32	497.50	499.32	497.97	498.70	499.14	498.36	499.09	499.45
	10	0.5	-	500.00	500.00	500.00	500.00	500.00	500.00	500.00	500.00	500.00	500.00
		0.7	-	500.00	500.00	500.00	500.00	500.00	500.00	500.00	500.00	500.00	500.00
		0.9	-	499.72	499.94	499.83	500.00	499.94	500.00	500.00	499.94	500.00	500.00
		0.95	-	496.80	498.87	498.39	499.94	499.39	499.24	499.94	499.86	499.89	499.95

Table C.6.: Incomplete Preferences, 200x200 - 500x500 Users

Size	MGS	PD	Opt	DA	RSMA	GS-Modified	Király	Mc-Dermid	Shift	GA	TA	GATA	GATA-MIXED
10x50	2	0.5	10.00	10.00	10.00	10.00	10.00	10.00	10.00	10.00	10.00	10.00	10.00
		0.7	10.00	10.00	10.00	10.00	10.00	10.00	10.00	10.00	10.00	10.00	10.00
		0.9	9.88	9.83	9.87	9.87	9.88	9.88	9.87	9.87	9.87	9.87	9.88
		0.95	9.19	9.08	9.17	9.13	9.19	9.14	9.18	9.18	9.18	9.18	9.19
	5	0.5	10.00	10.00	10.00	10.00	10.00	10.00	10.00	10.00	10.00	10.00	10.00
		0.7	10.00	10.00	10.00	10.00	10.00	10.00	10.00	10.00	10.00	10.00	10.00
		0.9	9.95	9.93	9.94	9.95	9.95	9.94	9.95	9.95	9.94	9.95	9.95
		0.95	9.29	9.16	9.28	9.26	9.28	9.27	9.28	9.29	9.28	9.29	9.29
	10	0.5	10.00	10.00	10.00	10.00	10.00	10.00	10.00	10.00	10.00	10.00	10.00
		0.7	10.00	10.00	10.00	10.00	10.00	10.00	10.00	10.00	10.00	10.00	10.00
		0.9	9.97	9.92	9.96	9.97	9.97	9.96	9.97	9.96	9.97	9.96	9.97
		0.95	9.29	9.17	9.28	9.29	9.29	9.27	9.29	9.29	9.29	9.29	9.29
10x100	2	0.5	10.00	10.00	10.00	10.00	10.00	10.00	10.00	10.00	10.00	10.00	10.00
		0.7	10.00	10.00	10.00	10.00	10.00	10.00	10.00	10.00	10.00	10.00	10.00
		0.9	10.00	10.00	10.00	10.00	10.00	10.00	10.00	10.00	10.00	10.00	10.00
		0.95	9.96	9.94	9.96	9.95	9.95	9.95	9.96	9.96	9.96	9.96	9.96
	5	0.5	10.00	10.00	10.00	10.00	10.00	10.00	10.00	10.00	10.00	10.00	10.00
		0.7	10.00	10.00	10.00	10.00	10.00	10.00	10.00	10.00	10.00	10.00	10.00
		0.9	10.00	10.00	10.00	10.00	10.00	10.00	10.00	10.00	10.00	10.00	10.00
		0.95	9.94	9.93	9.94	9.94	9.94	9.94	9.94	9.94	9.94	9.94	9.94
	10	0.5	10.00	10.00	10.00	10.00	10.00	10.00	10.00	10.00	10.00	10.00	10.00
		0.7	10.00	10.00	10.00	10.00	10.00	10.00	10.00	10.00	10.00	10.00	10.00
		0.9	10.00	10.00	10.00	10.00	10.00	10.00	10.00	10.00	10.00	10.00	10.00
		0.95	9.91	9.90	9.91	9.91	9.91	9.91	9.91	9.91	9.91	9.91	9.91
20x50	2	0.5	20.00	20.00	20.00	20.00	20.00	20.00	20.00	20.00	20.00	20.00	20.00
		0.7	20.00	20.00	20.00	20.00	20.00	20.00	20.00	20.00	20.00	20.00	20.00
		0.9	19.87	19.71	19.83	19.80	19.83	19.86	19.83	19.87	19.86	19.87	19.87
		0.95	17.78	17.31	17.60	17.61	17.76	17.59	17.71	17.75	17.64	17.75	17.78
	5	0.5	20.00	20.00	20.00	20.00	20.00	20.00	20.00	20.00	20.00	20.00	20.00
		0.7	20.00	20.00	20.00	20.00	20.00	20.00	20.00	20.00	20.00	20.00	20.00
		0.9	19.87	19.64	19.85	19.86	19.86	19.83	19.87	19.87	19.87	19.87	19.87
		0.95	18.23	17.56	18.14	18.05	18.19	18.09	18.17	18.21	18.16	18.21	18.22
	10	0.5	20.00	20.00	20.00	20.00	20.00	20.00	20.00	20.00	20.00	20.00	20.00
		0.7	20.00	20.00	20.00	20.00	20.00	20.00	20.00	20.00	20.00	20.00	20.00
		0.9	19.84	19.59	19.82	19.84	19.84	19.83	19.84	19.84	19.83	19.84	19.84
		0.95	18.08	17.34	18.01	17.93	18.06	18.00	18.04	18.07	18.03	18.07	18.08
20x100	2	0.5	20.00	20.00	20.00	20.00	20.00	20.00	20.00	20.00	20.00	20.00	20.00
		0.7	20.00	20.00	20.00	20.00	20.00	20.00	20.00	20.00	20.00	20.00	20.00
		0.9	20.00	20.00	20.00	20.00	20.00	20.00	20.00	20.00	20.00	20.00	20.00
		0.95	19.88	19.85	19.86	19.87	19.88	19.85	19.87	19.88	19.86	19.88	19.88
	5	0.5	20.00	20.00	20.00	20.00	20.00	20.00	20.00	20.00	20.00	20.00	20.00
		0.7	20.00	20.00	20.00	20.00	20.00	20.00	20.00	20.00	20.00	20.00	20.00
		0.9	20.00	20.00	20.00	20.00	20.00	20.00	20.00	20.00	20.00	20.00	20.00
		0.95	19.88	19.81	19.88	19.87	19.88	19.88	19.88	19.88	19.88	19.88	19.88
	10	0.5	20.00	20.00	20.00	20.00	20.00	20.00	20.00	20.00	20.00	20.00	20.00
		0.7	20.00	20.00	20.00	20.00	20.00	20.00	20.00	20.00	20.00	20.00	20.00
		0.9	20.00	20.00	20.00	20.00	20.00	20.00	20.00	20.00	20.00	20.00	20.00
		0.95	19.91	19.87	19.91	19.91	19.91	19.90	19.91	19.91	19.91	19.91	19.91

Table C.7.: Incomplete Preferences, Asymmetric Sides, 10x50 - 20x100 Users

Size	MGS	PD	Opt	DA	RSMA	GS-Modified	Király	Mc-Dermid	Shift	GA	TA	GATA	GATA-MIXED
50x10	2	0.5	10.00	10.00	10.00	10.00	10.00	10.00	10.00	10.00	10.00	10.00	10.00
		0.7	10.00	10.00	10.00	10.00	10.00	10.00	10.00	10.00	10.00	10.00	10.00
		0.9	9.89	9.87	9.87	9.89	9.89	9.88	9.89	9.89	9.87	9.89	9.89
		0.95	9.24	9.13	9.18	9.21	9.23	9.17	9.24	9.23	9.18	9.22	9.24
	5	0.5	10.00	10.00	10.00	10.00	10.00	10.00	10.00	10.00	10.00	10.00	10.00
		0.7	10.00	10.00	10.00	10.00	10.00	10.00	10.00	10.00	10.00	10.00	10.00
		0.9	9.94	9.90	9.93	9.93	9.94	9.94	9.94	9.94	9.93	9.94	9.94
		0.95	9.09	8.98	9.09	9.09	9.09	9.09	9.09	9.09	9.09	9.09	9.09
	10	0.5	10.00	10.00	10.00	10.00	10.00	10.00	10.00	10.00	10.00	10.00	10.00
		0.7	10.00	10.00	10.00	10.00	10.00	10.00	10.00	10.00	10.00	10.00	10.00
		0.9	9.95	9.91	9.95	9.94	9.95	9.95	9.95	9.95	9.95	9.95	9.95
		0.95	9.29	9.15	9.28	9.29	9.29	9.28	9.29	9.29	9.29	9.29	9.29
50x100	2	0.5	50.00	50.00	50.00	50.00	50.00	50.00	50.00	50.00	50.00	50.00	50.00
		0.7	50.00	50.00	50.00	50.00	50.00	50.00	50.00	50.00	50.00	50.00	50.00
		0.9	50.00	49.97	50.00	50.00	50.00	50.00	50.00	50.00	50.00	50.00	50.00
		0.95	49.45	48.82	49.21	49.12	49.34	49.32	49.26	49.43	49.29	49.43	49.45
	5	0.5	50.00	50.00	50.00	50.00	50.00	50.00	50.00	50.00	50.00	50.00	50.00
		0.7	50.00	50.00	50.00	50.00	50.00	50.00	50.00	50.00	50.00	50.00	50.00
		0.9	50.00	49.98	50.00	50.00	50.00	50.00	50.00	50.00	50.00	50.00	50.00
		0.95	49.65	48.81	49.56	49.51	49.63	49.59	49.63	49.65	49.62	49.65	49.65
	10	0.5	50.00	50.00	50.00	50.00	50.00	50.00	50.00	50.00	50.00	50.00	50.00
		0.7	50.00	50.00	50.00	50.00	50.00	50.00	50.00	50.00	50.00	50.00	50.00
		0.9	50.00	49.99	50.00	50.00	50.00	50.00	50.00	50.00	50.00	50.00	50.00
		0.95	49.65	48.80	49.60	49.59	49.63	49.59	49.65	49.65	49.63	49.65	49.65

Table C.8.: Incomplete Preferences, Asymmetric Sides, 50x10 and 50x100 Users

Size	MGS	PD	Opt	DA	RSMA	GS-Modified	Király	Mc-Dermid	Shift	GA	TA	GATA	GATA-MIXED
10x10	2	0.5	9.76	9.23	9.41	9.44	9.52	9.43	9.61	9.61	9.63	9.57	9.70
		0.7	8.76	8.24	8.38	8.52	8.60	8.43	8.59	8.63	8.65	8.64	8.74
		0.9	5.41	5.29	5.33	5.37	5.41	5.37	5.41	5.41	5.40	5.39	5.41
		0.95	3.58	3.55	3.56	3.58	3.58	3.55	3.58	3.58	3.58	3.58	3.58
	5	0.5	9.99	9.29	9.79	9.71	9.93	9.79	9.94	9.93	9.93	9.95	9.97
		0.7	9.08	8.19	8.81	8.68	8.90	8.75	8.90	8.93	8.98	8.91	9.03
		0.9	5.62	5.35	5.58	5.57	5.61	5.50	5.62	5.61	5.62	5.58	5.62
		0.95	3.65	3.55	3.60	3.64	3.65	3.63	3.64	3.65	3.65	3.65	3.65
	10	0.5	9.97	9.28	9.85	9.77	9.94	9.85	9.97	9.95	9.95	9.93	9.95
		0.7	9.18	8.32	8.93	8.78	9.06	8.96	9.12	9.05	9.10	9.04	9.15
		0.9	5.74	5.47	5.66	5.67	5.72	5.65	5.72	5.73	5.73	5.73	5.73
		0.95	3.44	3.39	3.42	3.44	3.44	3.43	3.44	3.44	3.44	3.44	3.44
20x20	2	0.5	19.96	19.48	19.51	19.58	19.72	19.60	19.82	19.77	19.67	19.75	19.87
		0.7	19.34	18.33	18.55	18.54	18.75	18.52	18.84	18.90	18.78	18.81	19.00
		0.9	15.00	14.29	14.63	14.72	14.89	14.58	14.82	14.88	14.75	14.85	14.96
		0.95	11.12	10.68	10.90	10.94	11.06	10.95	11.04	11.09	10.98	10.98	11.11
	5	0.5	20.00	19.42	19.80	19.84	19.95	19.78	19.97	19.98	19.94	19.98	20.00
		0.7	19.87	18.30	19.29	19.17	19.58	19.14	19.45	19.67	19.53	19.65	19.77
		0.9	15.65	14.36	15.06	15.03	15.36	15.17	15.29	15.39	15.15	15.28	15.54
		0.95	10.83	10.29	10.65	10.68	10.80	10.67	10.74	10.82	10.74	10.77	10.83
	10	0.5	20.00	19.42	20.00	19.95	19.99	19.99	20.00	20.00	20.00	20.00	20.00
		0.7	19.92	18.33	19.61	19.39	19.68	19.56	19.70	19.78	19.72	19.76	19.87
		0.9	15.61	14.06	14.99	15.04	15.41	15.10	15.14	15.33	15.16	15.28	15.52
		0.95	10.92	10.38	10.71	10.75	10.87	10.69	10.83	10.90	10.83	10.86	10.90
50x50	2	0.5	50.00	49.83	49.91	49.85	49.89	49.84	49.98	49.99	49.89	49.99	49.99
		0.7	49.93	49.01	49.25	49.14	49.41	49.15	49.53	49.60	49.27	49.57	49.69
		0.9	46.85	43.94	44.67	44.66	45.24	44.62	44.98	45.48	44.87	45.34	45.70
		0.95	39.62	37.43	38.26	38.54	38.99	38.29	38.43	39.03	38.36	38.80	39.24
	5	0.5	50.00	49.81	49.92	49.92	49.96	49.94	50.00	50.00	49.93	50.00	50.00
		0.7	50.00	48.96	49.54	49.46	49.84	49.48	49.92	49.96	49.73	49.95	49.98
		0.9	48.87	43.80	46.43	46.03	47.37	46.58	46.04	47.22	47.13	47.27	47.65
		0.95	41.56	37.49	39.69	39.65	40.58	39.50	39.45	40.63	40.05	40.36	40.94
	10	0.5	50.00	49.79	50.00	49.98	50.00	49.98	50.00	50.00	50.00	50.00	50.00
		0.7	50.00	48.99	49.94	49.83	50.00	49.96	50.00	50.00	49.99	50.00	50.00
		0.9	49.19	43.89	47.87	46.53	48.14	47.95	46.58	48.11	48.13	48.22	48.54
		0.95	41.63	37.17	39.74	39.60	40.74	40.06	39.47	40.70	40.19	40.58	41.14
100x100	2	0.5	100.00	99.95	99.95	99.96	99.99	99.94	99.99	99.99	99.94	99.99	100.00
		0.7	99.99	99.61	99.60	99.61	99.71	99.68	99.95	99.96	99.59	99.96	99.97
		0.9	99.15	94.88	95.40	95.71	96.29	95.52	96.10	96.66	95.57	96.51	96.87
		0.95	93.26	87.08	88.55	88.70	89.93	88.46	88.46	90.10	88.98	89.74	90.47
	5	0.5	100.00	99.98	99.98	99.99	100.00	100.00	100.00	100.00	99.97	100.00	100.00
		0.7	100.00	99.60	99.85	99.77	99.97	99.83	100.00	100.00	99.89	100.00	100.00
		0.9	99.94	94.72	96.98	97.02	98.51	97.42	97.06	98.57	98.31	98.61	98.74
		0.95	97.71	87.08	92.10	91.93	94.35	92.72	90.35	93.86	93.94	93.91	94.75
	10	0.5	100.00	99.97	100.00	99.99	100.00	100.00	100.00	100.00	100.00	100.00	100.00
		0.7	100.00	99.58	99.97	99.89	99.99	99.98	100.00	100.00	100.00	100.00	100.00
		0.9	99.99	94.90	99.41	98.16	99.68	99.43	97.92	99.64	99.71	99.69	99.82
		0.95	98.26	87.06	95.02	92.72	95.92	94.93	91.05	95.38	95.85	95.62	96.41

Table C.9.: Incomplete and Correlated Preferences

Appendix D.

Extended Results for Preference Manipulation

Pseudocode of Probe-and-Adjust Learning

Algorithm 6: Pseudocode of Probe and Adjust

```
Data: True Preference Profile
Result: Manipulated Preference Profile
begin
    Create initial neighborhood from true preference profile;
    for j ← 1to explorationRounds do
        randomly select preferences from neighborhood;
        submit these preferences to the matching algorithm, and save
        outcome;
    end
    for i ← 1to steps do
        create neighborhood based on current preference profile;
        for j ← 1to explorationRounds do
            randomly select preferences from neighborhood;
            submit these preferences to the matching algorithm, and save
            outcome;
        end
        select best performing preferences as new current profile;
    end
    return current best (manipulated) preference profile;
end
```

Table D.1.: Absolute Preference Gain for Truncation Strategies, 1-10 Manipulating Users, 20x20 Users

Number Man. Users	Truncation Degree	DA	RSMA	Király	Shift	GATA
1	0.95	-8.83	-6.52	-8.06	-7.19	-8.52
	0.9	-4.59	-2.68	-3.43	-2.77	-4.10
	0.8	-0.23	1.22	0.53	1.20	-0.05
	0.7	0.43	2.05	1.15	1.38	0.42
	0.6	0.57	2.06	1.02	1.36	0.52
	0.5	0.75	1.80	0.91	1.29	0.53
	0.4	0.49	1.33	0.72	1.00	0.24
	0.3	0.51	1.21	0.52	0.65	0.22
	0.2	0.37	0.90	0.38	0.58	0.14
	0.1	0.14	0.47	0.14	0.18	0.05
2	0.95	-7.86	-6.40	-6.81	-7.12	-8.40
	0.9	-4.78	-3.31	-3.44	-3.65	-4.92
	0.8	0.23	1.12	0.86	0.89	-0.51
	0.7	1.53	2.20	1.84	1.57	0.32
	0.6	1.55	2.20	1.66	1.40	0.28
	0.5	1.52	1.92	1.59	1.25	0.35
	0.4	1.09	1.30	1.19	0.88	0.18
	0.3	0.81	1.10	0.84	0.67	0.16
	0.2	0.44	0.49	0.50	0.35	0.00
	0.1	0.23	0.21	0.26	0.13	-0.04
4	0.95	-6.98	-6.03	-6.13	-6.30	-7.68
	0.9	-2.95	-2.02	-1.94	-2.18	-3.77
	0.8	0.51	1.65	1.21	0.86	-0.57
	0.7	1.60	2.38	1.73	1.58	0.23
	0.6	1.58	2.33	1.67	1.40	0.23
	0.5	1.47	2.05	1.48	1.31	0.34
	0.4	1.08	1.47	0.98	0.94	0.17
	0.3	0.83	1.31	0.75	0.66	0.14
	0.2	0.43	0.60	0.30	0.41	-0.13
	0.1	0.12	0.31	0.06	0.18	-0.05
6	0.95	-6.05	-4.85	-4.94	-5.66	-6.83
	0.9	-2.21	-0.75	-1.27	-1.64	-3.13
	0.8	0.61	1.89	1.33	0.82	-0.23
	0.7	1.66	2.84	1.97	1.52	0.29
	0.6	1.63	2.63	1.89	1.37	0.42
	0.5	1.50	2.35	1.59	1.15	0.34
	0.4	1.04	1.79	1.18	0.80	0.14
	0.3	0.81	1.44	0.82	0.57	0.01
	0.2	0.53	0.89	0.45	0.33	-0.06
	0.1	0.22	0.45	0.21	0.06	-0.05
8	0.95	-5.29	-3.98	-4.62	-5.21	-6.27
	0.9	-1.74	-0.44	-0.94	-1.54	-2.70
	0.8	0.86	2.16	1.64	0.99	-0.16
	0.7	1.80	2.85	2.15	1.55	0.62
	0.6	1.82	2.73	2.10	1.44	0.51
	0.5	1.59	2.45	1.75	1.23	0.36
	0.4	1.27	1.89	1.35	0.93	0.23
	0.3	1.01	1.49	1.03	0.70	0.12
	0.2	0.61	0.91	0.67	0.45	0.16
	0.1	0.16	0.45	0.25	0.12	0.13
10	0.95	-4.30	-3.25	-3.68	-4.37	-5.46
	0.9	-1.03	-0.04	-0.51	-1.26	-2.43
	0.8	1.22	2.21	1.68	1.23	-0.06
	0.7	2.13	3.02	2.39	1.92	0.62
	0.6	2.15	2.94	2.30	1.73	0.67
	0.5	1.98	2.64	2.00	1.40	0.45

Table D.2.: Absolute Preference Gain for Truncation Strategies, 10-20 Manipulating Users, 20x20 Users

Number Man. Users	Truncation Degree	DA	RSMA	Király	Shift	GATA
10	0.4	1.76	2.18	1.60	1.07	0.24
	0.3	1.38	1.85	1.22	0.85	0.09
	0.2	0.91	1.30	0.84	0.57	0.11
	0.1	0.47	0.49	0.31	0.19	0.10
12	0.95	-3.82	-2.87	-3.28	-4.06	-5.17
	0.9	-0.85	0.23	-0.17	-0.93	-1.99
	0.8	1.46	2.42	1.97	1.35	0.01
	0.7	2.26	3.20	2.61	1.89	0.84
	0.6	2.26	3.10	2.52	1.75	0.78
	0.5	2.04	2.73	2.06	1.46	0.44
	0.4	1.69	2.30	1.65	1.13	0.35
	0.3	1.41	1.94	1.26	0.87	0.22
	0.2	0.97	1.39	0.89	0.59	0.06
	0.1	0.35	0.58	0.27	0.19	0.04
14	0.95	-3.96	-2.72	-3.35	-3.96	-5.17
	0.9	-0.74	0.44	0.04	-0.62	-2.02
	0.8	1.29	2.41	1.90	1.35	0.04
	0.7	2.08	3.08	2.43	1.96	0.59
	0.6	2.12	3.01	2.42	1.77	0.67
	0.5	1.91	2.74	2.08	1.49	0.38
	0.4	1.54	2.30	1.64	1.20	0.22
	0.3	1.21	1.92	1.25	0.90	0.01
	0.2	0.91	1.48	0.91	0.66	0.00
	0.1	0.34	0.68	0.34	0.26	-0.04
16	0.95	-3.29	-2.21	-2.90	-3.49	-4.83
	0.9	-0.49	0.57	0.23	-0.47	-1.70
	0.8	1.51	2.60	2.00	1.49	0.30
	0.7	2.23	3.14	2.56	1.94	0.73
	0.6	2.25	3.17	2.52	1.85	0.76
	0.5	2.08	2.92	2.19	1.60	0.57
	0.4	1.68	2.46	1.73	1.26	0.38
	0.3	1.32	2.01	1.41	0.92	0.24
	0.2	0.87	1.46	1.03	0.60	0.07
	0.1	0.36	0.68	0.54	0.30	0.02
18	0.95	-3.19	-2.21	-2.96	-3.46	-4.79
	0.9	-0.35	0.70	0.44	-0.26	-1.62
	0.8	1.53	2.56	2.06	1.59	0.25
	0.7	2.14	3.15	2.57	2.01	0.66
	0.6	2.17	3.13	2.57	1.96	0.69
	0.5	2.04	2.85	2.30	1.75	0.53
	0.4	1.75	2.44	1.90	1.44	0.35
	0.3	1.31	1.97	1.51	1.05	0.20
	0.2	0.84	1.37	0.99	0.73	-0.06
	0.1	0.38	0.70	0.48	0.38	-0.03
20	0.95	-2.71	-1.77	-2.68	-3.22	-4.36
	0.9	0.01	0.96	0.68	-0.03	-1.29
	0.8	1.79	2.82	2.21	1.63	0.36
	0.7	2.43	3.32	2.64	2.06	0.83
	0.6	2.42	3.22	2.60	1.96	0.76
	0.5	2.24	3.01	2.40	1.72	0.57
	0.4	1.89	2.62	1.94	1.47	0.37
	0.3	1.47	2.08	1.53	1.06	0.14
	0.2	1.05	1.50	1.07	0.77	0.01
	0.1	0.52	0.81	0.50	0.39	-0.16

References

Abdulkadiroğlu, A., P. A. Pathak, and A. E. Roth (2009). Strategy-proofness versus efficiency in matching with indifferences: Redesigning the nyc high school match. *American Economic Review 99*(5), 1954–78.

Abdulkadiroğlu, A. and T. Sönmez (2003). School choice: A mechanism design approach. *American Economic Review 93*(3), pp. 729–747.

Abdulkadiroglu, A. and T. Sönmez (2010). Matching markets: Theory and practice. Prepared for the Econometric Society World Congress, China (2010).

Adar, E. and B. A. Huberman (2000). Free riding on gnutella. *First Monday 5*(10).

Alcalde, J. and S. Barberà (1994). Top dominance and the possibility of strategy-proof stable solutions to matching problems. *Economic Theory 4*(3), 417–435.

Aldershof, B. and O. M. Carducci (1999). Stable marriage and genetic algorithms: A fertile union. *Journal of Heuristics 5*(1), 29–46.

Anagnostakis, K. G. and M. B. Greenwald (2004). Exchange-based incentive mechanisms for peer-to-peer file sharing. In *Distributed Computing Systems, 2004. Proceedings. 24th International Conference on*, pp. 524–533. IEEE.

Anderson, D. and G. Fedak (2006). The computational and storage potential of volunteer computing. In *Cluster Computing and the Grid, 2006. CCGRID 06. Sixth IEEE International Symposium on*, Volume 1, pp. 73 –80.

Anderson, D. P. (2004). Boinc: A system for public-resource computing and storage. In *Grid Computing, 2004. Proceedings. Fifth IEEE/ACM International Workshop on*, pp. 4–10. IEEE.

Anderson, D. P., J. Cobb, E. Korpela, M. Lebofsky, and D. Werthimer (2002). Seti@ home: an experiment in public-resource computing. *Communications of the ACM 45*(11), 56–61.

Andreoni, J. and J. Miller (2002). Giving according to garp: An experimental test of the consistency of preferences for altruism. *Econometrica 70*(2), pp. 737–753.

Antikainen, M. (2011). *Facilitating customer involvement in collaborative online innovation communities*. Ph. D. thesis, Tampere University of Technology.

Antoniadis, P. (2004). Comparing economic incentives in peer-to-peer networks. *Computer Networks 46*(1), 133–146.

Ariely, D., A. Bracha, and S. Meier (2009). Doing good or doing well? image motivation and monetary incentives in behaving prosocially. *American Economic Review 99*(1), 544–555.

Armbrust, M., A. Fox, R. Griffith, A. D. Joseph, R. Katz, A. Konwinski, G. Lee, D. Patterson, A. Rabkin, I. Stoica, et al. (2010). A view of cloud computing. *Communications of the ACM 53*(4), 50–58.

Arrow, K. J. (1972). Gifts and exchanges. *Philosophy and Public Affairs 1*(4), 343–362.

Ashlagi, I. and F. Klijn (2012). Manipulability in matching markets: conflict and coincidence of interests. *Social Choice and Welfare 39*(1), 23–33.

Asvanund, A., K. Clay, R. Krishnan, and M. D. Smith (2004). An empirical analysis of network externalities in peer-to-peer music-sharing networks. *Information Systems Research 15*(2), 155–174.

Axelrod, R. (1997). The evolution of strategies in the iterated prisoner's dilemma. In *The dynamics of norms*, pp. 1–16.

Axelrod, R. and W. Hamilton (1981). The evolution of cooperation. *Science 211*(4489), 1390–1396.

Axtell, R. L. and S. O. Kimbrough (2008). The high cost of stability in two-sided matching: How much social welfare should be sacrificed in the pursuit of stability? In *Proceedings of the 2008 World Congress on Social Simulation (WCSS-08)*.

Babaoglu, O., M. Marzolla, and M. Tamburini (2012). Design and implementation of a p2p cloud system. In *Proceedings of the 27th Annual ACM Symposium on Applied Computing*, pp. 412–417. ACM.

Backstrom, L., P. Boldi, M. Rosa, J. Ugander, and S. Vigna (2012). Four degrees of separation. In *Proceedings of the 3rd Annual ACM Web Science Conference*, pp. 33–42. ACM.

Balinski, M. and T. Sönmez (1999). A tale of two mechanisms: student placement. *Journal of Economic Theory 84*(1), 73–94.

Baumgart, I., B. Heep, and S. Krause (2007). Oversim: A flexible overlay network simulation framework. In *IEEE Global Internet Symposium, 2007*, pp. 79–84.

Belk, R. (2010). Sharing. *Journal of Consumer Research 36*(5), pp. 715–734.

Belk, R. (2013). You are what you can access: Sharing and collaborative consumption online. *Journal of Business Research*.

Bénabou, R. and J. Tirole (2003). Intrinsic and extrinsic motivation. *The Review of Economic Studies 70*(3), 489–520.

Bénabou, R. and J. Tirole (2006). Incentives and prosocial behavior. *American Economic Review 96*(5), pp. 1652–1678.

Berg, J., J. Dickhaut, and K. McCabe (1995). Trust, Reciprocity, and Social History. *Games and Economic Behavior 10*(1), 122–142.

Bishop, J. (2007). Increasing participation in online communities: A framework for human-computer interaction. *Computers in Human Behavior 23*(4), 1881–1893.

Bolton, G. and A. Ockenfels (2000). ERC: A theory of equity, reciprocity, and competition. *American Economic Review 90*(1), 166–193.

Botsman, R. and R. Rogers (2010). *What's mine is yours: The rise of collaborative consumption*. HarperCollins.

Boudreau, J. (2011). A note on the efficiency and fairness of decentralized matching. *Operations Research Letters 39*(4), 231–233.

Boudreau, J. W. and V. Knoblauch (2010). Marriage matching and intercorrelation of preferences. *Journal of Public Economic Theory 12*(3), 587–602.

Buyya, R. and M. Murshed (2002). Gridsim: A toolkit for the modeling and simulation of distributed resource management and scheduling for grid computing. *Concurrency and Computation: Practice and Experience (CCPE) 14*(13), 1175–1220.

Calheiros, R. N., R. Ranjan, A. Beloglazov, C. A. F. De Rose, and R. Buyya (2011). Cloudsim: a toolkit for modeling and simulation of cloud computing environments and evaluation of resource provisioning algorithms. *Software: Practice and Experience 41*(1), 23–50.

Cappos, J., I. Beschastnikh, A. Krishnamurthy, and T. Anderson (2009). Seattle: a platform for educational cloud computing. In *ACM SIGCSE Bulletin*, Volume 41, pp. 111–115. ACM.

Casanova, H., A. Legrand, and M. Quinson (2008). Simgrid: A generic framework for large-scale distributed experiments. In *Computer Modeling and Simulation, 2008. UKSIM 2008. Tenth International Conference on*, pp. 126–131. IEEE.

Caton, S., C. Dukat, T. Grenz, C. Haas, M. Pfadenhauer, and C. Weinhardt (2012). Foundations of Trust: Contextualising Trust in Social Clouds. In *2nd International Conference on Social Computing and Its Applications (SCA 2012)*, pp. 424–429.

Caton, S., C. Haas, K. Chard, K. Bubendorfer, and O. Rana (2014). A social compute cloud: Allocating and sharing infrastructure resources via social networks. *IEEE Transactions on Services Computing (forthcoming)*.

Celik, O. B. and V. Knoblauch (2007). Marriage matching with correlated preferences. *Economics Working Papers*, Paper 200716.

Chan, C., M. Bhandar, L.-B. Oh, and H.-C. Chan (2004). Recognition and participation in a virtual community. In *System Sciences, 2004. Proceedings of the 37th Annual Hawaii International Conference on*, pp. 1–10.

Chard, K. and K. Bubendorfer (2008). A distributed economic meta-scheduler for the grid. In *Proceedings of the 8th IEEE International Symposium on Cluster Computing and the Grid (CCGRID)*, Lyon, France, pp. 542 – 547.

Chard, K., K. Bubendorfer, S. Caton, and O. F. Rana (2012). Social cloud computing: A vision for socially motivated resource sharing. *IEEE Transactions on Services Computing* 5(4), 551–563.

Chard, K., S. Caton, O. Rana, and K. Bubendorfer (2010). Social Cloud: Cloud Computing in Social Networks. In *2010 IEEE 3rd International Conference on Cloud Computing (CLOUD)*, pp. 99–106.

Chard, K., S. Caton, O. Rana, and D. Katz (2012). A social content delivery network for scientific cooperation: Vision, design, and architecture. In *High Performance Computing, Networking, Storage and Analysis (SCC), 2012 SC Companion:*, pp. 1058–1067.

Charness, G. and M. Rabin (2000). Social preferences: Some simple tests and a new model. Technical report, University of California at Berkeley.

Cheng, R. and J. Vassileva (2006). Design and evaluation of an adaptive incentive mechanism for sustained educational online communities. *User Modeling and User-Adapted Interaction 16*(3-4), 321–348.

Cime, W. and K. Marzullo (1999). The computational co-op: Gathering clusters into a metacomputer. In *Parallel and Distributed Processing, 1999. 13th International and 10th Symposium on Parallel and Distributed Processing*, pp. 160 –166.

Clary, E. G., M. Snyder, R. D. Ridge, J. Copeland, A. A. Stukas, J. Haugen, and P. Miene (1998). Understanding and assessing the motivations of volunteers: A functional approach. *Journal of Personality and Social Psychology 74*(6), 1516.

Coleman, J. S. (1990). *Foundations of Social Theory*, Volume 69. Harvard University Press.

Cropanzano, R. and M. S. Mitchell (2005). Social exchange theory: An interdisciplinary review. *Journal of Management 31*(6), 874–900.

Cuevas, R., M. Kryczka, A. Cuevas, S. Kaune, C. Guerrero, and R. Rejaie (2010). Is content publishing in bittorrent altruistic or profit-driven? In *Proceedings of the 6th International COnference*, pp. 11. ACM.

Curry, R., C. Kiddle, N. Markatchev, R. Simmonds, T. Tan, M. Arlitt, and B. Walker (2008). Facebook Meets the Virtualized Enterprise. In *Proceedings of the 12th International IEEE Enterprise Distributed Object Computing Conference (EDOC '08)*, Washington, DC, USA, pp. 286–292. IEEE.

De Jong, K. A. and W. M. Spears (1991). An analysis of the interacting roles of population size and crossover in genetic algorithms. In *Parallel Problem Solving from Nature*, pp. 38–47. Springer.

De Roure, D., C. Goble, and R. Stevens (2009). The design and realisation of the myexperiment virtual research environment for social sharing of workflows. *Future Generation Computer Systems 25*(5), 561–567.

Deci, E. L. and R. M. Ryan (1985). *Self-Determination*. Wiley Online Library.

Deterding, S., D. Dixon, R. Khaled, and L. Nacke (2011). From game design elements to gamefulness: Defining "gamification". In *Proceedings of the 15th International Academic MindTrek Conference: Envisioning Future Media Environments*, MindTrek '11, New York, NY, USA, pp. 9–15. ACM.

Deterding, S., M. Sicart, L. Nacke, K. O'Hara, and D. Dixon (2011). Gamification. using game-design elements in non-gaming contexts. In *CHI '11 Extended Abstracts on Human Factors in Computing Systems*, CHI EA '11, New York, NY, USA, pp. 2425–2428. ACM.

Diebold, F., H. Aziz, M. Bichler, F. Matthes, and A. Schneider (2014). Course allocation via stable matching. *Business & Information Systems Engineering* 6(2), 97–110.

Dueck, G. and T. Scheuer (1990). Threshold accepting: A general purpose optimization algorithm appearing superior to simulated annealing. *Journal of Computational Physics 90*(1), 161 – 175.

Duffy, J. (2006). Chapter 19 agent-based models and human subject experiments. In L. Tesfatsion and K. Judd (Eds.), *Handbook of Computational Economics*, Volume 2, pp. 949 – 1011. Elsevier.

Echenique, F., A. J. Wilson, and L. Yariv (2009). Clearinghouses for two-sided matching: An experimental study. *Social Science Working Paper, 1315.*

Echenique, F. and L. Yariv (2011). An experimental study of decentralized matching. Technical report, Working paper.

Ehlers, L. (2008). Truncation strategies in matching markets. *Mathematics of Operations Research 33*(2), 327–335.

Elnaffar, S., Z. Maamar, and Q. Z. Sheng (2013). When clouds start socializing: The sky model. *International Journal of E-Business Research (IJEBR) 9*(2), 1–7.

Elnozahy, E. M., M. Kistler, and R. Rajamony (2003). Energy-efficient server clusters. In *Power-Aware Computer Systems*, pp. 179–197. Springer.

Emerson, R. M. (1976). Social exchange theory. *Annual Review of Sociology 2*, 335–362.

Endress, M. (2012). Trust and the dialectic of the familiar and unfamiliar within the life-world. *Interaction and everyday life: Phenomenological and Ethnomethodological essays in honor of George Psathas*, 115–133.

Erdil, A. and H. Ergin (2006). Two-sided matching with indifferences. Technical report, Harvard Business School.

Erdil, A. and H. Ergin (2008). What's the matter with tie-breaking? Improving efficiency in school choice. *American Economic Review 98*(3), 669–689.

Falk, A. and U. Fischbacher (2006). A theory of reciprocity. *Games and Economic Behavior 54*(2), 293 – 315.

Feder, T. (1992). A new fixed point approach for stable networks and stable marriages. *Journal of Computer and System Sciences 45*(2), 233 – 284.

Fehr, E. and U. Fischbacher (2003). The nature of human altruism. *Nature 425*(6960), 785–791.

Fehr, E. and K. Schmidt (2000). Theories of fairness and reciprocity - evidence and economic applications. Technical report, Institute for Empirical Research in Economics - University of Zurich.

Fehr, E. and K. M. Schmidt (2006). The economics of fairness, reciprocity and altruism - experimental evidence and new theories. In S.-C. Kolm and J. M. Ythier (Eds.), *Handbook on the Economics of Giving, Reciprocity and Altruism*, Volume 1 of *Handbook on the Economics of Giving, Reciprocity and Altruism*, Chapter 8, pp. 615–691. Elsevier.

Feldman, M., K. Lai, I. Stoica, and J. Chuang (2004). Robust incentive techniques for peer-to-peer networks. In *Proceedings of the 5th ACM Conference on Electronic Commerce - EC '04*, pp. 102. ACM.

Festinger, L. (1954). A theory of social comparison processes. *Human Relations 7*(2), 117–140.

Foa, E. B. and U. G. Foa (2012). Resource theory of social exchange. In *Handbook of Social Resource Theory*, pp. 15–32. Springer.

Fogg, B. and D. Eckles (2007). The behavior chain for online participation: How successful web services structure persuasion. In Y. Kort, W. IJsselsteijn, C. Midden, B. Eggen, and B. Fogg (Eds.), *Persuasive Technology*, Volume 4744 of *Lecture Notes in Computer Science*, pp. 199–209. Springer Berlin Heidelberg.

Foster, I. (2011). Globus online: Accelerating and democratizing science through cloud-based services. *IEEE Internet Computing 15*(3), 70–73.

Foster, I. and C. Kesselman (2003). *The Grid 2: Blueprint for a new computing infrastructure*. Elsevier.

Frey, B. S. and R. Jegen (2001). Motivation crowding theory. *Journal of Economic Surveys 15*(5), 589–611.

Gale, D. and L. Shapley (1962). College admissions and the stability of marriage. *American Mathematical Monthly 69*(1), 9–15.

Ganley, D. and C. Lampe (2009). The ties that bind: Social network principles in online communities. *Decision Support Systems 47*(3), 266 – 274.

Garland, R. (1991). The mid-point on a rating scale: Is it desirable. *Marketing Bulletin 2*(1), 66–70.

Gelain, M., M. S. Pini, F. Rossi, K. B. Venable, and T. Walsh (2013). Local search approaches in stable matching problems. *Algorithms 6*(4), 591–617.

Gent, I. P. and P. Prosser (2002). An empirical study of the stable marriage problem with ties and incomplete lists. In *ECAI - 15th European Conference on Artificial Intelligence*, pp. 141–145.

Golbeck, J. A. (2005). *Computing and Applying Trust in Web-based Social Networks*. Ph. D. thesis, University of Maryland.

Goldberg, D. E. (1989). *Genetic Algorithms in Search, Optimization and Machine Learning*. Addison-Wesley Longman Publishing Co., Inc.

Golle, P., K. Leyton-Brown, I. Mironov, and M. Lillibridge (2001). Incentives for sharing in peer-to-peer networks. In *Electronic Commerce*, pp. 75–87. Springer.

Gosling, S. D., P. J. Rentfrow, and W. B. Swann Jr (2003). A very brief measure of the big-five personality domains. *Journal of Research in Personality 37*(6), 504–528.

Gracia-Tinedo, R., M. Sanchez-Artigas, and P. Garcia-Lopez (2012). F2box: Cloud-ifying f2f storage systems with high availability correlation. In *Cloud Computing (CLOUD), 2012 IEEE 5th International Conference on*, pp. 123–130.

Granovetter, M. (1985). Economic action and social structure: The problem of embeddedness. *American Journal of Sociology 91*(3), 481–510.

Granovetter, M. (2005). The Impact of Social Structure on Economic Outcomes. *Journal of Economic Perspectives 19*(1), 33–50.

Granovetter, M. S. (1973). The strength of weak ties. *The American Journal of Sociology 78*(6), 1360–1380.

Guo, Z., R. Singh, and M. Pierce (2009). Building the polargrid portal using web 2.0 and opensocial. In *Proceedings of the 5th Grid Computing Environments Workshop (GCE '09)*, New York, NY, USA, pp. 1–8. ACM.

Gusfield, D. (1987). Three fast algorithms for four problems in stable marriage. *SIAM Journal on Computing 16*(1), 111–128.

Gusfield, D. and R. W. Irving (1989). *The Stable Marriage Problem: Structure and Algorithms*. Cambridge, MA: MIT Press.

Haas, C., S. Caton, K. Chard, and C. Weinhardt (2013). Co-Operative Infrastructures: An Economic Model for Providing Infrastructures for Social Cloud Computing. In *Proceedings of the Forty-Sixth Annual Hawaii International Conference on System Sciences (HICSS). (Grand Wailea, Maui, USA)*, pp. 729–738.

Haas, C., S. Caton, D. Trumpp, and C. Weinhardt (2012). A Simulator for Social Exchanges and Collaborations - Architecture and Case Study. In *Proceedings of the 8th IEEE International Conference on eScience (eScience 2012)*.

Haas, C., S. Caton, and C. Weinhardt (2011). Engineering incentives in social clouds. In *Proceedings of the 11th IEEE/ACM International Symposium on Cluster, Cloud and Grid Computing (CCGrid 2011)*, pp. 572–575.

Haas, C., S. O. Kimbrough, S. Caton, and C. Weinhardt (2013). Preference-based resource allocation: Using heuristics to solve two-sided matching problems with indifferences. In J. Altmann, K. Vanmechelen, and O. Rana (Eds.), *GECON 2013, LNCS 8193*, pp. 149–160. Springer International Publishing Switzerland.

Haas, C., S. O. Kimbrough, and C. van Dinther (2013). Strategic learning by e-service suppliers in service value networks. *Journal of Service Research 16*(3), 259 – 276.

Halldórsson, M., K. Iwama, S. Miyazaki, and H. Yanagisawa (2007). Improved approximation results for the stable marriage problem. *ACM Transactions on Algorithms (TALG) 3*(3), 30. Article 30.

Halldórsson, M. M., R. W. Irving, K. Iwama, D. F. Manlove, S. Miyazaki, Y. Morita, and S. Scott (2003). Approximability results for stable marriage problems with ties. *Theoretical Computer Science 306*(1-3), 431 – 447.

Harper, F. M., S. X. Li, Y. Chen, and J. A. Konstan (2007). Social comparisons to motivate contributions to an online community. In *Persuasive Technology*, pp. 148–159. Springer.

Hars, A. and S. Ou (2001). Working for free? Motivations of participating in open source projects. In *System Sciences, 2001. Proceedings of the 34th Annual Hawaii International Conference on.*

Häsel, M. (2011). Opensocial: an enabler for social applications on the web. *Communications of the ACM 54*(1), 139–144.

Hearne, R. (2006). SERP click through rate of google search results. Red Cardinal. August 12, 2006. http://www.redcardinal.ie/google/12-08-2006/clickthrough-analysis-of-aol-datatgz/ – last accessed April 2014.

Henrich, J., R. Boyd, S. Bowles, C. Camerer, E. Fehr, H. Gintis, and R. McElreath (2001). In search of homo economicus: Behavioral experiments in 15 small-scale societies. *American Economic Review 91*(2), pp. 73–78.

Holland, J. H. (1992). *Adaptation in natural and artificial systems.* MIT Press.

Inamura, T., T. Shibata, H. Sena, T. Hashimoto, N. Kawai, T. Miyashita, Y. Sakurai, M. Shimizu, M. Otake, K. Hosoda, et al. (2010). Simulator platform that enables social interaction simulation - sigverse: Sociointelligenesis simulator. In *System Integration (SII), 2010 IEEE/SICE International Symposium on*, pp. 212–217. IEEE.

Iriberri, A. and G. Leroy (2009). A life-cycle perspective on online community success. *ACM Computing Surveys (CSUR) 41*(2), 11:1–11:29.

Irving, R. and P. Leather (1986). The complexity of counting stable marriages. *SIAM Journal on Computing 15*(3), 655–667.

Irving, R. W. (1994). Stable marriage and indifference. *Discrete Applied Mathematics 48*(3), 261 – 272.

Irving, R. W., P. Leather, and D. Gusfield (1987). An efficient algorithm for the optimal stable marriage. *Journal of the ACM 34*(3), 532–543.

Irving, R. W. and D. F. Manlove (2008). Approximation algorithms for hard variants of the stable marriage and hospitals/residents problems. *Journal of Combinatorial Optimization 16*(3), 279–292.

Irwin, D., J. Chase, L. Grit, and A. Yumerefendi (2005). Self-recharging virtual currency. In *Proceedings of the 2005 ACM SIGCOMM Workshop on Economics of Peer-to-peer Systems*, P2PECON '05, New York, NY, USA, pp. 93–98. ACM.

Iwama, K., S. Miyazaki, Y. Morita, and D. Manlove (1999). Stable marriage with incomplete lists and ties. In J. Wiedermann, P. Emde Boas, and M. Nielsen (Eds.), *Automata, Languages and Programming*, Volume 1644 of *Lecture Notes in Computer Science*, pp. 443–452. Springer Berlin Heidelberg.

Iwama, K., S. Miyazaki, and H. Yanagisawa (2010). Approximation algorithms for the sex-equal stable marriage problem. *ACM Transactions on Algorithms (TALG) 7*(1), 2.

Iwama, K., S. Miyazaki, and H. Yanagisawa (2014). A 25/17-approximation algorithm for the stable marriage problem with one-sided ties. *Algorithmica 68*(3), 758–775.

Jackson, M. O. (2003). Mechanism theory. In U. Derigs (Ed.), *Encyclopedia of Life Support Systems*. EOLSS Publishers: Oxford UK.

Javadi, B., D. Kondo, J. Vincent, and D. Anderson (2011). Discovering statistical models of availability in large distributed systems: An empirical study of seti@home. *Parallel and Distributed Systems, IEEE Transactions on PP*(99), 1.

Javadi, B., D. Kondo, J.-M. Vincent, and D. P. Anderson (2009). Mining for statistical models of availability in large-scale distributed systems: An empirical study of seti@ home. In *Modeling, Analysis & Simulation of Computer and Telecommunication Systems, 2009. MASCOTS'09. IEEE International Symposium on*, pp. 1–10. IEEE.

John, K., K. Bubendorfer, and K. Chard (2011). A social cloud for public eresearch. In *E-Science (e-Science), 2011 IEEE 7th International Conference on*, pp. 363 –370.

John, O. P., E. M. Donahue, and R. L. Kentle (1991). The big five inventory - versions 4a and 54. *Berkeley: University of California, Berkeley, Institute of Personality and Social Research.*

Jones, Q. and S. Rafaeli (1999). User population and user contributions to virtual publics: a systems model. In *Proceedings of the International ACM SIGGROUP Conference on Supporting Group Work*, GROUP '99, New York, NY, USA, pp. 239–248. ACM.

Jøsang, A., R. Ismail, and C. Boyd (2007). A survey of trust and reputation systems for online service provision. *Decision Support Systems 43*(2), 618–644.

Kagel, J. H. and A. E. Roth (2000). The dynamics of reorganization in matching markets: A laboratory experiment motivated by a natural experiment. *The Quarterly Journal of Economics 115*(1), 201–235.

Kamvar, S. D., M. T. Schlosser, and H. Garcia-molina (2003). The Eigen-Trust Algorithm for Reputation Management in P2P Networks. In *Proceedings of the 12th International World Wide Web Conference, Budapest, Hungary*, pp. 640–651.

Karau, S. J. and K. D. Williams (1993). Social loafing: A meta-analytic review and theoretical integration. *Journal of Personality and Social Psychology 65*(4), 681.

Kesten, O. (2012). On two kinds of manipulation for school choice problems. *Economic Theory 51*(3), 677–693.

Khan, A. M., L. Navarro, L. Sharifi, and L. Veiga (2013). Clouds of small things: Provisioning infrastructure-as-a-service from within community networks. In *Wireless and Mobile Computing, Networking and Communications (WiMob), 2013 IEEE 9th International Conference on*, pp. 16–21. IEEE.

Kimbrough, S. and A. Kuo (2010). On heuristics for two-sided matching: revisiting the stable marriage problem as a multiobjective problem. In *Proceedings of the 12th Annual Conference on Genetic and Evolutionary Computation*, pp. 1283–1290. ACM.

Kimbrough, S. O. and F. H. Murphy (2009). Learning to Collude Tacitly on Production Levels by Oligopolistic Agents. *Computational Economics 33*(1), 47–78.

Király, Z. (2011). Better and simpler approximation algorithms for the stable marriage problem. *Algorithmica 60*(1), 3–20.

Klaus, B. and F. Klijn (2006a). Median stable matching for college admissions. *International Journal of Game Theory 34*(1), 1–11.

Klaus, B. and F. Klijn (2006b). Procedurally fair and stable matching. *Economic Theory 27*, 431–447.

Klimeck, G., M. McLennan, S. P. Brophy, G. B. Adams, and M. S. Lundstrom (2008). nanoHUB.org: Advancing Education and Research in Nanotechnology. *Computing in Science and Engineering 10*, 17–23.

Knuth, D. E. (1976). *Marriages Stables.* Montreal, Canada: Les Presses de l'Université de Montreal.

Knuth, D. E. (1997). *Stable Marriage and Its Relation to Other Combinatorial Problems: An Introduction to the Mathematical Analysis of Algorithms*, Volume 10 of *CRM Proceedings & Lecture Notes, Centre de Recherches Mathématiques Université de Montréal*. Providence, RI: American Mathematical Society. Originally published as Knuth (1976).

Koh, J., Y. Kim, B. Butler, and G. Bock (2007). Encouraging participation in virtual communities. *Communications of the ACM 50*(2), 68–73.

Kojima, F. and P. A. Pathak (2009). Incentives and stability in large two-sided matching markets. *American Economic Review 99*(3), pp. 608–627.

Kollock, P. (1999). The economies of online cooperation: Gifts and public goods in cyberspace. In P. Kollock and M. Smith (Eds.), *Communities in Cyberspace*, pp. 219–240. Routledge.

Kourtellis, N. (2012). *On the Design of Socially-Aware Distributed Systems*. Ph. D. thesis, University of South Florida.

Kourtellis, N., J. Finnis, P. Anderson, J. Blackburn, C. Borcea, and A. Iamnitchi (2010). Prometheus: User-controlled p2p social data management for socially-aware applications. In I. Gupta and C. Mascolo (Eds.), *Middleware 2010*, Volume 6452 of *Lecture Notes in Computer Science*, pp. 212–231. Springer Berlin Heidelberg.

Krishnan, R., M. Smith, and R. Telang (2006). The economics of peer-to-peer networks. *Journal of Information Technology Theory and Application (JITTA) 5*, 31–44.

Lakhani, K. R. and E. von Hippel (2003). How open source software works: "free" user-to-user assistance. *Research Policy 32*(6), 923 – 943.

Lakhani, K. R. and R. G. Wolf (2005) Why hackers do what they do: Understanding motivation and effort in Free/Open source software projects. In J. Feller, B. Fitzgerald, S. A. Hissam, and K. R. Lakhani (Eds.), *Perspectives on Free and Open Source Software*, pp. 3–21. Cambridge, Massachusetts: The MIT Press.

Lampe, C., R. Wash, A. Velasquez, and E. Ozkaya (2010). Motivations to participate in online communities. In *Proceedings of the SIGCHI Conference on Human Factors in Computing Systems*, CHI '10, New York, NY, USA, pp. 1927–1936. ACM.

Law, A. M. (2007). *Simulation modeling and analysis* (4. ed. ed.). McGraw-Hill series in industrial engineering and management science. McGraw-Hill.

Lazar, J. and J. Preece (2002). Social Considerations in Online Communities: Usability, Sociability, and Success Factors. In H. Van Oostendorp (Ed.), *Cognition in a Digital World*. Mahwah: NJ: Lawrence Erlbaum Associates Inc. Publishers.

Lee, S. (2011). Incentive compatibility of large centralized matching markets. *Job market paper*.

Levine, M. (2009). Share my ride. New York Times Magazine. March 9, 2009.

Liao, R. R.-F., R. H. Wouhaybi, and A. T. Campbell (2002). Incentive engineering in wireless LAN based access networks. In *10th IEEE International Conference on Network Protocols, 2002. Proceedings.*, pp. 58–67. IEEE.

Manlove, D. F., R. W. Irving, K. Iwama, S. Miyazaki, and Y. Morita (2002). Hard variants of stable marriage. *Theoretical Computer Science 276*(1), 261 – 279.

Mao, Y., J. Vassileva, and W. Grassmann (2007). A system dynamics approach to study virtual communities. In *System Sciences, 2007. HICSS 2007. 40th Annual Hawaii International Conference on*.

Markus, M. L. (1987). Toward a "critical mass" theory of interactive media: Universal access, interdependence and diffusion. *Communication Research 14*(5), 491–511.

Mas-Colell, A., M. D. Whinston, J. R. Green, et al. (1995). *Microeconomic Theory*, Volume 1. Oxford university press, New York.

McDermid, E. (2009). A 3/2-approximation algorithm for general stable marriage. In *Automata, Languages and Programming*, pp. 689–700. Springer.

Mell, P. and T. Grance (2011). The nist definition of cloud computing. Technical Report 800-145, National Institute of Standards and Technology (NIST), Gaithersburg, MD.

Michalk, W. and C. Haas (2011). Incentives in service level agreement establishment the case of economic and social aspects. In *Requirements Engineering for Social Computing (RESC), 2011 First International Workshop on*, pp. 30–33.

Mohaisen, A., H. Tran, A. Chandra, and Y. Kim (2011). SocialCloud: Using Social Networks for Building Distributed Computing Services. Technical report, Cornell University.

Montresor, A. and M. Jelasity (2009). Peersim: A scalable p2p simulator. In *Peer-to-Peer Computing, 2009. P2P'09. IEEE Ninth International Conference on*, pp. 99–100. IEEE.

Mowbray, M., F. Brasileiro, N. Andrade, J. Santana, and W. Cirne (2006). A Reciprocation-Based Economy for Multiple Services in Peer-to-Peer Grids. In *Sixth IEEE International Conference on Peer-to-Peer Computing (P2P'06)*, pp. 193–202. IEEE.

Muck, P. M., B. Hell, and S. D. Gosling (2007). Construct validation of a short five-factor model instrument: A self-peer study on the german adaptation of the ten-item personality inventory (tipi-g). *European Journal of Psychological Assessment 23*(3), 166.

Nakamura, M., K. Onaga, S. Kyan, and M. Silva (1995). Genetic algorithm for sex-fair stable marriage problem. In *Circuits and Systems, 1995. ISCAS '95, 1995 IEEE International Symposium on*, Volume 1, pp. 509 –512 vol.1.

Neumann, D. G. (2004). *Market Engineering: A structured design process for electronic markets*. Univ.-Verlag Karlsruhe.

Nisan, N. and A. Ronen (1999). Algorithmic mechanism design. In *Proceedings of the Thirty-First Annual ACM Symposium on Theory of Computing*, pp. 129–140. ACM.

Nobel Prize Committee (2012). Alvin E. Roth and Lloyd S. Shapley: Stable allocations and the practice of market design. Technical report, Royal Swedish Academy of Sciences.

Nov, O. (2007). What motivates wikipedians? *Communications of the ACM 50*(11), 60–64.

Nov, O., D. Anderson, and O. Arazy (2010). Volunteer computing: a model of the factors determining contribution to community-based scientific research. In *Proceedings of the 19th International Conference on World Wide Web*, WWW '10, New York, NY, USA, pp. 741–750. ACM.

Nov, O., M. Naaman, and C. Ye (2010). Analysis of participation in an online photo-sharing community: A multidimensional perspective. *Journal of the American Society for Information Science and Technology 61*, 555–566.

Odlyzko, A. (2003). The case against micropayments. In R. Wright (Ed.), *Financial Cryptography*, pp. 77–83. Springer.

Pais, J. (2008). Random matching in the college admissions problem. *Economic Theory 35*(1), 99–116.

Paluch, K. (2012). Faster and simpler approximation of stable matchings. In *Approximation and Online Algorithms*, pp. 176–187. Springer.

Parkes, D. C. (2001). *Iterative combinatorial auctions: Achieving economic and computational efficiency*. Ph. D. thesis, University of Pennsylvania.

Pavlou, P. A. and D. Gefen (2004). Building effective online marketplaces with institution-based trust. *Information Systems Research 15*(1), 37–59.

Petri, I., O. F. Rana, Y. Regzui, and G. C. Silaghi (2012). Risk assessment in service provider communities. In *Economics of Grids, Clouds, Systems, and Services*, pp. 135–147. Springer.

Petri, I., O. F. Rana, Y. Rezgui, and G. C. Silaghi (2012). Trust modelling and analysis in peer–to–peer clouds. *International Journal of Cloud Computing 1*(2), 221–239.

Pini, M. S., F. Rossi, K. B. Venable, and T. Walsh (2011a). Manipulation complexity and gender neutrality in stable marriage procedures. *Autonomous Agents and Multi-Agent Systems 22*(1), 183–199.

Pini, M. S., F. Rossi, K. B. Venable, and T. Walsh (2011b). Weights in stable marriage problems increase manipulation opportunities. In *Proceedings of the 13th Conference on Theoretical Aspects of Rationality and Knowledge*, TARK XIII, New York, NY, USA, pp. 200–204. ACM.

Porter, J. (2010). *Designing for the social web*. Peachpit Press.

Porter, P. K. and G. W. Scully (1987). Economic efficiency in cooperatives. *Journal of Law and Economics 30*(2), pp. 489–512.

Preece, J. and D. Maloney-Krichmar (2003). *Online communities: focusing on sociability and usability*. Lawrence Erlbaum Publishers, Mahwak: NJ.

Priedhorsky, R., J. Chen, S. T. K. Lam, K. Panciera, L. Terveen, and J. Riedl (2007). Creating, destroying, and restoring value in wikipedia. In *Proceedings of the 2007 International ACM Conference on Supporting Group Work*, GROUP '07, New York, NY, USA, pp. 259–268. ACM.

Rafaeli, S. and Y. Ariel (2008). Online motivational factors: Incentives for participation and contribution in wikipedia. In A. Barak (Ed.), *Psychological Aspects of Cyberspace*. New York, NY: Cambridge University Press.

Ranganathan, K., M. Ripeanu, A. Sarin, and I. Foster (2004). Incentive mechanisms for large collaborative resource sharing. In *IEEE International Symposium on Cluster Computing and the Grid, 2004. CCGrid 2004*, pp. 1–8. IEEE.

Ranjan, R., L. Zhao, X. Wu, A. Liu, A. Quiroz, and M. Parashar (2010). Peer-to-peer cloud provisioning: Service discovery and load-balancing. In *Cloud Computing*, pp. 195–217. Springer.

Ren, Y., R. Kraut, and S. Kiesler (2007). Applying common identity and bond theory to design of online communities. *Organization Studies 28*(3), 377–408.

Ren, Y. and R. E. Kraut (2011). A simulation for designing online community: Member motivation, contribution, and discussion moderation. Unpublished.

Rheingold, H. (1993). *The virtual community. Homesteading on the electronic frontier.* New York,: Addison-Wesley.

Rifkin, J. (2000). *The age of access : the new culture of hypercapitalism, where all of life is a paid-for experience.* New York, NY: Jeremy P. Tarcher/Putnam.

Romero-Medina, A. (2001). Sex-equal'stable matchings. *Theory and Decision 50*(3), 197–212.

Roth, A. (1982). The economics of matching: Stability and incentives. *Mathematics of Operations Research 7*(4), 617–628.

Roth, A. (2008). Deferred acceptance algorithms: History, theory, practice, and open questions. *International Journal of Game Theory 36*(3), 537–569.

Roth, A. and M. Sotomayor (1992). *Two-sided matching: A study in game-theoretic modeling and analysis*, Volume 18. Cambridge University Press.

Roth, A. E. (1985). The college admissions problem is not equivalent to the marriage problem. *Journal of Economic Theory 36*(2), 277–288.

Roth, A. E. and U. G. Rothblum (1999). Truncation strategies in matching markets-in search of advice for participants. *Econometrica 67*(1), pp. 21–43.

Roth, A. E., U. G. Rothblum, and J. H. V. Vate (1993). Stable matchings, optimal assignments, and linear programming. *Mathematics of Operations Research 18*(4), pp. 803–828.

Rothblum, U. G. (1992). Characterization of stable matchings as extreme points of a polytope. *Mathematical Programming 54*(1-3), 57–67.

Roure, D. D., C. Goble, and R. Stevens (2009). The design and realisation of the myexperiment virtual research environment for social sharing of workflows. *Future Generation Computer Systems 25*(5), 561–567.

Ryan, R. M. and E. L. Deci (2000). Intrinsic and extrinsic motivations: Classic definitions and new directions. *Contemporary Educational Psychology 25*(1), 54 – 67.

Sabater, J. and C. Sierra (2002). Social ReGreT, A reputation model based on social relations. *ACM SIGecom Exchanges 3*(1), 44–56.

Schnell, R., P. B. Hill, and E. Esser (2011). *Methoden der empirischen Sozialforschung*. Oldenbourg Verlag.

Scott, S. (2005). *A study of stable marriage problems with ties*. Ph. D. thesis, University of Glasgow.

Seuken, S., D. Charles, M. Chickering, and S. Puri (2010). Market design & analysis for a p2p backup system. In *Proceedings of the 11th ACM Conference on Electronic Commerce*, pp. 97–108. ACM.

Seuken, S., K. Jain, D. Tan, and M. Czerwinski (2010). Hidden markets: Ui design for a p2p backup application. In *Proceedings of the 28th International Conference on Human Factors in Computing Systems*, pp. 315–324. ACM.

Sexton, R. J. (1986). The formation of cooperatives: A game-theoretic approach with implications for cooperative finance, decision making, and stability. *American Journal of Agricultural Economics 68*(2), 214–225.

Shampanier, K., N. Mazar, and D. Ariely (2007). Zero as a special price: The true value of free products. *Marketing Science 26*(6), 742–757.

Skinner, B. F. (1953). *Science and Human Behavior*. New York, NY: Macmillan.

Smith, V. L. (1982). Microeconomic systems as an experimental science. *American Economic Review 72*(5), 923–955.

Sönmez, T. (1999). Can pre-arranged matches be avoided in two-sided matching markets? *Journal of Economic Theory 86*(1), 148–156.

Spear, R. (2000). The co-operative advantage. *Annals of Public and Cooperative Economics 71*(4), 507–523.

Stephen, A. T. and O. Toubia (2010). Deriving Value from Social Commerce Networks. *Journal of Marketing Research 47*(2), 215–228.

Streitberger, W. and T. Eymann (2009). A simulation of an economic, self-organising resource allocation approach for application layer networks. *Computer Networks 53*(10), 1760–1770.

Suls, J., R. Martin, and L. Wheeler (2002). Social comparison: Why, with whom, and with what effect? *Current Directions in Psychological Science 11*(5), 159–163.

Swamynathan, G., C. Wilson, B. Boe, K. Almeroth, and B. Y. Zhao (2008). Do social networks improve e-commerce?: a study on social marketplaces. In *Proceedings of the First Workshop on Online Social Networks*, WOSN '08, New York, NY, USA, pp. 1–6.

Tapscott, D. and A. D. Williams (2007). *Wikinomics: How Mass Collaboration Changes Everything*. New York: Penguin.

Tedjamulia, S., D. Dean, D. Olsen, and C. Albrecht (2005). Motivating content contributions to online communities: Toward a more comprehensive theory. In *System Sciences, 2005. HICSS '05. Proceedings of the 38th Annual Hawaii International Conference on*.

Thal, R. (2013). Representing Agreements in Social Clouds. Master's thesis, Karlsruhe Institute of Technology.

Thaufeeg, A., K. Bubendorfer, and K. Chard (2011). Collaborative eResearch in a social cloud. In *E-Science (e-Science), 2011 IEEE 7th International Conference on*, pp. 224 –231.

Thorndike, E. L. (1927). The Law of Effect. *American Journal of Psychology 39*, 212–222.

Tran, D. N., F. Chiang, and J. Li (2008). Friendstore: Cooperative online backup using trusted nodes. In *Proceedings of the 1st International Workshop on Social Network Systems (SocialNet'08)*, Glasgow, Scotland.

van Dijck, J. (2009). Users like you? Theorizing agency in user-generated content. *Media, Culture & Society 31*(1), 41–58.

Van Slyke, C., V. Ilie, H. Lou, and T. Stafford (2007). Perceived critical mass and the adoption of a communication technology. *European Journal of Information Systems 16*(3), 270–283.

Vande Vate, J. H. (1989). Linear programming brings marital bliss. *Operations Research Letters 8*(3), 147 – 153.

Vargo, S. L. and R. F. Lusch (2004). Evolving to a new dominant logic for marketing. *Journal of Marketing 68*, 1–17.

Vassileva, J. (2012). Motivating participation in social computing applications: a user modeling perspective. *User Modeling and User-Adapted Interaction 22*(1-2), 177–201.

Venkatesh, V., M. G. Morris, G. B. Davis, and F. D. Davis (2003). User acceptance of information technology: Toward a unified view. *MIS Quarterly 27*(3), 425–478.

Vien, N. A. and T. C. Chung (2006). Multiobjective fitness functions for stable marriage problem using genetic algrithm. In *SICE-ICASE, 2006. International Joint Conference*, pp. 5500 –5503.

Walter, F. E., S. Battiston, and F. Schweitzer (2008). A model of a trust-based recommendation system on a social network. *Autonomous Agents and Multi-Agent Systems 16*(1), 57–74.

Wang, H., J. E. Chung, N. Park, M. L. McLaughlin, and J. Fulk (2012). Understanding online community participation: A technology acceptance perspective. *Communication Research 39*(6), 781–801.

Watts, D. J. and S. H. Strogatz (1998). Collective dynamics of 'small-world' networks. *Nature 393*(6684), 440–442.

Weijters, B., E. Cabooter, and N. Schillewaert (2010). The effect of rating scale format on response styles: The number of response categories and response category labels. *International Journal of Research in Marketing 27*(3), 236–247.

Weinhardt, C., C. Holtmann, and D. Neumann (2003). Market-Engineering. *Wirtschaftsinformatik 45*(6), 635–640.

Westland, J. C. (2010). Critical mass and willingness to pay for social networks. *Electronic Commerce Research and Applications 9*(1), 6 – 19. Special Issue: Social Networks and Web 2.0.

Wigfield, A. and J. S. Eccles (2000). Expectancy-value theory of achievement motivation. *Contemporary Educational Psychology 25*(1), 68 – 81.

Williams, R. L. and J. Cothrel (2000). Four smart ways to run online communities. *Sloan Management Review 41*(4), 81–92.

Xiang, R., J. Neville, and M. Rogati (2010). Modeling relationship strength in online social networks. In *Proceedings of the 19th International Conference on World Wide Web*, WWW '10, New York, NY, USA, pp. 981–990. ACM.

Xiaohui, W., D. Zhaohui, Y. Shutao, H. Chang, and L. Huizhen (2006). CSF4: A WSRF Compliant Meta-Scheduler. In *In Proceedings of World Congress in Computer Science, Computer Engineering, and Applied Computing*, pp. 61–67.

Xiong, L. and L. Liu (2004). Peertrust: Supporting reputation-based trust for peer-to-peer electronic communities. *IEEE Transactions On Knowledge and Data Engineering 16*(7), 843–857.

Xu, S. and M. Yung (2010). Socialclouds: Concept, security architecture and some mechanisms. In L. Chen and M. Yung (Eds.), *Trusted Systems*, Volume 6163 of *LNCS*, pp. 104–128. Springer.

Zhang, K., N. Antonopoulos, and Z. Mahmood (2009). A review of incentive mechanism in peer-to-peer systems. In *Advances in P2P Systems, 2009. AP2PS '09. First International Conference on*, pp. 45–50.

Zhou, R. and K. Hwang (2007). Powertrust: A robust and scalable reputation system for trusted peer-to-peer computing. *IEEE Transactions on Parallel and Distributed Systems 18*(4), 460–473.

Zhuang, Y., A. Rafetseder, and J. Cappos (2013). Experience with Seattle: A Community Platform for Research and Education. In *Research and Educational Experiment Workshop (GREE), 2013 Second GENI*, pp. 37–44. IEEE.